New Edition

Viewfinder

Topics

Resource Book

Ireland

by
Peter-J. Rekowski

Langenscheidt

Berlin · München · Wien · Zürich · New York

Viewfinder

Topics

Resource Book

Ireland

A Story of Beauty and Hope

Herausgeber:
Prof. em. Dr. Dr. h.c. mult. Peter Freese, Paderborn

Autor:
Dr. Peter-J. Rekowski, Kirchhain

Projekt-Team:
Dr. Martin Arndt, Münster
David Beal, M. A., Bochum
Dr. Peter Dines, Cert. Ed., Ludwigsburg
Prof. i.R. Dr. Hanspeter Dörfel, Ludwigsburg
Prof. Dr. Sabine Doff, Frankfurt am Main
OStR Dieter Düwel, Castrop-Rauxel
Prof. em. Dr. Dr. h.c. mult. Peter Freese, Paderborn
Dr. Carin Freywald †
Jennifer von der Grün, B. A., Castrop-Rauxel
OStR Reimer Jansen, Bremen
Dr. Michael Mitchell, M. A., Reken und Warwick
Prof. Dr. Michael Porsche, Paderborn
StD i.E. Detlef Rediker, Lippstadt
StD Dr. Peter-J. Rekowski, Kirchhain
OStR i.K. Peter Ringeisen, M. A., Amberg
Karl Sassenberg, Münster
StD Henning Scholz †
StD Dr. Annegret Schrick, Gevelsberg
OStR Ekkehard Sprenger, Olympia, USA
StD Dr. Dietrich Theißen, Gütersloh
Donald Turner, M. A. †
Prof. Dr. Laurenz Volkmann, Jena
Philip Wade, M. A., Cert. Ed., Amberg

Verlagsredaktion: Sibylle Freitag, Dr. Beatrix Finke

Layout und Produktion: kaltnermedia GmbH, Bobingen

Umwelthinweis: Gedruckt auf chlorfrei gebleichtem Papier.

1. Auflage 2006

Printed in Germany

ISBN-13: 978-3-526-51005-5
ISBN-10: 3-526-51005-9

1 2 3 4 5 / 08 07 06

Contents

Course Manager

Teaching Resources

** Title provided by the editor*

Info Sheets

Course Manager

The Theme

Although interest has been focused recently on other English-speaking countries apart from the U.S. or the United Kingdom – like Australia, New Zealand or African or Caribbean cultures, Ireland has, over the years, always been a favourite topic in the field of cultural and historical background studies (*Landeskunde*) in the German advanced EFL-classroom. Of course, what has drawn attention to this small, English-speaking country at the periphery of Europe, was more than anything else, the so-called Northern Ireland conflict, and indeed, this conflict is the island's most characteristic, though also most depressing, feature. Yet, within the last ten or so years, the Irish conflict has slowly but gradually been transformed into what has come to be known as the Irish peace process. This astonishing change might be reason enough to conduct some in-depth studies of the divided island. However, there is more to this island than that. Both the Republic of Ireland and Northern Ireland are countries in transition and have their own stories to tell but they also have much in common. Many current curricula demand that "Ireland" or "Northern Ireland" should be studied in the upper grades of the German *Gymnasium*.

This is why part II of this *Viewfinder* volume also offers various texts that might allow young German readers possible access to what is often euphemistically called 'The Troubles' and now 'The Irish Peace Process', but it really puts the accent on part I, which deals with the 'other' Ireland. Ireland is not Northern Ireland, but again, what is going on in Northern Ireland cannot be understood without a deeper insight into the historical, cultural, political, social, and economic background of the island as a whole. This *Viewfinder* anthology on Ireland tries to tell this story and it is a "story of beauty and terror" as the first edition of this anthology was called, or today "the story of beauty and hope." Regardless of the reasons why visitors choose to come to Ireland, they cannot fail to be impressed by the beauty of the island; the particular lifestyle of the people; the island's cultural richness, especially its literature and music; the scars of a troubled history; the omnipresence of a living religious faith; and the visible and impressive signs, in both the north and the south of the island, of a return to peace and normality.

For this reason, this study book about Ireland first offers a variety of texts that mirror the different factors that have shaped the history and culture of the island. With this background information in mind the student may then examine the sectarian violence marked by bullets and bombs that make other, less knowledgeable people, shake their heads about this island and wonder whether a lasting peace will ever be possible there.

The two terms in the subtitle, "beauty" and "hope", that divide this anthology into two main parts, imply a division that is more notional than real. "Beauty" refers, of course, to the "beauty" of Ireland as a whole including Northern Ireland; and "hope", while focusing mainly on the end of the conflict in Northern Ireland, points to a political dimension that has significance for the Republic of Ireland as well.

These two main parts are again sub-divided into the six sequences

- **The Emerald Isle**
- **A Look Back in Anger**
- **The Celtic Heritage**
- **Ireland on Fast-Forward**
- **Northern Ireland and the Story Behind It**
- **Peace in Ireland?**

which structure the anthology so that the above-mentioned aims may become more obvious. They must, however, be understood as heuristic selections from a much more complex context that cannot be dealt with in the framework of such an anthology.

All the texts in this volume have been selected on the premise that they reveal as many facets, and are as representative of the aspect of Irish life they describe, as possible. According to the new notion of *Landeskunde* as cross-cultural or intercultural learning, this publication on Ireland presents a new and challenging educational strategy which involves the *hic et nunc* of German students and continually confronts them with questions about their own experience, value system and knowledge of the world.

Because of that, this *Viewfinder* volume does not limit itself to providing facts and figures and expository texts about Ireland, but also contains a number of literary ones. This was motivated by the desire first to pay tribute to Ireland's great literary tradition and, second, to present different forms of imaginative treatment of the Irish experience. On the basis of an innovative and motivating methodological approach that allows the students more self-determination and expects more responsibility in dealing with the texts, the author hopes to help the students

- to develop an open-minded, informed and critical attitude in the debate about the Irish question
- to gain experience and develop skills in the analysis of fictional and non-fictional texts,
- to have lively and constructive discussions that may open their minds to the common "human condition"[1] in all the concepts presented in the texts,

[1] G.B. Madison, *Understanding. A Phenomenological Pragmatic Analysis* (Westport/Connecticut and London/England: Greenwood Press, 1982), pp. 130f.

- to increase their command of the English language,
- and, finally, experience the charm of a beautiful country, despite what is going on "over there".

The Texts

The **Students' Book** consists of **16 texts**, representing different types of text: feature, poem, essay, pamphlet, documentation, letter, folksong, newspaper article, travel report, short story, political speech, newspaper headline, political commentary, novel, interview and **55 thematically related illustrations**, which correspond to the eight visual text types of photograph, postcard, collage, map, drawing, cartoon, portrait, graph.

The current *Lehrpläne* for advanced students of English and contemporary EFL-methodology demand that academic and scholarly methods as well as communicative methods of foreign language learning be brought into the classroom. In compliance with these two basic requirements, the Study Texts contain strictly authentic texts that have not been tampered with for specific didactic purposes. Each text is presented in its original wording, omissions are marked by [...], titles provided by the editor are signalled by *, and complete bibliographical data is given to make it easy for the reader to check the context of the excerpts. In order not to interfere with the authenticity of the texts, no annotations are given; explanatory material is provided separately in the Study Aids. The 16 texts vary in difficulty from * (easily accessible) to *** (rather demanding). The grading is determined by

- the number of unknown words,
- the syntactic complexity,
- the amount of background information required for the text to be properly understood, and
- the intellectual level of the text.[2]

This *Viewfinder* volume progresses in a carefully structured way, but it is also sub-divided into six sections or sequences, each of which can be studied separately. The individual teacher can thus decide which sub-groups of texts he/she will deal with in a given course and in which order.

The **Study Aids** offer

- **vocabulary:** explanations of unknown words and phrases with information about grammatical forms, and where necessary, register and pronunciation,
- **explanations:** information about historical persons and events, geographical, biographical, literary and other such 'culture-bound' ingredients necessary for a full understanding of a text,
- **Info boxes:** information about important concepts and names connected with the topics of the texts,
- **bibliographical information** about the authors,
- **selected additional texts and illustrations**, and
- carefully structured sets of **questions and tasks**.

The Study Aids thus serve as a reference section on the Study Texts and may be used both as a dictionary and encyclopaedia by the students. In addition, they provide methodological support for the teacher.

The following synopsis provides an introductory survey of all texts and illustrations in the Study Texts with regard to their

- text type,
- length,
- degree of difficulty, and
- theme.

It also gives a summary of the contents of each text with some preliminary analysis. In addition, the teacher will find in the Course Manager references to the supplementary material contained in the Study Aids, as well as to the Information Sheets in this Resource Book. The information in this synopsis will help teachers to define their objectives and strategies with respect to the small sequences and the individual texts.

The Structure of the Anthology

As has been said earlier, this anthology forms a unit in itself, yet the teacher might want to select only individual sections from this volume. For this reason the anthology has been sub-divided and the texts have been arranged in the following sequences:

The Emerald Isle (Title Page; Introduction; Text 1)
A Look back in Anger (Texts 2–5)
The Celtic Heritage (Texts 6–7)
Ireland on Fast-Forward (Texts 8–10)
Northern Ireland and the Story Behind It (Texts11–13)
Peace in Ireland? (Texts 14–16)

Sequence One: The Emerald Isle

The Introductory Section

This section, which is meant to create some initial interest in the studies of the culture and history of Ireland that this anthology offers, opens with a brief introductory text and 14 photographs which are intended to alert the students to the various aspects which make up the idiosyncrasy of this island.

text type: introduction
length: 412 words
degree of difficulty: *; 0 annotations and 0 explanations
theme: the various faces of Ireland

Irish "motifs"
text type: photographs

[2] As reference has also been made to American sources in the selection of texts, it was decided to adhere to American spelling conventions in both these particular texts and the relevant Study Aids.

1 | Makki Marseilles "Impressions of Ireland"

text type: (excerpt from) feature
length: 875 words
degree of difficulty:***; 28 annotations and 41 explanations
theme: an ardent 'declaration of love' by an Ireland enthusiast that provides a fine overview of the characteristic traits of Ireland

"Céad Mile Fajlte"
text type: postcard

landscape in Co. Galway
text type: photograph

Living culture on a Dublin pavement
text type: photograph

Grafton Street, Dublin
text type: photograph

2 | Collage

text type: different types of text and photographs
length: 677 words
degree of difficulty: *
41 annotations and 9 explanations
theme: a visual and verbal panorama of Ireland's past and present

stamp in Gaelic
what's what called?
coat of arms of the four provinces of Ireland
Ireland meets industrialisation
map of Ireland
statistics about Ireland (2004)
a singing pub
a modern industrial estate
Seamus Heaney, "Digging"
the Cross of Muiredach, Monasterboice
famous Irish writers
an Irishman's approach to a problem
St Kevin's Church (Glendalough)
Irish humour
Irish sport: Hurling
Irish saying
Rock of Cashel, Co. Tipperary
traditional Irish recipe: Irish Stew

An introduction to Ireland could start by dealing with the romantic picture of Ireland that is suggested by the term 'Emerald Isle'. This side of Ireland does of course exist, but students should be made aware that there is more to Ireland. This is why Sequence One approaches the topic from different perspectives:

The Introductory Section presents photographs and some remarks which are intended to introduce the theme, arouse the students' interest in it and get the course started.

The illustrations symbolise the two faces of Ireland: its natural beauty and rich cultural life are sharply contrasted with the remorseless forces of terror that have, over time, left their scars on the face of the island. But they also offer symbols of hope that Ireland needs so much.

A discussion of the Introductory Section should make clear that this is a rather simplified presentation of Ireland's characteristic features and is only intended to create a first general awareness of the topic.

Makki Marseilles' article has deliberately been chosen for its typically enthusiastic outside perspective on Ireland. His readers' approach to Ireland, however, is more intellectual than that of the normal tourist, which tends to be rather romantic. Marseilles' article informs that the Emerald Isle has always enchanted its visitors and it critically introduces them to some well-known stereotypes about the Republic of Ireland as a country. The author himself is obviously fascinated by Ireland's rich cultural, and in particular literary, heritage, but he also presents Ireland as an island with a modern look. The information contained in this article serves as basic knowledge for many of the texts in the anthology.

The collage is intended to allow a third, more visually-oriented approach to Ireland. It takes up some points from Marseilles' article and adds others in order to complete an overall view of Ireland's characteristic traits. Although the visual element dominates, the collage also contains some basic statistics, a famous Irish recipe, and some jokes. It also contains an explanation of the different names for Ireland, which often cause irritation, and a poem by the Nobel Prize winner, Seamus Heaney, which establishes a link with the second sequence.

Sequence Two: A Look Back in Anger

2 | John Tarver "What's up in Ireland?"

text type: (extract from) historical essay
length: 1460 words
degree of difficulty: **; 38 annotations and 32 explanations
theme: a survey of Ireland's history from the beginning to the present day

Percentage of land owned by native Irish in the 17th century
text type: map

3 | Jonathan Swift *A Modest Proposal*

text type: pamphlet
length: 747 words
degree of difficulty: **; 28 annotations and 5 explanations
theme: an ironic proposal to solve the problem of poverty and hunger in Ireland; in fact, an urgent appeal for economic reforms; Swift at his best as a pamphleteer

An Irish scene during the times of eviction; poor Irish family
text type: drawing

Poor Irish farmer's cottage
text type: photograph

additional information about satire

4 | Cecil Woodham-Smith *The Great Hunger*

text type: documentation
length: 1304 words
degree of difficulty: **; 32 annotations and 12 explanations
theme: a moving account of the greatest tragedy in Irish history, based on contemporary sources

"Searching for potatoes"
text type: drawing

"The English labourer's burden"
text type: cartoon

5 | *Cragie Hills*

text type: (traditional) folk song
length: 286 words
degree of difficulty: *; 19 annotations and 6 explanations
theme: an Irish emigration song telling about the wishful thinking that accompanies such a decision

a Bodhran player; Emigrants leaving Cobh
text type: photograph

additional information about eviction and emigration

Whereas **Sequence One** has more of an introductory function and is meant to motivate the students by providing a first, partly more affective access to the theme of this anthology, **Sequence Two** is more concerned with the essential knowledge about Ireland's history which the student requires in order to gain some basic understanding of Ireland's situation today. History is probably more the heart of the matter than anything else when it comes to making sense of today's events in Ireland. For this reason, section two provides the students with a survey of Irish history and presents three texts about landmarks in Irish history, which will form an essential background to the rest of the material in this anthology.

John Tarver's informative short chronology of Irish history, which comes here in an abridged version, not only gives the students a good survey of Ireland's eventful history, but also serves as a framework for the following texts of this unit. Students will thus be able to study three decisive moments in Irish history in depth.

One of Ireland's best-known literary figures, the satirist Jonathan Swift, is the author of *A Modest Proposal*, a poignant pamphlet in which he scourges the social conditions of the poor Irish Catholic peasantry at the time of landlordism (18th century) by proposing that Irish parents should breed their children like cattle and sell them for food to the "fine gentlemen". Swift's outspoken criticism of English rule in Ireland, which is not only evident in this pamphlet, but in all his brilliant satirical writings, might make this text a good starting-point for exploring in more detail the tragic Anglo-Irish relations from their beginnings in 1170 till today.

The great catastrophe of the years 1845–49, known as The Famine or The Great Hunger is described here in an excerpt from Cecil Woodham-Smith's carefully researched book, in which she introduces her readers to the disaster by basing her account of the events on official letters. The impression of immediacy and authenticity conveyed here has a strong emotional appeal for the reader.

The final text in this section, an old folk song, is internally linked with the Famine text since it depicts the immediate consequence of this calamity for the Irish if they wanted to flee starvation: emigration. The folk song has been a particularly powerful medium both for deploring the fate of emigration in many variations and also for expressing the hopes placed in it. In order to deepen their understanding of both the impact of emigration on Irish society and the specific role of music in Irish cultural life, the students are expected

- to study the song and learn from the personal story it tells that unrealistic expectations are often linked to the decision to emigrate,
- to analyse a historical depiction of the often disastrous consequences that the decision to emigrate had for the immigrants to the New World.
- to learn about the importance of music as a means of expression in Ireland.

This last point connects this sequence with the topic of the next sequence, the Celtic Heritage, since love of public singing is also an important and distinguishing feature of the Celtic culture of the Irish.

The Study Aids provide brief additional information about **satire** on p. 19 for an adequate understanding of Swift's text, as do the information boxes on **emigration** and **eviction** on p. 26 for texts 4 and 5.
The Resource Book contains five optional Information Sheets:

Info 1: Swift's Ireland
Info 2: Mercantilism and Laissez-Faire
Info 3: Irish Immigration to the United States by Decade, 1820–1970
Info 4: Ulster-Scots
Info 5: Folklore in Ireland

Info 1 informs the students about Ireland's economic, cultural and political situation at the time of Swift's writing, Info 2 sketches the theoretical economic background to text 4. Statistical information about Irish emigration to the United States is given in Info 3, Info 4 provides additional information about a specific group of emigrants from Northern Ireland, the Ulster-Scots, and Info 5 informs about the tradition of folklore in Ireland. These information sheets help students to facilitate their work on texts 5 (and 6).

Sequence Three: The Celtic Heritage

6 | W. B. Yeats "The Wanderings of Oisin"

text type: (excerpt from) long poem
length: 360 words
degree of difficulty:**; 20 annotations and 8 explanations
theme: the clash between the wild, pagan world of the Celts and Christian Ireland at the time of St. Patrick

A Celtic Warrior (Cúchulainn)
text type: photograph of a mural in Belfast

Ringfort Grianán Ailigh
text type: photograph

additional information about the Celts

7 | James F. Clarity "Gaelic Now Trips off Ireland's Silver Tongues"

text type: newspaper article
length: 704 words
degree of difficulty: *; 13 annotations and 5 explanations
theme: the astonishing revival of the Gaelic language in Ireland

A Gaelic signpost; a road sign indicating you are entering the Ghaeltacht area (where Irish is spoken); a prohibition sign at the beach; another road sign which warns the driver he is approaching a school
text type: photographs

map of the Ghaeltacht areas in the Study Aids, p. 32
text type: map

In this third sequence the students are now given the opportunity to learn about the Celtic roots of Ireland, which make up much of the specific character of Irish life and culture. Since space is limited in this brief anthology, only two documents (three if one counts the folk song in the second section) have been picked to explain the ways in which the Celtic heritage is still alive in modern Ireland. One is an excerpt from a classic of Irish literature; the other is a 1994 newspaper article on the revival of the Irish language.

W. B. Yeats' "The Wanderings of Oisin" depicts a world in the distant Celtic past. It is the world of pre-Christian warriors (Fionn mac Cumhaill and his Fianna) and the people of the Otherworld who live a free and independent life full of earthly joys. Oisin, who was taken to the Otherworld and spent 300 years there, returns to and rejects the Christian Ireland of the present and praises the pagan Celtic Ireland of the Fianna.

In their further studies of W. B. Yeats, the students will learn more about the so-called 'Celtic Revival' that inspired a humiliated Ireland of the 19th century through writings like "The Wanderings of Oisin".

James F. Clarity's article in the *New York Times* points out the surprising fact that the Irish language, which had only been preserved in some so-called Ghaeltacht-areas on the west coast and other pockets in Ireland, is gaining more and more popularity among the Irish.

The illustrations and texts of this sequence will give students a vivid impression of the living traditions of the Irish and will also explain differences between the lifestyle of the Celtic peoples and that of other nations in Western Europe.

An information box about **The Celts** on p. 29 in the Study Aids includes the translation of the Gaelic version of the emblematic poem of the nation of Ireland, which was originally part of the mural on p. 28 in the Study

Texts. Extra information on **'An Ghaeltacht'**, the areas where Irish is still spoken, can be found as part of the Study Aids on p. 32. In addition, the Resource Book contains three optional Information Sheets:

Info 6: Celtic Mythology
Info 7: A Province of Myth and Legend
Info 8: Irish Bilingualism

Info 6 is a synopsis of the mythical history of Ireland, mainly of the three Irish Cycles of mythical stories. Info 7 gives information about some mythological phenomena and Info 8 explains why many people in Ireland speak two languages, Irish and English.

Sequence Four: Ireland on Fast-Forward

8 | Richard Conniff "God Bless You, Father"*

text type: (excerpt from) travel report
length: 677 words
degree of difficulty: **; 24 annotations and 3 explanations
theme: an outsider's personal encounter with the influence of the Catholic Church in Ireland

a bare-footed pilgrim at Croagh Patrick; forty shades of green
text type: photograph

"... and if they allow contraception"
text type: cartoon

an Irish blessing
text type: blessing

additional information about Saint Patrick

9 | Rita Kelly "The Cobweb Curtain"

text type: (excerpt from) short story
length: 2257 words
degree of difficulty: **; 57 annotations and 1 explanation
theme: a reunion with people from her past forces the female protagonist to defend her life

Dilapidated house in the country; another Irish country cottage with peat
text type: photograph

10 | Mary McAleese "Hopes for the New Millenium"

text type: political speech
length: 514 words
degree of difficulty: *; 14 annotations and 4 explanations
theme: The address of the second female Irish president on the occasion of the turn of the millennium

President Mary McAleese
text type: photograph

After looking into the past in the previous two sequences of texts, **Sequence Four** now takes the students into the world of today, allowing them to see the Republic of Ireland in a remarkable transitional phase at the beginning of the 21st century.

No better introduction to this sequence could be found than Makki Marseilles' words in text 1: "A stranger to Ireland might be forgiven if he formed the opinion that Ireland was a wild and distant country wrapped in the misty vapours of North Europe ..." (p. 6). Of course, Ireland may have had the reputation of being on the periphery of Europe and backward when compared to other European countries. However, it would be a grievous error to hang on to this outdated stereotypical image. Since 1973, when the Republic of Ireland joined the E.C., today European Union, Ireland has changed rapidly. EU money has, over the years, helped to modernise the country's infrastructure, and changes in attitude, especially among the well-educated younger population, are gradually turning Ireland into a modern, self-confident, open and pluralistic European country.

This transformation has been taken into consideration when the sequence of texts in this section were arranged.

Richard Conniff's "God Bless You, Father" refers to the fact that roughly 95% of the population in the republic are Catholic and that the Catholic Church has traditionally exerted an enormous influence on Irish society. Yet this influence is being challenged by a growing secularization, mostly among the more cosmopolitan and Europe-oriented younger generation. Richard Conniff's article reveals how profoundly Catholic morality has shaped Irish life.

Although Rita Kelly's short story "Cobweb Curtain" has nothing to do with the Catholic Church as such, it has something in common with text 8 in that it, too, looks at traditions and forms of dealing with them in modern Ireland. Only in this case the text introduces the students to the problem of the position of women in the Republic of Ireland, particularly that of women in rural Ireland. Whereas Mrs Scott represents the traditional role of the farmer's wife and the children's mother, her daughter Julie is clear-eyed, practical and is building up an existence in England. Kate, the apparent protagonist of the story, is caught up in conflicting feelings as to whether she belongs to this or the other world - until she is finally forced to make a decision. The story affords a good opportunity for the students to discuss this issue on the premise of its intercultural relevance.

The final text in this section deals with the reflections of the President of the Republic of Ireland, Mary McAleese, the second female president of Ireland after President Mary Robinson. McAleese looks into the promising future of a fast-developing Ireland with new hopes and perspectives.

The Study Aids provide background information on **Saint Patrick** (p. 35) and on **narrative techniques** (p. 40).

Sequence Five: Northern Ireland and the Story Behind It

11 | "No More Terror?"

text type: political commentary
length: 84 words
degree of difficulty: *; 4 annotations and 2 explanations
theme: a hopeful but sceptical first evaluation of the IRA ceasefire announcement of 31 August 1994

"It's Over"
text type: newspaper front-page

12 | The Good Friday Agreement

text type: legal document
length: 1091 words
degree of difficulty: ***; 39 annotations and 8 explanations
theme: key points of the Good Friday Agreement

"Confidence essential"
text type: editorial

"The Agreement"
text type: photograph

"Confidence in Peace"
text type: graph

13 | Bernard MacLaverty *Cal*

text type: (excerpt from) novel
length: 1172 words
degree of difficulty: **; 55 annotations and 7 explanations
theme: a young boy's nervous wait for an imminent terrorist attack on him

"The Christian Churches in Northern Ireland (2001)"
text type: chart

"Sniper at work"
text type: photograph

Memorial in Belfast
text type: photograph

"Battle of the Boyne"
text type: photograph of a mural

Text 11 of **Sequence Five** marks the beginning of part II of this anthology, which focuses on what usually is the main reason why international attention is turned on Ireland: the situation in Northern Ireland.

Having dealt with sections 1 to 4, the students will have gained some basic knowledge about the common historical and cultural roots of the southern and the northern part of the island. Part II now gives them an opportunity to deepen their understanding of what is happening in Northern Ireland. This fifth section is intended to convey something of the atmosphere in an area of this world that has learned to live between hate and hope, whereas Sequence Six, apart from an interview with representatives of the younger generation, provides the students with two texts that demand a more analytical approach.

The front page of the *Belfast Telegraph* of 31 August 1994, the day of the IRA ceasefire announcement, reveals both the excitement and the scepticism aroused by the announcement of a possible peace.

The Good Friday or Belfast Agreement has become the cornerstone of a peaceful future of Northern Ireland and is the background against which any form of negotiation or its outcome is seen.

Bernard MacLaverty's *Cal* has already become a classic and is used in this sequence because the excerpt chosen is a dramatic depiction of the stifling atmosphere of fear and omnipresent danger which prevail in parts of Northern Ireland.

For extra information on the **IRA**, the **Fenians** and the **Twelfth of July**, see Study Aids pp. 52 ff. To help students understand the complicated background of the Northern Ireland conflict better, the Resource Book includes the following Information Sheets:

Info 9: The 1994 Ceasefire Statements
Info 10: IRA Statement, 28 July 2005
Info 11: Chastelain Report on IRA Decommissioning, 26 September 2005
Info 12: A Short History of the Conflict in Northern Ireland
Info 13: Who is Who? The Four Major Players
Info 14: Jet Log: Irish Murals Illustrate History and Tensions

Info 9 contains the authentic wording of the 1994 ceasefire statements of the IRA and the Loyalist Military Command, while Info 10 is the IRA's proclamation of ending its "armed struggle." Info 11 contains the so-called Chastelain Report, i.e. the International Decommissioning Commission's determination that the IRA has put its weapons beyond use, one of the main demands of the Belfast Agreement. Info 12 looks at the most important historical events that led to the conflict in Northern Ireland. Info 13 presents four short texts which show the historical positions the four main parties in the conflict came from. They are, however, in a process of change as the peace process goes on. Finally, Info 14 allows a look into a private diary which describes the impressions the Belfast murals leave on an overseas visitor.

Sequence Six: Peace in Ireland?

14 | Michael Elliott "Overburdened with History"

text type: monograph
length: 796 words
degree of difficulty: ***; 23 annotations and 25 explanations
theme: a critical comment on the over-emphasis on historic events and their significance for life today in Northern Ireland

Oliver Cromwell mural
text type: mural

Two ladders
text type: cartoon

15 | Interviews with Students from Methodist College

text type: interview
length: 1277 words
degree of difficulty: *; 9 annotations and 7 explanations
theme: a talk about young life in Belfast

The interviewees; building of Methodist College Belfast
text type: photographs

Being Young in Belfast
text type: poems

16 | A Farewell to Arms? From Long War to Uncertain Peace in Northern Ireland

text type: article from non-fictional book
length: 727 words
degree of difficulty: **; 18 annotations and 3 explanations
theme: introduction to a non-fictional book which prepares the ground for a detailed analysis of the Irish peace process and its chances of realization

Sniper: Job Seeking; Peace Memorial, Belfast
text type: photographs

Sequence Six concludes this *Viewfinder* volume first with Michael Elliott's shrewd meditations on the tragic effects that overemphasizing history and tradition might have. What follows is a refreshing interview with young fourth and sixth formers from Methodist College Belfast, a distinguished grammar school with a reputation for academic excellence which is open to all students irrespective of their denomination or ethnic background. This is accompanied by some moving poems by three second formers at the same school. The final text in this sequence and of the anthology as a whole is an extract from the introduction to an in-depth scientific analysis of the situation in Northern Ireland after the Good Friday Agreement which discusses the chances of lasting peace there.

This final section will acquaint the students with the particular difficulties which a peaceful island still has to face but also the hopes which must be nursed to believe in this peace, especially among the younger generation of the troubled province of Northern Ireland. And, indeed, there are initiatives to change things for the better, as the additional material of this section reveals.

The Resource Book contains the following optional Information Sheets:

Info 15: What Foreigners Think of Ireland
Info 16: Building the Peace. A Community Relations Project in Belfast
Info 17 Education for Mutual Understanding and Cultural Heritage
Info 18: Millward Brown Ulster Opinion Poll March 2005
Info 19: Irish WWW-Sites of Interest
Info 20: Glossary and Abbreviations

Info 15 contains extracts from a newspaper article about guest workers in the Republic of Ireland and what they have to say about their experiences there. Info 16 gives the name, address and aims of a Belfast Community Relations Group as an example of constructive grassroots peace work. Info 17 focuses on the curricular elements of the special Northern Ireland programme of Education for Mutual Understanding (EMU). Info 18 provides information on a 2005 public opinion poll in Northern Ireland about the peace process and how it affects their lives. Info 19 lists some interesting Irish Internet Sites which might provide useful information, particularly for project work. Finally, Info 20 helps students to better understand the many terms, names and short forms of organizations, etc in the Northern Ireland context.

To sum up: the Students' Book and the Resource Book provide a wide range of carefully related building blocks which can be combined in numerous ways to suit the specific needs of any given course. It should be stressed again that there is a logical progression in the sequences so that the course would profit most if the sequences were followed in the given order. However, it is perfectly possible for each section to be worked independently if this fits in with the requirements of particular classes.

The so-called Northern Ireland conflict and its recent development towards a peaceful future might therefore be dealt with separately by only working on the texts of part II (Sequences Five and Six), as they can be regarded as a self-contained unit. If, however, the students are to acquire a comprehensive understanding of the issue and to realize the degree to which present problems are conditioned by past events and developments, at least Sequences One and Two should be studied first, because they provide the relevant background knowledge for part II.

A teacher might well prefer to begin with Ireland's Celtic background and work his/her way up chronologically, following the material on Irish history provided in the Students' Book.

Another possibility might be to begin with texts 9 and 10, which both give the female perspective special emphasis and thus allow quite a different approach to the topic.

Teaching Strategies

The study of *Ireland – A Story of Beauty and Hope* is intended to combine foreign language learning with a deeper insight into Irish cultural phenomena and attitudes. The Cultural Studies concept followed in this *Viewfinder* collection might be called cross-cultural or intercultural learning as it brings the students into contact with foreign culture by permanently confronting them with their own personal and cultural frame of reference. It leads them to question their own familiar modes of thought and assumptions and thus helps create an awareness of other cultural values and the 'relativity' of their own culture. One hopes, all this will contribute to the creation of intercultural understanding which is essential in a world where nations are becoming more and more interrelated.

Bearing that in mind, texts, whether they are expository statements or literary accomplishments, cannot simply be taken as different forms of information about an unfamiliar culture. Texts become vehicles for self-reflection and possible change in that they are not only 'texts about' something, but texts that, in the medium of language or illustration, determine and change perceptions and thus change reality since they also explore the assumptions and beliefs that the students and the teacher bring to the class. In other words, during their studies of the individual texts of this volume, students will again and again – and from very different perspectives – be required to compare the issues addressed in the texts with their situation in their own cultural context.

The successful exploration of the interplay between the foreign-language text and its cultural and historical background presupposes considerable knowledge that the learner, of course, cannot have. This is why the Resource Book puts the main accent on the 'what' and not on the 'how' of teaching. It provides short but detailed commentaries on each text as well as relevant information about its cultural context, while abstaining from giving all-too-obvious methodological advice.

However, the *Viewfinder* concept sets out a basic scheme to make course work easier for students and teachers alike and provide procedural recommendations for classroom activities and home assignments where they seem advisable. By putting the accent on student-oriented, oral, pair or group work, the task sections of the Study Aids are designed to invite students to develop responses to them and to encourage the comparative approach explained above.

It can be assumed that the practising EFL-teacher will be aware of the range of approaches and strategies designed to allow reflection and lively classroom discussions and also promote understanding of the given texts. Still, it might be worth mentioning some of the less commonly used approaches to texts in order to promote more flexibility and creativity in the work on the texts as well as advance the interaction between the students themselves and the students and the teacher:

- plenary or group 'brainstorming' sessions,
- individual reading on the basis of pre-reading tasks involving deduction of meanings from contexts,
- mind-mapping or topic-mapping,
- cloze procedure,
- affective approaches and creative responses,
- staging of texts, using acting, miming, music, dance,
- interactive group work on text fragments,
- multi-media presentation,
- integrating exterior elements like illustrations, different text types, relevant internet information, etc.

It should go without saying that every practising teacher knows that whatever recommendations are made, they need to be modified to suit the needs of the particular course, individual learners and, of course, the personality of the teacher. It is up to the teacher to decide upon the most effective and appropriate methods of achieving the aims set out in this anthology. The same is true for the use of the task sections, as it is not necessary for all the questions and tasks to be dealt with. It is for the teacher and the students to decide which ones they wish to concentrate on.

The questions and tasks following each text are carefully structured in six phases. They form a progression from an opening phase intended to create an awareness of the topic of the text via comprehension and analysis, to a point where students are able to formulate their personal opinions. Additional projects provide opportunities for independent activities, in which students are intellectually and creatively challenged.

Awareness

For students to understand, interpret and appreciate a text, it has come to be recognised that pre-reading tasks and activities have an important role to play. They are meant to let the interpretation of the following text unfold within the intellectual, emotional and experiential horizon of each individual reader. Since advanced foreign language learners are expected to deal with

- texts that are written in a foreign language (linguistic distance)
- texts that belong to a strange and only partly understood culture (cultural distance), and
- texts that refer to an unfamiliar historical and geographical context (historical distance) it may be advisable not to let them approach these texts without some preparatory activities.

In addition, pre-reading activities are intended to make the students aware of their previous knowledge (or lack of it), recognise their expectations and prejudices, and increase the scope of their imagination when embarking on a new text. It should be mentioned at this point that awareness tasks in this *Viewfinder* collection are particularly designed to emphasise the affective approach to the various texts by taking into account a holistic approach to learning and, wherever possible, aiming at a personal involvement of the students in the topic. Nevertheless, the tasks offered under 'awareness' should be understood as general suggestions that might be tailored to the given course and the specific situation.

Comprehension

When a student approaches a text that is written in a foreign and only partly mastered language, it is essential to understand the linguistic and cultural elements in this text before forming judgments about it. In order to make this task easier for the students, the Study Aids provide an extensive 'vocabulary' and detailed cultural and historical 'explanations'. Regardless of this immediate help, it is suggested, however, that students should be trained in the use of appropriate monolingual dictionaries or in the deduction of meanings from contexts. As 'comprehension' in this limited sense is the precondition for any textual analysis, it is not dealt with in the Resource Book in detail, but since the Study Aids contain relevant 'comprehension' questions students might organise their ideas and allow the teacher to check whether basic understanding of the text has been achieved.

Analysis

The ability to analyse a text plays an important role in the requirements of the Abitur, where students are expected to demonstrate their ability not only to comprehend but also to examine a given text with regard to both what it says and how it is said. Consequently, text analysis is the basis of interaction with the text and forms the centre of course work. Since it is meant to be done within a Cultural Studies approach, it cannot be limited to intrinsic aspects alone, but must consider the text as the articulation of particular cultural values in a certain historical context. For this phase, too, 'analysis' questions are provided.

Opinion

If text analysis is considered as a transactional activity against the individual reader's experiential background, it is equally important that the students are given the opportunity, and are encouraged, to voice their reactions and opinions. Since this can easily be misunderstood as the voicing of an unconsidered reaction or prejudice, the 'opinion' questions in the *Viewfinder* series are designed to guide the students towards a well-considered presentation of their opinions and judgments in an adequately verbalised way, either individually or through negotiation and discussion.

Projects

Finally, it is often desirable and possible to go beyond the analysis of a text and the formulation of a personal view, to carry out further research or initiate an activity in the form of a project. This can involve further individual work or group activity for which the individuals or groups take fuller responsibility. In its simpler forms, this may just call for extra reading or library work or – as 'projects' in the true sense of the term – lead to activities outside the classroom, such as the interviewing of relevant persons, the putting together of a newspaper, conducting a survey or organizing an exhibition. This type of work offers scope for variety and individual initiative as well as a more holistic approach towards the issue, and deepens the sense of involvement with the material. Such activities, of course, depend on the individual teaching situation, but here, too, the Study Aids offer some suggestions, and the Resource Book provides further material to help carrying them out. In addition, in the new edition a number of internet-based projects enlarge the scope of more student-centered activities which also meet the need for practising independent research and study work as demanded in new examination forms like *Präsentationsprüfung*, for example. Moreover, they are meant not only to introduce modern forms of learning into the classroom but also to acquaint the students with both the enormous opportunities and the potential pitfalls which Internet-based research entails.

The questions and tasks for each text therefore constitute an elementary guideline, which might be suitably combined with the further material provided in the Study Aids and the optional Information Sheets contained in the Resource Book.

Getting the Course Started

There are, of course, many different ways of beginning a course on Ireland. Which of them proves most appropriate will depend on the abilities and limitations of the members of a given course, on the themes with which the course has dealt, and on their familiarity with Irish issues in particular. Issues in the news or current concerns may provide a suitable opening, but the teacher or the members of the course may have their own reasons why and how they should embark upon this topic.

One rather unusual but promising way of starting this topic is to begin with a fantasy journey that, in the form of a simulation supported by music and words, takes the students into an imaginative situation in Ireland, such as a walk along the coast or a visit to an old monastery, and prepares them on a more affective level to open their minds for the rewarding exploration of the fascinating idiosyncrasy of a foreign country.

For teachers who have neither the time nor the inclination to engage in this or other preparatory activities but prefer to enter in *medias res*, an interpretation of the Title Page and the introductory section with its many visual stimulations on pp. 4 and 5 might prove the shortest introduction to the material in that students try to work out the meaning of the different aspects presented in the title, the text and the photos. For detailed information about the introductory part see "Teaching Resources" in this Resource Book. To structure this approach, the teacher might find it useful to draw the students' attention to the awareness tasks of text 1 and thus help them find their way into the topic. In order to present a more differentiated picture of the country, the course might well first continue the visual encounter with Ireland by exploiting the collage on pp. 8 and 9, before starting the text work of text 1.

Starting the course using the title page will allow the students to get an initial idea of the beauty and tranquility of the landscape along the west coast of Ireland. It is here where visitors to Ireland feel they have finally arrived in Ireland. The colour photograph presents an idealistic and tranquil rural scene with an old white cottage overlooking the quiet blue sea on a beautiful summer day. This is exactly the cliché that is so widespread among foreigners and that is therefore favoured by the advertising industry. However, it cannot be denied that this is Ireland, since travelling along the Irish west coast the visitor will indeed see this scene again and again or others of equally romantic charm. The picture is meant to stand not only for Ireland's scenic beauty but Ireland's beauty in a more sophisticated sense as can then be seen on pp. 4 and 5: its cultural achievements like its literature, music and art, its old customs, its mysterious language, and its architecture, which includes both Dublin's Georgian houses and the ruins of old monasteries far out in the country. Apart from that, it also refers to the highly praised friendliness, hospitality and sociability of the Irish.

Nevertheless, there is also the other face of the island as the big rocks in the foreground of the title page photo already indicate, and which the students will become fully aware of when they see the gunman on top of p. 5 with his gun pointing right at them, or the IRA-writing on the wall warning England not to believe the war in Northern Ireland is over. However, it is the word *Hope* that dominates the page and it is the "hands across the divide" that directs the students to the more recent developments on the island which are dealt with in the last part of this anthology.

Another, yet more sophisticated and challenging opening of a unit on Ireland on the basis of this Viewfinder anthology, may be an exploration of the famous line "A terrible beauty is born" from W. B. Yeats' poem **"Easter 1916"** as it directs the students towards a milestone of Irish history and one of the crucial events that has left its scars on the island until today. The quotation is actually the last line of three stanzas and also the final line of the poem. Yeats wrote this poem on 25 April 1916, shortly after the Easter Rebellion of April 1916, in the aftermath of which, 15 men, among them their leaders James Connolly and Patrick Pearse, were executed. It is the irony of a heroic but finally pointless sacrifice that Yeats wants to reveal and that comes up in many of his other poems. He, in fact, wrote a letter to his long-time friend, Maude Gonne, mentioning "both the 'lunacy' and the 'heroic, tragic' aspect of the rebels' action and their fate."[3] What had happened?

When the First World War broke out in 1914, a strong Irish resistance movement against British influence in Ireland, mainly borne by The Irish Republican Brotherhood, saw an opportunity to take action. Among them was Patrick Pearse, who, in particular, argued that a blood sacrifice would inspire the Irish to a final struggle for freedom. An IRB military council finally decided on Easter Monday 1916 as the time for the insurrection. Armed rebels from across Ireland went to Dublin to reinforce the revolutionaries led by Connnolly and Pearse, whose task it was to divert the attention of British troops until the rebels' arrival. But when the British discovered the twenty thousand rifles that the rebels had secretly ordered in Germany the orders for the Easter Rising were countermanded by the chief of staff of the rebel army. Pearce and Connolly, however, decided to continue their part of the action and seized the General Post Office in Dublin and some other public buildings around it, with some eighteen hundred soldiers. Pearce proclaimed an independent Republic of Ireland. Their action was doomed to failure from the beginning because of bad organization and little support from a stupefied Dublin population. However, the brutal execution of the 15 leaders of the rebellion by the British increased anti-British sentiment. The Easter Rising, famed in song and poem, was followed by a bloody War of Independence against the British, which, accompanied by a Civil War, finally brought the division of Ireland with the Irish Free State in the south, and Northern Ireland a part of Britain.

Yeats reacted strongly to the event and the executions. His poem "Easter 1916" was written in honour of the rebels, among whom were personal friends, but he also feared the violence and extremism that they had fostered among those Irishmen who looked on the rebels as martyrs so that he withheld his poem from general publication for a number of years.

[3] William H. O'Donnell, *The Poetry of William Butler Yeats. An Introduction* (New York: Ungar, 1986), p. 75.

The rather ambiguous refrain "A terrible beauty is born" that also ends the poem, must primarily be understood in the light of Yeats' view of the rebels. The complete sense unit reads as follows:

"I write it out in verse –
MacDonagh and MacBride,
And Connolly and Pearse
Now and in time to be,
Are changed, changed utterly:
A terrible beauty is born."[4]

In these lines, Yeats is summing up what he is predominantly occupied with in his poem, namely the various changes that the rebels' death has brought about, most of all for themselves: "The refrain suggests [...] some of those changes are favorable and some are distinctly unfavorable. The only certainty is that Easter 1916 was the occasion for profound change. The poem leaves as an open question the extent to which the named rebels should be regarded as heroes who have won immortal fame or as impractical fools who are dead."[5]

But the event also brought change to Ireland. And just as change for the executed rebels was favourable and unfavourable at the same time, the ambiguity of the refrain suggests that the future of Ireland cannot be predicted. The final lines of the first stanza "All changed, changed utterly: /A terrible beauty is born" unequivocally point to the enigmatic uncertainty that Ireland has faced since the events of 1916. Still, the rebels' death will never be forgotten in Ireland.

> Der Aufstand verhalf dem irischen Freiheitskampf zu Märtyrern, und Yeats' Gedicht trug viel dazu bei, sie unsterblich zu machen; es personalisiert den Aufstand, mythisiert Geschichte, schafft Schönheit aus Schrecken.[6]

Looking at some ninety years of Irish history from today's point of view, one has to acknowledge Yeats' impressive poetical insight in these two lines. Yeats' ambiguous words expressing his hopes and fears about the effects of the rebels' actions might be understood as still valid for the situation in Ireland today as Part Two (Texts 11–16) will reveal.

[4] W. B. Yeats, *The Collected Works of W. B. Yeats, vol. I. The Poems Revised*, ed. Richard J. Finneran (New York: Macmillan, 1990), p. 182.
[5] William H. O'Donnell, *The Poetry of William Butler Yeats*, p. 82.
[6] Bruno von Lutz, "'Terrible Beauty'", *Neue Zürcher Zeitung*, 28./29. September 1996, p. 51.

Media

A wide range of visual materials on Ireland is available on the internet or from video shops in Ireland or the U.K. and even Germany at reasonable prices. The British Council Centre have videotapes or DVDs that may be ordered for use at schools; see www.brithishcouncil.de for details.

Three thematically related videos should be mentioned more specifically, however. There is the widely acclaimed four part 1995 documentary on the Irish Famine (see text 4) (abbreviated version, 1h) *When Ireland Starved*, produced by Radharc/RTE Radharc Films and distributed by Chart Records, 5/6 Lombard St. East Dublin 2, available now at http://www.irishmusicmail.com. A multimedia version, which includes a complete teaching unit on this topic with teaching strategies and activities, can be found on the internet under http://www.irishhistorydvd.org/Famine/. Secondly *Out of Ireland. The Story of Irish Emigration to America* by Paul Wagner, Shanachie Entertainment, U.S.A. (111 minutes), is available at http://www.amazon.com. Thirdly George Morrison's acclaimed 1959 *Mise Éire*, based on the Patrick Pearse poem "Mise Éire", which deals with the revolutionary movement in Ireland between 1896 and 1918.

Other documentaries worth mentioning for use in the classroom are *The Celts – Rich Traditions & Ancient Myths* (1987), Director: David Richardson, or Gil Rosselioni's *The Kickhams* (http://www.rottentomatoes.com/m/enemy_mine_northern_ireland_the_kickhams/), a documentary about a tightknit nationalist community in loyalist North Belfast that could expand the disussion about MacLaverty's *Cal*. The sequence "Peace in Ireland"? could be enriched with *Sons of Derry*, a documentary on the efforts of Glen Barr, a Protestant, and Paddy Doherty, a Catholic, to overcome the bitterness of the past in Derry. An ITV production from 1993, *When Did You Last See Your Father?*, brings the viewer face to face with the aftermath of many of those murders in Northern Ireland that are only too easily forgotten (see Text 13, Analysis 9).

Apart from these documentary films, there are some recommendable "edutainment" films, such as Jim Sheridan's *The Field*, which looks at such aspects as the Famine, evictions or land reform from an Irish peasant's point of view, or John Ford's *The Quiet Man* (1952; released on video 1985). Set in a rural community in the twenties, *The Quiet Man* follows the fortunes of Paddy Bawn Enright, who returned to Ireland after having made his way in America. The film is a classic and has moulded the vision of Ireland, its people and its countryside for many people outside Ireland. The picture *Into the West* tells, in a modern version, the old Oisin and Neamh story (see text 6), whereas Thaddeus O'Sullivan's *December Maid* (1990) might underline the message of Rita Kelly's "Cobweb Curtain" (see text 9). It is a film about a strong young woman who, at the turn of the century, fights for her way of life against the moral standards of her time. *Far and Away*, starring Tom Cruise, takes up the story of the emigration song *Cragie Hills* and portrays a young Irish couple that fight their way through the hardships suffered by Irish newcomers to the U.S.A. during the 1800s. Among the most successful Irish films R. J. Flaherty's *Man of Aaran* (1934) and Jim Sheridan's *In the Name of the Father* (1993) must be included. One should not forget to mention Neil Jordan's award-winning *Michael Collins* (1996), the epic portrayal of the controversial life and death of this Irish patriot and founding father of the Free Irish State (1922). The problems of modern Ireland are masterly (and amusingly) depicted in the three films based on Roddy Doyle's successful novels *The Commitments*, *The Snapper*, and *Fish and Chips*. One of the most successful films about the Irish in recent years and a fine analysis of the Irish character was *Long Live Ned Devine* (also known as *Waking Ned Devine*) (1998). For more information about Irish fiction films see *The Irish Filmography: Fiction Films 1896–1996* (Dublin: Red Mountain Media, 1996).

Among many others, the following cassettes might be useful as far as modern Irish literature is concerned: Seamus Heaney, *The Spirit Level*, read by Seamus Heaney (London: Faber and Penguin Audiobooks, 1996), *Classic Irish Short Stories*, read by T. P. McKenna (London: CSA Telltapes, 1996), *Woman's Hour Short Stories*, BBC Radio Collection (London: BBC Worldwide, 1996). A cassette which offers an authentic account on "Growing up in Derry in the '60s" by Sean Mullan is available from the author as may be others, for example, on "Living in Donegal" or a full recording of the interviews with the students from Methodist College Belfast (see Text 15).

One should not forget the almost endless number of Irish folksongs and also Irish rock music that have much to contribute to educational purposes on this level. The texts of hundreds of folksongs make many references to Irish history, specific events and Irish dreams, frustrations, hopes and hardships. Irish folk festivals in Germany provide another chance of experiencing the fact that in Ireland history and song are one. CDs of almost any Irish group or singer can be obtained at CeDisc, Am Hirtenberg 14, 37136 Bösinghausen. Among many others, the following songbooks might help with the texts: *Irish Songs Of Resistance 1169–1923*, by Patrick Galvin (New York: OAK Publications, 1962); Frederik Hetmann, *Irische Lieder und Balladen* (Frankfurt am Main: Fischer Taschenbuch, 1979); Jake Walton, *Keltische Folksongs* (Fischer Taschenbuch, 1983).

Finally, with the growth of the internet, many interesting internet projects on Ireland or the events in Northern Ireland have been worked on and uploaded by school classes. Teachers may wish to search the internet for up-to-date examples, or refer to the **LINKFINDER** (www.langenscheidt.de/elt).

Those schools or teachers that are hooked up to a satellite dish may profit from live radio programs on RTE Cork on channel 26 or Irish Sat Radio on channel 27, both on satellite frequency band 11538 via the Astra satellite.

Internet Projects

All the websites (URLs) mentioned as sources of information for project work have been carefully researched. There can, however, due to the nature of their complexity and subjection to changes at source, be no guarantee once they have been printed that they remain constant. Should anyone experience difficulty, VIEWFINDER offers a a unique service supporting the series with an index of interesting websites relevant to the Topics and Literature titles and themes. LINKFINDER is an online library available via the Langenscheidt homepage in which all Internet addresses are checked and updated on a regular basis. The list includes all those URLs suggested as sources for project work.

Access to LINKFINDER can be gained either via search engines and the word *Linkfinder* or via the Langenscheidt homepage: www.langenscheidt.de/elt, then *Lehrwerke – Viewfinder* and the *More Infos* button. Then *Linkfinder*.

Teaching Resources

Introduction
Ireland – A Story of Beauty and Hope

The Text

This short introductory text, enriched by a collage of significant Irish motifs, is divided into two parts: the first part depicts an Ireland that is much cherished by the romanticists, whereas the second part on p. 5 shows a more realistic side of this island. Ireland is changing and the visitor who is looking for the thatched cottage that used to be so typical of Ireland in former years will have problems finding one, because Ireland has made great leaps forward within the last 25 years or so. The same change will be realized when looking at Northern Ireland that has so long been recognized for its incomprehensible conflict only. Considerable progress has been made towards a lasting peace in the never-ending story of this conflict. The Republic of Ireland is in transition. It has come forward to play an important role in Europe and the world and the efforts for an end of the Northern Ireland conflict seem to be crowned with success. Yet, Ireland would not be Ireland, if things just went straight in this country. This island will always be a little paradise for many people, as the first part on p. 4 claims and it will always have to nurse the hope that one day there will be lasting peace in Northern Ireland, which is rather fragile at the time being. Anyhow, after centuries of war and poverty Ireland's hopes are gradually coming true. This introductory text hints at all the aspects that will be dealt with in detail in the following texts and offers a first overview to students of what they will expect in the course of this anthology.

The Photos

The 14 photos have been chosen to underline the message of the text. They are meant to enable the students to "see" what the title of this anthology *Ireland – A Story of Beauty and Hope* implies and what the text tries to convey. At the same time they hint at many of the topics discussed in the following texts of this anthology.

- The central photo shows the beauty of the Irish countryside on a wonderful early morning and illustrates the first keyword of the title: "beauty". It is characteristic of the Irish countryside with its water, moorland and rolling hills in the background.
- At the top of p. 4 students will see two photos which indicate the deep religiosity of many Irish people. Celtic crosses can be found all over Ireland and are characteristic of Irish cemeteries. The idea of the design is a relict from Celtic times but has been taken into Christian cemetery culture. One of the oldest Celtic crosses is the Cross of Muiredach in Monasterboice in the east of Ireland (more about that cross can be found on p. 12 in the Students' Book). The photo next to it shows a glassbowl with a plastic replica of the Holy Mary. This kind of grave decoration may look naïve, especially as it is often made of plastic, like plastic flowers or red plastic hearts, but it shows a special religious dedication that is deeply felt. The photo of the fuchsias has been picked for the rich fauna of Ireland and particularly the fuchsia could be called the "national" flower of the Republic of Ireland (which, of course, is the shamrock) as fuchsias grow wild in Ireland and, unlike other countries of less favourable climate, this plant can be found all around Ireland, even alongside the roads.
- Lower left is the memorial of James Joyce as it can be seen in one of the Dublin streets. Joyce stands for the rich Irish culture, in particular its contributions to world literature which go along with names like Swift, Joyce, Yeats, O'Casey, Beckett, Heaney, and many more.
- The photo in the right hand corner of p. 4, the colourful houses, vividly illustrates the love of colour of the Irish. It may well be – as some people say – that the Irish like to use bright colours to cheer up surroundings that are often made grey and gloomy by rain and fog.
- Looking at the photos on p. 5 from bottom to top we come across a Gaelic greeting that the visitor will see at Galway airport. It points to text 7 in which students will learn more about the native language of the Irish.
- Irish hospitality, love of socializing, drink and music are symbolized in the three photos of Leo's Tavern in Crolly, Co. Donegal, a so-called singing-pub, home of world-famous singer Enya and the folk band "Clannad", the eye-catching, manifold display of pub-signs which are very common all over Ireland and a street musician, an Irish institution in many a town.
- Finally, and that points to the main message of p. 5 and the second part of the book, students are confronted with the situation in Northern Ireland. The word "hope" stands out on this page and corresponds with the photo entitled "Hands across the divide". This is a memorial situated in Londonderry and is, indeed, intended to raise hopes for better understanding and peace between the two communities in Northern Ireland. But it is only hope and hopes can be thwarted. There are still manifestations of the conflict in the Northern Ireland of 2005 as the photo of the gunman (a mural in the Protestant Shankill area of Belfast) and the graffiti on a wall in Londonderry demonstrate. (See also Information Sheet 14: "Jet Log: Irish murals illustrate history and tensions.") Peace in the troubled province

is fragile, just like the dove of peace in the small picture on the right is, but the dove also symbolizes hope and hope is what Northern Ireland needs as President McAleese says: "I have a deep hope it is a journey many more will commit to as we attempt to build new friendships and partnerships ..." (see, Students' Book, p. 42, ll. 45–47)

1 Makki Marseilles "Impressions of Ireland"

text type: (excerpt from) feature
length: 875 words
degree of difficulty: ***; 28 annotations and 41 explanations
theme: an ardent 'declaration of love' by an Ireland enthusiast that provides a fine overview of the characteristic traits of Ireland

related visual material: postcard "Céad Mile Fajlte", a common greeting in Ireland; photograph of a landscape in Co. Galway, an island off the Irish west coast; photograph of a metal inscription on a Dublin pavement referring to James Joyce's *Ulysses*; photograph of Grafton Street, Dublin

additional material: collage
text type: collage
length: 677 words
degree of difficulty: *; 41 annotations and 9 explanations
theme: a visual and verbal kaleidoscope of Ireland's past and present.
Visual material: stamp in the Gaelic language; the coat of arms of the four provinces of Ireland; photograph of cattle in front of a modern plant; map of Ireland; photograph of musicians playing traditional Irish music in a singing pub; photograph of a modern industrial estate; photograph of the Cross of Muiredach, Monasterboice, Co. Louth, one of the most beautiful Irish High Crosses; collection of paintings of famous Irish writers; photograph of St Kevin's Church (Glendalough, Co. Wicklow), a monastic site from the sixth century; photograph of a hurling match, a widely played Irish sport; drawing of Irish saying; photograph of the Rock of Cashel, Co. Tipperary, a centre of religious and secular power.
Written material: information box about the different names for Ireland; traditional Irish recipe: Irish Stew; statistics about Ireland (2003); poem "Digging" by Nobel Prize winner Seamus Heaney; joke about "an Irishman's approach to a problem"; Irish humorous saying about the climate in Ireland

The preceding observations on creating a general awareness of the topic will have made apparent that if we talk about Ireland we must take a closer and a more differentiated look at it in order not to simply understand it as just another troublespot in the world. It makes sense now to turn to some facts and figures about Ireland as a whole, the Republic and Northern Ireland, the land and the people, and the question why Ireland has such "seductive powers" as Makki Marseilles states in his text.

Background to the Text: Basic Information about Ireland

Ireland is an island situated in the north-west of Europe, west of Britain with the Irish Sea between them. The total area is 84,421 square kilometres, of which 70,282 square kilometres belong to the Republic and 14,139 square kilometres to Northern Ireland. Mountainous coastal regions and hills in the interior parts surround a large central lowland with its characteristic areas of bog and loughs.

The island's climate is mainly influenced by the Gulf Stream, which, together with the winds predominantly from the south-west, allows a mild climate that enables palm trees to grow in the south-west. The annual rainfall between 800 and 1200 mm is often exaggerated as typical of Ireland while the average 5 to 7 hours of sunshine per day in May and June, for example, are not too well known among foreigners.

Ireland is part of the so-called 'Celtic fringe' that forms a crescent running from the south-west to the north of the British Isles, including Cornwall, Wales, Ireland, and Scotland. Historically, this is the part of the British Isles that neither the Romans nor the Germanic invaders of the post-Roman times (from about 449 A.D. onwards), the Angles, Saxons, and Jutes, ever conquered. Accordingly, Celtic culture and even the Celtic language, the Gaelic, or Goidelic, was able to survive in some pockets in this 'Celtic fringe' until today. Of all the constituent parts of the United Kingdom it was only the Republic of Ireland that broke away from the British state, first as the Irish Free State in 1922, and then by the Republic of Ireland Act in 1948, as the fully independent and sovereign Republic of Ireland, while Northern Ireland, like Scotland and Wales, is part of the United Kingdom.

Northern Ireland came into existence when in 1921, after a brutal war of independence against Britain, the Anglo-Irish Treaty gave the six Ulster counties, where most of the Protestants were afraid of being a minority in a Catholic country, the right to opt out of the Irish Free State. This was the name given to the twenty-six counties of 'Southern Ireland' which had voted for Sinn Féin (republican) candidates. The parliament in Belfast immediately took advantage of this option and continued in political union with Britain as 'Northern Ireland'. Ever since, Ireland, that is the island of Ireland, has been politically divided into a southern part, the Republic of Ireland (Eire), and a northern part, Northern Ireland or simply (and geographically as well as politically not quite correctly) called Ulster. Just as the political split over the treaty led Ireland into civil war as an immediate reaction, the over 80 years of division in Ireland have split the North and the South in many important questions, such as identity, peripherality and Celticism.

The Republic of Ireland's economy has traditionally been based on agriculture with most of the population living in rural areas. Especially as a result of massive aid from the European Union since it joined the European Community in 1973, the Republic's manufacturing and service industries have been increasing in importance and have helped modernise the country. Today about half of the Republic's workers are employed in such services as education, health care, insurance, real estate, or tourism-related businesses like hotels or restaurants. Trade, transport, and communication have also contributed to the hitherto unknown economic prosperity of the South. Northern Ireland, on the other hand, after its industrialisation in the 19th century provided its population with great wealth compared to the poor rural south, has been undergoing a long and deep economic recession since about the mid-1970s. Along with rival ethnic, religious, cultural and social thinking the high unemployment rate must be considered one of the main causes of the permanent threat of violence in Northern Ireland.

More and more people from abroad find their way to the Emerald Isle. Tourism is a growing economic sector with expenditure by tourists to the Republic of Ireland in 2004 of almost € 4.2 billion. Whereas in 1994, 3.6 million overseas visitors came to the island, in 2004 6.5 million visitors from other countries came over. Tourism has turned out to be especially important to the formerly disadvantaged areas mainly along the west coast which, for geographical reasons, could neither be used for agriculture nor industrial development. (The Irish Tourist Board (Bord Fáilte Éireann) is the main government agency for the marketing of tourism abroad.)

Most people, of course, come for the natural beauties of the country, chiefly in the 'wild west'. Their destinations are rugged Donegal, the supreme scenic grandeur of Connemara, stretching westwards of Galway City to the sea, the breathtaking Cliffs of Moher in Co. Clare or the number one tourist spot, the Ring of Kerry in the south-west. Thousands of less known areas all over the country like the many lakes, the hills, the moors, the River Shannon are beauty spots that only the unhurried visitor will find and fall in love with immediately. Hundreds of abbeys, monastic sites, churches, Celtic crosses, Round Towers, but also castles, still in operation or as ruins, fortresses and even pre-historic stone battlements are signs of a living past that attract other tourists. Others come for quite different reasons: to listen to Irish folk music in the so-called 'Singing Pubs' or to visit the many folk festivals around the country, or they may wish to learn the Gaelic language in a summer course at University College Galway or do the famous Dublin Literary Pub Crawl. In addition, they might wish to go to the world-famous Abbey Theatre or to see one of the great treasures of the world, the illuminated Book of Kells in Trinity College, itself an architectural jewel in the European City of Culture of 1991.

The Text and the Collage

Makki Marseilles was born a Greek, but was educated in Britain; his wife is Irish. He may therefore be seen as a fine example of the outside beholder of Ireland, just like any visitor to the country, but one with a profound knowledge of its distinctive features. He, too, is fascinated by this country, but unlike many tourists who will leave Ireland with only a more or less superficial impression of a "beautiful country" he is able to tell us why. His is a more intellectual approach that answers the question why, apart from its natural beauty, it is worthwhile putting Ireland not only on one's travel agenda but also why one should turn one's attention to Irish Studies as a multifarious programme of learning.

Marseilles' article in *Practical English Teaching*, a British magazine for teachers of English all over the world, gives a fine overview of the characteristic features of Ireland today and serves as a framework for many of the texts in this anthology.

The article has a very simple logical structure. The author introduces the reader to the country by giving prominence to something that most of its visitors will have noticed themselves: Ireland's "seductive powers" (ll. 5f.) which have influenced almost everybody who has ever set foot on Irish soil, even its conquerors. The author then summarises the most prominent features of a country that many believe they know but only a few really do. The changes that have taken place in recent years in Ireland will cause visitors to at least review long-fostered stereotypes about this "wild and distant country wrapped in the misty vapours of North Europe" (ll. 11f.), although some of those stereotypes, such as the talkativeness of the Irish, for example, cannot be denied. Before he tells us more about these changes in the part of the text entitled "Great returns", however, the author paints in bright colours what he obviously considers to be the heart of Ireland: Dublin. Dublin's conspicuous position among Irish towns as the gateway to the world has brought its own cosmopolitan flavour to this city. Apart from its great architecture, it is in particular its living literary tradition that is characteristic of Dublin. A long line of writers has not only enriched the cultural life of Dublin and Ireland but also contributed impressively to world literature in general. Marseilles lists the names of the many famous literary figures that Ireland has brought forth, while he pays only little tribute to the Ireland beyond Dublin. In the next paragraph he refers to a well-known tourist attraction, the "gift of the gab" (l. 83), that many visitors hope to achieve by kissing the Blarney Stone at Blarney Castle, near Cork. Marseilles asserts that just as it is impossible to really acquire "the gift of the gab", i.e. the eloquence that the Irish are famous for, it is almost impossible for a foreigner to understand the Irish outlook on life. In the final part of his feature the author again takes up the point he made at the beginning of the text and briefly explains why the new Ireland has a right to be looked at as a modern and future-oriented European country.

Although this summary cannot go into the above-mentioned aspects in detail, it should have become clear by now that Ireland as a topic of cultural background studies needs a differentiated and more cautious treatment than is often adopted. In order to support this predominantly educational aim, students should be made aware of the fact that when talking about "the essence of Irishness" for example (**Analysis 6**), they are dealing with the difficult subject of national character. It should be made clear at this point that there is, indeed, something like the phenomenon of 'Irishness', as many attempts to define it indicate[7], and it possibly includes some of the attitudes mentioned by Marseilles, but by no means must his tongue-in-cheek interpretation of Irish attitudes be regarded as a definitive description of the Irish character, let alone of particular individuals! What is behind Marseilles' enumeration of more unfavourable attributes when he tries to elucidate Irish attitudes to life is a somewhat benelovent, if not even envious, view of an easygoing and off-hand way of life that has been lost in most western societies. Often the Irish have been blamed for this and been called lazy or even "thick", and poking fun at them was quite common among the British as can be seen in the cartoon in the Study Aids on p. 17 ("Irish"). Hundreds of anti-Irish jokes helped to cement the stereotype of the cloth-capped Irishman whose most outstanding characteristics are his stupidity and ignorance. The normative power of stereotypical jokes is only too well known from jokes about other minorities or special ethnic groups, so that students should be careful to distinguish between truth and fiction. Whatever the term 'Irishness' may imply, an explanation should be based on factual information about ethnic background, culture, language, way of life, etc. Makki Marseilles' favourable use of this term becomes obvious in the the rest of this paragraph (ll. 88ff.) in which he ascribes "love, indulgence and humour" (l. 89) to the Irish as prevailing character traits of the race. It must be these liberal qualities which sometimes make the Irish accept a more negative self-image than is objectively true.

In answering **Analysis 9** students might find a first clue in the last sentence of "Essence of Irishness". Marseilles honours the Irish when he says that they are "a race that has excelled in every aspect of human endeavour" (l. 90f.). His ironical description of the foreigner's outdated, stereotypical image of poor Ireland with its "uneducated and untrained people" (ll. 21f.) shows us very clearly that he is not only giving necessary information but is also defending the country against the stranger who has formed that wrong opinion. Formulations in his article like "confirming the genius of the race ..." (l. 31), "Dublin [...] is now the beneficiary of a great architectural tradition" (ll. 39ff.), "the visitor cannot help but fall under the city's magic spell and has difficulty choosing what to admire first ..." (ll. 44f.) or "you'll go away believing in miracles" (ll. 72f.) reveal his own fascination with Ireland, the Irish, and above all Dublin, and are intended to arouse curiosity in the reader and the wish to experience the same. The stylistic device of appealing directly to the reader as in ll. 69ff. ("... the portraits [...] will furnish you with an instant passport to history"), ll. 71ff. ("and if you enter a pub [...] you'll go away believing in miracles") or ll. 79ff. ("if you are brave enough [...] you may deservedly acquire ...") follows the same aim and motivates the reader to assume a positive attitude to the country and its people. This more personal part in his feature about Ireland is, however, embedded in reliable, objective information about the country and its people.

The last observation is without doubt true of his remarks on Dublin's renowned architecture, the great tradition of Irish literature, and the changes going on in the Irish economy. Since this last aspect will be dealt with in detail in text 10, it is suggested that the topic be disregarded here.

Dublin's **architecture** is indeed superb, although most of its impressive buildings do not date back further than the 17th century. In fact, it is only Dublin Castle where architectural elements of the other two influences, the Norse and the Norman, can still be seen. Both the original Viking Christ Church Cathedral (1030) and St Patrick's Cathedral have been rebuilt over the centuries and were completely restored in the 19th century. What stands out in Dublin's architecture are, of course, the Palladian and Neoclassical buildings, excellent examples of the

---

[7] An Irish critic, Fintan O'Toole, then arts editor of the *Sunday Tribune*, turned the answer as to the nature of Irishness into questions: "'Defining 'Irishness' is of course a problem (...). Is it based on the Gaelic tradition? Or on the Catholic tradition? Is it the notion of a noble peasantry? Do you have to be a Gaelic-speaking Catholic peasant, not to fail as an Irishman?'" (Hedda Friberg, "Irish Writing in the Late 20th Century", *Moderna Sprak*, 80, 3 (1986), p. 210). See also R. Foster, "Varieties of Irishness" in *Cultural Traditions in Northern Ireland*, ed. by Maurna Crozier (Belfast: Institute of Irish Studies. The Queen's University of Belfast, 1989).

Georgian architectural styles of the early 18th century. Among them are, for example, the old Parliament House (1728, now the Bank of Ireland) and Leinster House (1745, now the seat of the Irish parliament). The best-known Neoclassical buildings are the Customs House (1781–91) and the Four Courts (1786–1802). Although founded as long ago as 1592, many of the buildings of famous Trinity College (University of Dublin) were only built at that time as well. Yet, to many overseas visitors it is the unique red-brick houses with their well-proportioned windows and colourful doors terraced along St Stephen's Green, for example, that make for Dublin's architectural attraction.

Besides architecture, Marseilles mentions, in the paragraph entitled "Famous names," the long line of renowned **literary figures** that Ireland has brought forth. Dublin, especially, has long been celebrated as a literary city and home of many outstanding writers, not only in Irish but predominantly in English, among them four Nobel Prize winners (W. B. Yeats [1923], G. B. Shaw [1925], Samuel Beckett [1969], Seamus Heaney [1995]). Their names and works are "in the air" when one walks through Dublin, and an official Dublin literary tour that takes visitors to places where the spirit of the great Irish literary tradition is still alive is only surpassed by the carnival-like celebration of Bloomsday, 16 June, the date when Leopold Bloom, immortalised in James Joyce's novel *Ulysses*, made his journey around the Dublin of 1904. On Bloomsday a full programme of activities attracts both Dubliners and Joyceans to re-enact and celebrate the greatest novel of the twentieth century. In 1991 the City of Dublin honoured its many famous literary sons and daughters with the opening of the Dublin Writers Museum. Annotations for the names mentioned in Marseilles' text are provided on p. 10f. in the Study Aids.

The **Collage** with its 15 illustrations and 6 short texts may be exploited in either group or whole class work or in individual short projects to be presented to the class in form of short reports. It may also serve as a basis for any form of individual writing in which all the aspects mentioned in the collage could be linked to present a valid picture of Ireland. Since most of the illustrations and texts are self-explanatory or annotated in the Study Aids, some illustrative remarks will be made here only on the Seamus Heaney poem.

Nobel Prize winner Seamus Heaney must be considered the most significant figure in recent Irish literature and is often called "a new Yeats". Born in the North in 1939 and growing up on his parents' farm near Castledawson, Co. Derry, he was deeply impressed by the moors and the life on the farm. Especially in his early poetry Heaney draws heavily on his early boyhood experiences in these surroundings, as can be seen in his first volume of poems, *Death of a Naturalist* (1966). It is this continuing search for answers from the past to questions of the present that made him write poems like "Bogland" or "Digging". While in the first one, published in his 1969 collection *Door into the Dark*, "he worked out resemblances [...] of early Iron Age atrocities in northern Europe and the killings, brutalities and rituals of the violence in Northern Ireland",[8] thus underlining his duty as a writer to publicly interfere in matters of human concern, his earliest published poem "Digging", from *Death of a Naturalist* (1966), digs up the past in a more private attempt to identify his role as a writer in the Irish context. Just as the peat layers in "Bogland" have preserved fragments of Irish realities and must be seen as an image of Irish history, Heaney compares his pen that digs into the past with his father's and grandfather's spades digging the soil for turf and potatoes, genuinely Irish elements throughout the years. What comes out is a fairly simple analogy in that he transfers the farm work of his ancestors to his imaginative work as a poet and thus weaves the past into the present and vice versa. It is this typically Irish tradition of 'digging', this "recapture of a lost time" in which his "freedom and joy of artistic creativity"[9] is rooted and which has brought forth "intense, lyrical works that seem suspended between contradictions – life and death, joy and grief, memory and loss."[10] Although Heaney has later criticised his poem as "a big, coarse-grained navvy of a poem"[11] and has become a more mature poet, it is not coincidental that "Digging" starts off both volumes of *Selected Poems* because Heaney respects his first phases just as a geologist would respect older rock strata.[12] A more detailed analysis of this poem with regard to its formal achievements is not intended in this context. However, students or the teacher may wish to gain some insight into this side of Seamus Heaney's work since he is famed for his refined use of language. Here is a short stylistic analysis of "Digging" taken from Bernard O'Donoghue's brilliant book *Seamus Heaney and the Language of Poetry*:

> The principal recurrent themes in *Death of a Naturalist* [the collection in which "Digging" first appeared, P.R.], as they bear on language, have frequently been noted. There is, first, a primitivism of subject, reflected in a primitivism of language. In "Digging", for example, there is the "coarse-grained" observation of manual labour, matched by the syntactic crudity of the verbless sentences, the child-language

[8] Maurice Harmon, "Contemporary Irish Poetry", in *Anglistik & Englischunterricht. Ireland: Literature, Culture, Politics*, ed. by Manfred Beyer et. al. (Heidelberg: Universitätsverlag C. Winter, 1994), p. 24.

[9] *The Oxford Companion to Irish Literature*, ed. by Robert Welch (Oxford: Clarendon Press, 1996), p. 240.

[10] Paul Gray, "A Poet of the Threshold", *Time*, 16 October 1995, p. 105.

[11] Seamus Heaney, *Preoccupations: Selected Prose 1968–1978* (London: Faber & Faber: 1980), p. 43.

[12] See Paul Ingendaay, "Spaten zu Federn", *Frankfurter Allgemeine Zeitung*, 6 October 1995.

> [...] and the awkward stress of the last line. Second, writing is already a conscious theme: the squat pen is already poised to dig metaphorically in "Digging". Third, there is a striking recurrence of a contrast between hard and soft materials and surfaces which the language used reflects (even in "Digging" the spade rasps into gravelly ground and the dug potatoes have a "cool hardness", in contrast with "the squelch and slap/Of soggy peat"). This type of contrast has obvious phonological application; by the time of *Field Work* (1979) Irish speech is described as "soft-mouthed" in "The Guttural Muse", and a contrast between hard, consonantal English and soft, vocalic Irish has been well established.[13]

The poem is also an excellent example of Heaney's permanent endeavour to define his position as a writer, particularly as an Irish writer in a political situation such as the one that is linked with his homeland Northern Ireland. Seamus Heaney has, like many other Irish writers before him, suffered from the dilemma of the "competing loyalties to his community and his craft,"[14] as especially his collection *Station Island* (1984) shows. In this work a relative who has been shot by terrorists appears in the poet's dreams and accuses him of escaping into poetry in the face of a kinsman's murder. When the Swedish Academy, however, awarded Seamus Heaney the 1995 Nobel Prize for Literature, it cited, among other reasons for choosing Heaney the fact that he "As an Irish Catholic, [...] has concerned himself with analysis of violence in Northern Ireland – with the express reservation that he wants to avoid the conventional terms."[15]

2 John Tarver "What's up in Ireland?"

text type: (extract from) historical essay
length: 1460 words
degree of difficulty: **; 38 annotations and 32 explanations
theme: a survey of Ireland's history from the beginning to the present day

related visual material: map of percentage of land owned by Irish natives in 1641 and 1688 in the Study Aids (p. 15); a cartoon "How the British saw the Irish" (Study Aids p. 17)

Background to the Text: A Survey of the History of Ireland

Talking about Ireland means talking about Irish history, since no other factor has contributed so much to the shaping of the island and its people as we meet them today, to Ireland's current problems, and to the ongoing pursuit of national identity. A whole range of books about Irish history[16] have been written to document and explain a national history that actually cannot be called a national history as it is foremost and fundamentally the history of Ireland's relations with its powerful neighbour in the east: England.

In the aftermath of the death of Brian Boru, the powerful first all-Ireland high king, in 1014, disunity among the Gaelic kings compelled one of them, Dermot MacMurrough, to seek allies in England. The Anglo-Norman king Henry II granted him this help and landed with his army at Waterford in October 1171. His well-trained and disciplined Norman foot-soldiers, archers and knights easily brought to bear their military superiority against the Irish. Beforehand, he had won the approval of Pope Adrian IV for the invasion of Ireland. In his bull *Laudabiliter*, the Pope recognised him as lord of Ireland and expected him to carry out religious reforms. It is this year, 1171, that is usually recognised as the beginning of English control of Ireland and the end of Celtic predominance on the island, an influence that brought an extraordinary cultural flowering to the area, at least in its Christian period and is sometimes also called "the 'Golden Age' of religion, art and scholarship."[17] For more details about early Celtic Ireland see text 6.

However, since the Anglo-Norman invaders were gradually assimilated into the original Irish population, the English conquest did not, in fact, have a marked effect on Ireland until the Tudor conquest and colonisation from about 1534 onwards. As a reaction to the rebellion of Hugh O'Neill, an Ulster chief who was able once more to unite the Irish against English ambitions to completely anglicise Ireland, the English government confiscated Ulster land and offered it to

[13] Bernard O'Donoghue, *Seamus Heaney and the Language of Poetry* (Hemel Hempstead: Harvester Wheatsheaf, 1994), pp. 46f.

[14] *The Oxford Companion to Irish Literature*, p. 241. See also the interview with Seamus Heaney "In der Falle sitzen ist irische Erfahrung", *Frankfurter Allgemeine Zeitung*, 6 October 1995.

[15] Paul Gray, "A Poet of the Threshold", p. 105.

[16] Among many others of equal quality the following might be useful for further and more detailed study: *A New History of Ireland*, ed. by Theodore William Moody, F. X. Martin, Francis Byrne, W. E. Vaughan (London: Oxford University Press, 1976ff.): this many-volumed edition is the standard work of reference on Irish history; a shorter version is T. W. Moody and F. X. Martin, *The Course of Irish History* (Cork: Mercier Press, rev. ed., 1996): although originally published in 1967, it is still the best-selling history of Ireland; Martin Wallace, *A Short History of Ireland* (Belfast: The Appletree Press, 1986): a concise but informative pocket reference book; John Ranelagh, *Ireland. An Illustrated History* (London: Collins, 1981) offers valuable visual historical material.

[17] *Ireland and Its Problems. Kursmaterialien für die Sekundarstufe II*, ed. by Terence Conway (Stuttgart: Klett, 1978), p. 7.

English and Scottish Protestants. After their surrender in 1603 O'Neill and more than ninety other Ulster chiefs went into exile on the continent (the 'flight of the earls'). This 'Ulster Plantation' as it came to be known must be seen as the beginning of today's marked difference between the north and the south of the island. Religious and social differences soon stood out especially sharply because Ulster was gradually dominated by zealous Scottish Calvinists and English followers of the Protestant Church of Ireland, formed after the Church of England, whereas the rest of the island remained Roman Catholic. The native Irish in Ulster, governed by English aristocratic landholders and deprived of substantial income by Scottish and English immigrant tenant farmers, were left dispossessed and were forced to carry out menial tasks.

Increasing religious turmoil and a violent attempt to re-establish Catholic power in Ireland in the rebellion of 1641 brought Oliver Cromwell onto Irish soil in 1649 in order to reconquer Ireland for England. A brutal occupation policy, in which he waged a ruthless campaign against the Irish, finally ended the Gaelic system and established a colonial relationship with Britain. Whereas Catholics owned about three-fifths of Ireland in 1641, they only held about one-fifth after the Act of Settlement (1662) and the Act of Explanation (1665) had been implemented. Compared with the impact of Cromwell's work another landmark in Irish history from that time that still has a singular effect on today's Irish life (at least in the north) is overemphasised: the Battle of the Boyne of 12 July (actually 1 July) 1690. When James II, a Catholic, became king of England in 1685, many English people feared a Catholic succession to the throne and persuaded William of Orange, a Protestant, to accept the throne of England. In the English Revolution of 1688 the Irish Roman Catholic population sided with James so that Catholic Ireland remained his only hope. After an unsuccessful siege of the Protestant towns of Enniskillen and Londonderry in Ulster the Protestant king William III, (formerly William of Orange) met the Catholic king James II on the battlefield at the river Boyne in eastern Ireland. William's larger forces defeated the Irish forces and Protestant control of Ireland was consolidated. Ireland was given over to the so-called Protestant ascendancy, i.e. the successors of Tudor and Stuart settlers from England. Only about one-seventh of Irish soil was left to the Catholics and with the Penal Laws enacted, which were mainly directed against Roman Catholics, they were excluded from parliament, the armed forces and any government service and from entering the legal or teaching professions. Apart from that, no Catholic was allowed to buy land. Irish commerce and trade was deliberately suppressed by the English. A gradual economic decline, which also affected the Protestants in Ireland, was the result of these measures.

On 1 January 1801 the Act of Union ended the last manifestation of Irish independence, the Irish parliament in Dublin, which had actually never been representative as it was exclusively an assembly of Protestant land owners. It finally secured British supremacy over Ireland. The Act of Union, which joined Ireland with Great Britain in the United Kingdom of Great Britain and Ireland, was a reaction to a growing Irish-Catholic emancipation movement under the influence of the French revolution. (A rebellion of the Society of United Irishmen under the leadership of Theobald Wolfe Tone in 1798 had, however, failed). Although Ireland was granted certain fundamental rights, among them the promise of emancipation for Roman Catholics and the right of Irish Catholics to sit at Westminster, the Union soon turned out to be a great disillusion for those who had hoped it would lead to an improvement of Anglo-Irish relations.

The history of Ireland, not only since the Union but particularly since that time, has been the history of struggle for civic and and religious freedom and for independence from Great Britain, and in a way still is. This is how, in 1848, the Irish patriot James Fintan Lalor put the Irish national question into words:

> Ireland her own – Ireland her own, and all therein from the sod to the sky. The soil of Ireland for the people of Ireland, to have and to hold from God alone who gave it – to have and to hold to them and their heirs for ever, without suit or service, faith or fealty, rent or render, to any power under Heaven, [...] the entire ownership of Ireland, moral and material, up to the sun and down to the centre, is vested of right in the people of Ireland.[18]

These words may have a solemn, even sentimental tone, yet they express the feeling of the time, the longing for national identity but also for the revival of a cultural heritage that had been suppressed even to the point of extinction. One has to acknowledge, however, that reforms were brought about in Ireland in the second part of the 19th century (Land Acts), partly in the wake of the calamity of the Famine, but the Irish answer, not only to the economic hardships but also to their national and cultural uprootal, was emigration. By 1850 the Irish population had, through starvation or emigration, been reduced by at least 2 million. Those who stayed fought their way through political, religious and economic struggles that finally led them to an Irish Free State with all the suffering born from that, even until today. For further information on Ireland's history in the 20th century see text 11.

[18] *James Fintan Lalor, Patriot and Political Essayist 1807–1849*, ed. by L. Fogarty (Dublin, 1921), p. 57; quoted from Priscilla Metscher, "In Pursuit of National Identity", *Gulliver 7: Literatur und Politik in Irland. Sean O'Casey zum 100. Geburtstag*, Argument-Sonderband AS 46, ed. by Gudrun Boch et. al. (Berlin: Argument-Verlag, 1980), p. 79.

The rather confusing history of Ireland, especially if it includes a differentiated look at the history of Ireland as such and that of Ulster or the later Northern Ireland in particular, might make it necessary to give students an overview of the most significant periods. Ireland's history is usually divided into the following periods:

- **Early Ireland**: from the Neolithic Age to the Iron Age; Early Celtic Ireland and Early Christianity ('The Golden Age'), including conversion, Irish monasticism, learning and art;
- **First Centuries of English Rule** (1166–1600), including the Anglo-Norman invasion, the Reformation period, and Ireland under Elizabeth I;
- **Modern Ireland under British rule** (17th century – the beginning of the 20th century), including, in the 17th century: the 'Ulster Plantations', Cromwell, James II, William of Orange, the Penal Laws; in the 18th century: the decline of the Irish economy, a patriotic movement to gain more independence from Britain, Grattan's parliament, the insurrection of Wolfe Tone and the United Irishmen; in the 19th century: the Act of Union (1801) and the Home Rule movement;
- **Independent Ireland and Northern Ireland** (from 1921 until today), including a) the establishment of the Irish Free State, De Valera's government, the establishment of the Republic of Ireland (1948); b) Northern Ireland's opting 'out' of the Free State, a relatively prospering economy, instability since the 1960s.

The Text

John Tarver's article appeared in a professional journal for teachers of English as a foreign language in 1995 in the light of the ceasefire announcements of the IRA (31 August 1994) and of the Combined Loyalist Military Command (13 October 1994). The essay provides a good overview of these decisive events in Irish history in a short and concise form and thus serves very well as an introduction to this complex and crucial constituent of the Irish situation today.

Students will presumably have acquired some basic knowledge of the history of England or later Britain in their previous studies in *Sekundarstufe I* so far, but it might be assumed they are not too well informed about Britain's influence on its western neighbour Ireland. (For reasons of historical correctness, students should know that one says England until 1707 whereas from that year on, after the Act of Union with Scotland, the correct name is Britain. Nevertheless, the term "Britain" is often used even when "England" is meant.)

As was illustrated in the background information, Ireland's history is mainly the history of its relations with Britain which have, over the centuries, been characterised by Irish resistance to British control of the country. In typically Irish manner, many historic events have found their way into song and story and have been handed down in this way from generation to generation. One can safely claim that "history and song are one"[19] in Ireland and no Irish Folk Festival passes without Irish rebel songs, which are also often significantly called 'national ballads' in Ireland, such as "The Wearing of the Green", "Foggy Dew" or "The Rising of the Moon," all of which have become fairly well known on the continent. The celebrated Irish folk bands *The Dubliners*, *The Wolfe Tones* and *The Clancy Brothers* have made Irish folk music and songs popular outside Ireland, as has Christy Moore with more reflective lyrics about the fate of the individual in Ireland's struggle of resistance. Thus it might be a good idea to start a unit on Irish history with one or two of these songs (see "Media" in the Course Manager); besides, students might have heard the one or the other rebel song before or even like Irish folk music in general. At the same time they might get a first idea of how meaningful history is in Ireland given the fact that the Irish have kept these songs alive for so long.

As has been said above, the author's interest in Ireland was apparently aroused by the surprising events in Northern Ireland in the autumn of 1994. In order to make them conceive the impact of a possible end to terror and bloodshed not only in Northern Ireland but also in Ireland as a whole (and even the mainland), Tarver helps his readers to understand the background to this event. It is quite obvious for a foreigner to primarily ask the question why terrorism actually exists in Northern Ireland and why Ireland is a country with such "complicated problems" (l. 7). Tarver's answer is summarised in one word: "England" (l. 11). In the following he unfolds in a succinct fashion why, to his mind, this is the case.

After the Celts had started to come to Ireland in the 4th century BC, they established a culture that "went from strength to strength" (l. 36). Neither the Romans nor the Anglo-Saxons disturbed this culture, and the Viking attacks around 1000 AD were resisted. Only the invasion of the Normans meant the end of this highly-developed culture, and a century-long foreign rule of the country followed. Ever since, England has found ways of securing its control over Ireland through "the policy of settling Protestants" (l. 78), Oliver Cromwell's "genocidal campaign" (l. 84) or finally the "Union of 1801" (l. 89). When, after the calamity of the Famine, mass emigration, a "powerful movement for Home Rule" (l. 102) and the Rising of 1916, Ireland was finally divided into the "Free State" and "Northern Ireland" (ll. 121f.), "the stage for bloodshed was set" (ll. 150f.) with a continuing "struggle for a united Ireland" (l. 136) between the IRA and the Protestants of Northern Ireland who wished to remain British. The point John Tarver

[19] Patrick Galvin, *Irish Songs of Resistance*, 1169–1923 (New York: Oak Publications, 1962).

makes is that "Ireland's modern tragedy [...] terrorism" (l. 125) is directly linked with a tragic history substantially shaped and dominated by Britain.

Although his essay objectively states facts about Irish history, the author does not refrain from taking sides in his depiction of Irish history as influenced by English power politics. It is his language that reveals his attitude. One can trace his sympathy for Ireland throughout the article in his use of language which praises the country and, at the same time, criticises England. Thus, for example, he talks of Ireland as "the jewel of Europe" (l. 9) whereas the critical tone towards England becomes evident in a formulation like "the so-called United Kingdom" (l. 13). The same is true of the passage in ll. 48f. ("In most aspects of life Ireland was ahead of England. Yet that was soon to change") in which he suggests a sombre, almost dangerous situation for Ireland with the coming of the Normans. The sneering term "Brits" of the paragraph heading, in which he describes the British impact on Ireland over the centuries, makes clear his cynical attitude towards the British just as the exclamation "Ah" and the following part of the sentence "no matter how sweet the cultural excellence of the Irish was" (ll. 65f.) shows his warmth towards the Irish and their cultural achievements. Even such matter-of-fact sentences as "[Protestants] got the best land" (l. 80) or "Irish people were shipped to America as virtual slaves" (ll. 87f.) show his animosity towards the British while an explicit reproach goes along with the information that "over a million Irish people died [during the catastrophe of the Famine] – although crops were still being exported to England" (ll. 97ff.) and the final sentence of this passage "London looked on" (l. 100). Tarver's critical attitude towards the British becomes most obvious in his remarks in ll. 119f. ("With typical cunning the British ruling class partitioned Ireland [...]") or ll. 122ff. ("Promises [...] were never kept") whereas an ironically implied critical opinion shines through in his formulation that "Northern Ireland has been governed by telephone from London" (ll. 160f.) after local government was suspended.

Although the article presents a matter-of-fact description of Irish history, it is also intended to reveal Britain's responsibility for the unhappy situation in Northern Ireland. By mingling hints of his personal evaluation with the facts he presents, Tarver insinuates in his essay that Britain might even be blamed for having contributed, through its century-long one-sided power politics, to the use of violence as a means of gaining political ends in Ireland. Although nothing is said about the facts and figures of Irish history which cannot be accepted as historically true, this is why one cannot say that the author presents an objective description of Irish history. It is through this 'personal touch' that rather dry subject-matter, namely the presentation of historical facts and figures about Ireland, becomes interesting and motivating for the students to study. In an intercultural expansion of the topic they will learn, maybe more than they have been aware of, that events in the past have an inevitable influence not only on later generations as a whole but on individuals. Opinion 13 will expand this idea.

3 | Jonathan Swift *A Modest Proposal*

text type: pamphlet
length: 747 words
degree of difficulty: **; 28 annotations and 5 explanations
theme: an ironic proposal to solve the problem of poverty and hunger in Ireland, in fact, an urgent appeal for economic reforms; Swift at his best as a pamphleteer

related visual material: drawing: an Irish scene during the times of eviction; drawing: poor Irish family; photograph: style of cottage of an Irish farmer in Swift's time

for extra information about satire see Study Aids p. 19; for additional background material see Information Sheet 1: "Swift's Ireland"

Now that some knowledge of Irish history and some insights into the role of Ireland's powerful neighbour Britain have been gained, it might be appropriate to examine a historical document from the time when Anglo-Irish relations had reached a dubious climax because they could practically be defined as those between an imperial power and its colony.

Background to the Text: Swift's Life and Times

Jonathan Swift was 23 when William of Orange defeated his Catholic rival for the throne of England, James II, at the Battle of the Boyne in 1690. This victory finally decided Ireland's future for the rest of the century and, in a way, until today. After the Stuart colonisation and the resulting creation of a Protestant ruling aristocracy had successfully been completed and Oliver Cromwell's brutal attack on Ireland had enabled his Protestant sympathisers to seize even more property and political power, William's victory then secured this power for the small Protestant group that followed. It left the Irish Catholics politically helpless, and particularly the indigent peasantry had to suffer from increasing economic hardships as the system of tenancy made them completely dependent on the landowners. The confiscations during the 17th century had made Ireland a land of great estates on which ordinary Irish people laboured as tenants. Only about one-seventh of Irish soil was left to the Catholics. Because of an increase in population the land that was given to the tenants was often subdivided and its productivity thereby curtailed. In addition, as tillage farming was replaced by pasturage in large parts of the south and the east, demand for labour declined and added to the poverty among the ordinary people. In 1707 an Irish petition for a union with England, as had successfully been established between Scotland and England before, was denied and consequently free trade, economic benefits, and representation in the British Parliament. What is more, in 1720 the Declaratory Act affirmed the right of the British Parliament to legislate for Ireland, and with the Penal Laws enacted, Roman Catholics were not only excluded from parliament, but also from the armed forces and any government service or from entering the legal or teaching professions. Apart from that, harsh restrictions on the ownership of property were imposed on Catholics. Irish commerce and trade was deliberately suppressed by the British and a gradual economic decline, that, by the way, also affected the Protestants in Ireland, resulted from these measures.

Into this Ireland was born the man who later became known as the most ardent critic of these circumstances and the greatest pamphleteer in Anglo-Irish literature, Jonathan Swift. Swift's life was influenced by his double consciousness first as a member of the privileged English governing classes and secondly by his resentment as an Irishman against the English subordination of Ireland, particularly against the treatment of the majority of the Irish population that was kept in utmost poverty and degradation. As Swift was born into the family of an English clergyman and received the best education available at that time, he had the opportunity of entering the English ruling classes when he was living with Sir William Temple, a retired Whig diplomat and distant relative of his mother at Moor Park, Surrey, during the time of political unrest at the end of the 1680s in Ireland. This decade between 1689 and 1699 saw his intellectually formative years. During this time he began to develop his literary talents with Temple's rich library at his disposal and his help with the editorial work on Temple's memoirs.

In his first major work, *A Tale of a Tub*, which apart from the Tales is made up of "The Battle of the Books" and "Discourse Concerning the Mechanical Operation of the Spirit", Swift already displays his outstanding satirical wit and his great mastery of stylistic effects. Swift was rewarded with the deanery of St Patrick's for his services as a political writer for the Tory government that had found his sympathy the moment they gave more support to the Church of England than the Whigs had done lately. In his convictions, however, he never renounced the Whiggish background that had implanted in him the firm belief that "the ultimate power [...] derived from the people as a whole and, in the English constitution, had come to be exercised jointly by king, lords, and the commons."[20]

Swift's career in England ended with Queen Anne's death and the end of the Tory government (1714). He withdrew to his deanery at St Patrick's, Dublin, and for many years lived in seclusion. It was only in 1720 that he regained interest in public affairs. That was when Ireland's economic decline and social deterioration made him turn to the pen again – his most powerful weapon. In his Irish pamphlets of that time he blames both the English government for their ill-treatment of Ireland and their ignorance about the real state of affairs in the country and the Irish themselves for too passively accepting their fate instead of trying to improve their situation on their own. Among his most well-known writings of that period is *A Modest Proposal* (1729). It shows Swift's grim irony at its best.

The Text

A Modest Proposal is a poignant pamphlet in which Swift castigates the social conditions of the poor Irish Catholic peasantry at the time of landlordism. Swift lets a "Projector" act as a public-spirited citizen who writes a letter of advice that Irish parents should breed their children like cattle and sell them for food to the "fine gentlemen". The narrator himself says in one of the following passages of his *Proposal* why he made this unusual, if not inhuman, proposition:

> But, as to my self; having been wearied out for many Years with offering vain, idle, visionary Thoughts; and at length utterly despairing of Success, I fortunately fell upon this Proposal; which, as it is wholly new, so it hath something solid and real, of no Expence, and little Trouble, full in our own Power; and whereby we can incur no Danger in disobliging ENGLAND: For, this Kind of Commodity will not bear Exportation; the Flesh being too tender a Consistence, to admit a long Continuance in Salt; although, perhaps, I could name a Country, which would be glad to eat up our whole Nation without it.[21]

Indeed, Swift had tried before to draw attention to Ireland's critical economic situation[22] by proposing many practical reforms such as the boycott of English goods and the launching of a kind of 'Buy-Irish' campaign by appealing to his countrymen and countrywomen to consume more home-made manufactures,[23] but these appeals for reform remained unheard. Thus, *A Modest Proposal* must be considered "the climax of accumulated rage and frustration"[24] about the suffering he witnessed

[20] "Swift, Jonathan" on *Britannica CD 2.0* (Chicago: Encyclopaedia Britannica, 1995).

[21] "A Modest Proposal" in *Swift's Irish Pamphlets*, ed. by Joseph McMinn (Gerrards Cross: Colin Smyth, 1991), p. 150.

[22] See e.g. *A Short View of the State of Ireland* (1728).

[23] See *A Proposal for the Universal Use of Irish Manufacture* (1720).

in "Wretched Dublin, in miserable Ireland".[25] Ireland's social and economic plight in the 1720s must, indeed, have been unbearable if one believes an anonymous pamphlet of those days called A Letter to the People of Ireland (1729) that reads:

> We...see...our Publick Streets crowded with living Spectres, Bodys of our Species with half Life, rambling about for Sustenance, in the most miserable Condition human Nature can be reduc'd to...If they happen to hear of the Death of a Horse, they run to it as to a Feast.[26]

As obviously none of his ordinary means of drawing attention to the Irish agony seemed to show the slightest effect, the Dean turned to the extraordinary, the unthinkable. In an advertisement that appeared in the *Dublin Intelligencer* of November 1729 a Dublin citizen driven by some seemingly patriotic concern offers a "wholly new scheme" which aimed "to alleviate the serious famine, restore a sense of national purpose, and, not the least, please the English landlords. At the center of this plan was cannibalism ... ."[27] Swift has met with both praise and condemnation for this portentous proposal, and the vast critical history of *A Modest Proposal* comprises such judgments as "an admirable specimen of comic humour" but also "Die Schrift ist schon vom Wahnsinn umdunkelt".[28] What has been commonly used as an excuse for this most inhuman scheme was, at least in twentieth-century literary criticism, Swift's strategy of 'irony' or 'satire' in order to underline the fact that Swift intended the opposite of what he said.[29]

What, then, was Swift's intention with this barbarous idea? It seems, at first sight, that Swift only wanted to pillory England for her purely economically orientated treatment of Ireland; and, indeed, what infuriated him was that England, contrary to his understanding of the constitutional equality of the two countries, treated Ireland as a colony and the Irish as slaves by draining all the goods and the money from the country. In the third of his famous *Drapier's Letters* he asks:

> Were not the People of Ireland born as Free as those of England? How have they forfeited their Freedom? [...] Are they not Subject of the same King? Does not the same Sun shine over them? And have they not the same God for their Protector? Am I a Free-man in England, and do I become a Slave in six Hours by crossing the Channel?[30]

His main attacks were directed against the landowners who neglected agriculture but exploited their tenants and against the evil of absenteeism, both of which he considered responsible for the lamentable state of the Irish peasantry and the fact that Irish money was spent in England rather than in Ireland itself. It was for this reason that he wrote in a letter to the Dean of Armagh that the economic breakdown of Ireland and its terrible manifestations among the Irish population were the "effects of English tyranny."[31] Ireland, Swift asserted, "can only prosper if she has political control over her own affairs."[32] However, he was just as unstinting in his criticism of the Irish. Apart from accusing them later in *A Modest Proposal*[33] of having ignored his sensible proposals in earlier writings he criticised their lethargy in changing things, and their defeatism.[34]

What comes into focus in a textual approach to this pamphlet is Swift's narrator or *persona*, the character of the Proposer. As W. A. Speck states in his interesting article on *A Modest Proposal*, "one of Swift's favourite targets was the economic projector who conjured up schemes for the improvement of man's lot."[35] Those economic projectors had been encouraged by the Royal Society, founded under Charles II, to offer schemes for the benefit of mankind. Swift had already ridiculed their more eccentric proposals in *Gulliver's Travels* (1726),[36] because the Dean disliked these "political arithmeticians [...] whose schemes were doomed to failure because they interfered too drastically with the course of nature."[37] He did not, however, criticise the accepted doctrines of the mercantilist theorists of his time, such as the maxims that "a country had to export more than it imported" or that "people are the riches of a country."[38] But driven by his strong patriotic, moral and Christian views, Swift makes the figure of the Proposer appear to be one of those coldly calculating political economists who reduce human suffering to statistics and no longer see the human

24 *Swift's Irish Pamphlets*, p. 17.

25 *The Correspondence of Jonathan Swift*, ed. by Harold Williams, *III: 1724-1731* (Oxford: Oxford University Press, 1965), p. 113.

26 Quoted from Oliver W. Ferguson, *Jonathan Swift and Ireland* (Urbana, Ill.,University of Illinois Press, 1962), p. 170.

27 *The Macmillan Dictionary of Irish Literature*, ed. by Robert Hogan (London: Macmillan, 1980), p. 645.

28 Quoted from Hermann J. Real, "*A Modest Proposal*. An Interpretation", *Englisch Amerikanische Studien*, 1, (1988), pp. 50ff.

29 See Hermann J. Real, p. 53f.

30 "Some Observations Upon a Paper, Call'd, The Report of the Committee of the Most Honourable the Privy-Council in England, Relating to Wood's Half-pence," in *The Drapier's Letters to the People of Ireland against receiving Wood's Halfpence by Jonathan Swift*, ed. by Herbert Davis (Oxford: Oxford University Press, 1935), p. 40.

31 *See Correspondence*, IV, p. 34.

32 *Swift's Irish Pamphlets*, p. 17.

33 See "A Modest Proposal", in *Swift's Irish Pamphlets*, p. 149.

34 See his pamphlet *A Proposal for the Universal Use of Irish Manufacture* (1720).

35 W. A. Speck, p. 31.

36 See Gulliver's account of the colleges of Balnibari in Part III, Chapter 4.

37 W. A. Speck, p. 31.

38 Quoted from Hermann J. Real, p. 57.

being behind the sums and figures ("a Boy or a Girl before twelve Years old, is no saleable Commodity; and will not yield above Three Pounds, or Three Pounds and half a Crown at most, on the Exchange" [ll. 2ff.] or "Many other Advantages might be enumerated. For Instance, the Addition of some Thousand Carcasses" [ll. 81f.]). The Proposer, knowledgeable, polite, skilled in economics and statistics, seems to act as a person motivated by a social conscience, but it is his language that gives him away as an arrogant and conceited "Mr Mercantilism Misapplied" who shows "the inhuman face of a system which practises, with ruthless logic, its tenets to the 'dead end.'"[39] Talking about human beings as "Commodity" (l. 4), or stating that "a young Child, well nursed, is, at a Year old, a most delicious, nourishing, and wholesome Food; whether *Stewed, Roasted, Baked*, or *Boiled*; and I make no doubt, that it will equally serve in a *Fricasie*, or *Ragoust*" (ll. 17ff.) must be considered an act of extreme inhumanity if not madness. "The Modest Proposer is Swift's impersonation of this madness *in actu*."[40] The Proposer's scheme to "render [the Irish children] plump, and fat for a good table" (ll. 27f.) or his formulation "A Child will make two Dishes at an Entertainment for Friends" (ll. 28f.) make the reader's blood freeze with horror at the nonchalance and matter-of-factness of this proposal. In addition, what occurs throughout the pamphlet is the equating of men and animals. The animal imagery in this extract, for example, includes such references as "the fore or hind Quarter" (l. 30), "Breeders" (l. 43), "the best Receipts for dressing it to Perfection" (ll. 61f.), "*bring the fattest Child to the Market* (ll. 75f.), "Men would become as *fond* of their Wives [...] as they are now of their *Mares* [...], their *Cows* [...], or Sows (ll.76ff.), *Carcasses* (l. 82), "barrelled Beef" (l. 83), "*Swines Flesh*" (l. 84), "good *Bacon*" (l. 85), "*Pigs*" (l. 86) apart from the various hints at the modes of cooking (see above). Swift's Proposer is no longer able to see his suffering fellow human being, but offers his new plan which he is sure "will not be liable to the least Objection" (ll. 14f.). His sarcastic suggestion about how to solve the problem of the famine in Ireland, namely by fattening the children of the poor to feed the rich, is Swift's desperate satirical answer to the above-mentioned combined forces of Ireland's plight: "Ireland's self-destructive tendencies and England's brutal obsessions."[41]

As W. A. Speck defines 'satire', it "traditionally takes two forms: it can either ridicule or punish its victims. One seeks to laugh, the other to lash men out of their follies and vices."[42] With Swift one finds out very soon that his main aim was to make the object of his satire appear ridiculous, and one of the strongest tools Swift has at his disposal for this is irony. The *Longman Dictionary of English Language and Culture* defines irony as "the use of words which are clearly opposite to one's meaning [...]." Swift often put this into practice in his writing by either assuming a false identity, supplying a pseudonym or using a persona or mask. This device allowed him to play a role and even to pretend to be an exponent of the views he was attacking. Accordingly, "the *Modest Proposal* purported to be the work of an economic projector, and the awful impact of it depends to a considerable extent upon his skill in conveying the impression that the 'author' of the ghastly scheme is in deadly earnest."[43]

What contributes to this impression is Swift's care with style in his pamphlets. "Their characteristic style, no matter what audience is addressed, is magisterial but direct, formal yet energetic [...] leavened by repeated use of anecdote and dramatic visual imagery."[44] Thus, when Swift creates the vision that "*Pigs*, too frequent at our Tables, [...] are no way comparable in Taste, or Magnificence, to a well-grown fat yearly Child; which roasted whole, will make a considerable Figure at a *Lord Mayor's Feast*, or any publick Entertainment" (ll. 86ff.), it is not argument any more but an appeal to the readers' imagination which must bring them to their senses. Swift's irony turns humour into horror and the Dean "lashes" his reading audience out of their lethargy and complacency. One has to focus on the Proposer's language to understand Swift's intention. It is "strictly 'functional', intensifying in its cold, precise and professional matter-of-factness the horror of Swift's indictment."[45] There are numerous examples in the extract to support this assessment, for example, when the Proposer enumerates the advantages of his proposal or when he rationally but cold-heartedly equates pregnant mothers with mares, cows or sows. Swift unmasks the hidden brutality of this friendly, well-educated, concerned citizen's proposal through his language. It is the tone of this pamphlet that makes the reader aware of the monstrosity of what he or she is reading and only gradually unfolds Swift's rectifying irony when he contrasts the Proposer's pseudo-scientific language, for example, with exaggerations that make any acceptance of this proposal impossible. Swift's irony serves one main aim: to awaken human compassion and to castigate those responsible for Ireland's calamity.

---

[39] Hermann J. Real, p. 62.
[40] Hermann J. Real, p. 62.
[41] Carole Fabricant, "Antipastoral Vision and Antipastoral Reality", in *Critical Essays on Jonathan Swift*, ed. by Frank Palmeri (New York: G. K. Hall& Co., 1993), p. 235.
[42] W. A. Speck, p. 36.
[43] W. A. Speck, p. 40.
[44] *Swift's Irish Pamphlets*, p. 18.
[45] Hermann J. Real, p. 65.

Although the Dean cannot be considered, as is often the case, the father of Irish nationalism,[46] Swift's outspoken criticism of English rule in Ireland, which is not only evident in this pamphlet but in all his brilliant satirical writings, might make this text a good starting-point for exploring in more detail the tragic course of Anglo-Irish relations from their beginnings in 1170 till today.

4 Cecil Woodham-Smith *The Great Hunger*

text type: documentation
length: 1304 words
degree of difficulty: **; 32 annotations and 12 explanations
theme: a moving account of the greatest tragedy in Irish history based on contemporary sources

related visual material: drawing "Searching for potatoes" and cartoon "The English Labourer's Burden"

for additional background material see Information Sheet 2: "Mercantilism and Laissez-Faire"

Whereas Jonathan Swift's pamphlet must be judged as an ironical form of literary protest against the miseries of Ireland, Cecil Blanche Woodham-Smith's *The Great Hunger* is a deadly serious account of Ireland's most tragic disaster: the great starvation. She approaches the issue from the perspective of an apparently unbiased scholar but by basing her chronicle of the events on written contemporary documents she is able to present a moving picture of the sufferings of the population and the cynicism of the authorities in charge.

Background to the Text: The Irish Famine of 1845–51

In his article "Muffling the Cry from a Hungry Past" in *The Guardian* of 17 June 1995, Seamus Deane asks why the dead of the Irish Famine of 1845–51 had to die:

> Did they die as a consequence of a natural disaster only, or were they the victims of a policy of genocide, or of an opportunist policy of exploiting the scarcity in order to clear the land and restructure the economy, or of a mix of incompetent administration, economic dogma and racist beliefs about their own irretrievably feckless nature? Who or what was to blame? The British government, the landlords, the economic system that was perhaps so ramshackle that it scarcely merited the name of a system? Or perhaps it was merely (!) a visitation from God, or a demonstration of the truth of Malthusian prophecies, an event that was in the inexorable nature of things.[47]

[46] See *Swift's Irish Pamphlets*, p. 19.

[47] Seamus Deane, "Muffling the Cry from a Hungry Past" in *The Guardian*, 17 June 1995.

One event has shaped Irish consciousness more than anything else: the great hunger period of 1845–51 that has gone down in history under the names of *An Gorta Mor*, the Irish Famine, the Great Hunger, the Great Starvation or simply the Famine. Apart from the fact that a potato disease killed the crop three years in a row and about one and a half million people died from hunger, this defining event in Irish history started a controversy that continues right up to the present day about who was to blame for that catastrophe. The discussion is very appropriately summarised in the above questions from the article in *The Guardian* as it demonstrates the two positions that the Irish nationalist and revolutionary John Mitchel put into the words: "God sent the blight, but the English made the Famine."[48] Although more circumspect historians have judged the situation in a more considered fashion and claim that the portrayal of the famine in some books is "grossly exaggerated",[49] the Irish version that has prevailed to the present day has it that the disaster was the climax of the arrogant and contemptuous colonial rule by the British of a conquered country.[50] Much embitterment and hate have been piled up in the 160 years in which people have tried to come to grips with this tragedy, and it is not only staunch nationalists who have found exceptional words to describe their feelings about this traumatic event. The Irish writer Brendan Behan once called it "the greatest disaster to happen to any one nation in Europe until the murder of six million Jews in the last war [...]."[51] The controversial debate about the truth should be left to the historians to decide. But what is undeniable is the memory of the enormous suffering of the population that has been kept alive through story, song and art[52] and which has found commemoration in the Famine Museum in Strokestown, Co. Roscommon.

[48] John Mitchel, *The Last Conquest of Ireland (Perhaps)*, 1861, here quoted from *The Canadian Journal of Irish Studies*, 20, 1 (July 1994), p. 46.

[49] See, for example, John Percival, *The Great Famine* (London: BBC Books, 1995) in his well-considered evaluation of the circumstances in the final chapter "Who is to blame?", pp. 162-186, here p. 180.

[50] See Seamus Deane's complete article in *The Guardian*, in which he sharply criticises the "irrational myth-making" in the interpretation of the Famine by "that monolithic group known as 'nationalists'."

[51] Brendan Behan, *Brendan Behan's Island – An Irish Sketchbook* (London: Corgi Books, 1962), p. 185. A very critical assessment of this view is adopted by Terry Eagleton, "Die Geister der Toten. Ein Lehrstück: Der Holocaust und die große irische Hungersnot", in *Frankfurter Allgemeine Zeitung*, 18 October 1996, and Seamus Deane, "Muffling the Cry from a Hungry Past".

[52] See specifically Liam O'Flaherty's classic historical novel *Famine* (1937); a more recent novel that examines the modern heritage of the 1840s famine period is Kenny Sean's *The Hungry Earth* (Dublin: Wolfhound Press, 1995). On a teenage level, Colette McCormack's *Mary-Anne's Famine* (Dublin: Attic Press, 1995) and the sequel, *After the Famine* (Dublin: Attic Press, 1996) are recommended.

Perhaps the internationally known Irish singer Sinéad O'Connor points in the right direction when she sings of the commemoration of the 150th anniversary of the catastrophe:

> And if there ever is gonna be healing
> There has to be remembering
> And then grieving
> So that there then can be forgiving
> There has to be knowledge and understanding.[53]

What are the facts? In August 1845 the appearance of the fungus *phytophthora infestans* was reported from parts in Europe that grew potatoes like Belgium, Germany and Holland. In the same year half of Ireland's potato harvest was devastated by the blight and 8.3 million people were in danger of starvation, as the potato was the basic source of nourishment in this country. The crop of the following years was either completely destroyed, like the one in 1846, or so highly infected that the situation could not be improved until 1849. The final death toll was more than one million people, another million were able to escape through emigration, mainly to America. Figures are not certain[54] but it is said that Ireland's population was reduced by a third in the years of the Famine.

Ireland had been integrated into the United Kingdom by the Act of Union (1801) and was dependent on government aid granted from London. The Tory administration of Sir Robert Peel managed to meet the first attack of 1845 by importing maize, but Lord John Russell's Whig Government's relief measures of public works and free soup kitchens proved completely inadequate. Private aid from other countries of about one million pounds in 1847 was extraordinary when compared to only eight million pounds of government money in 5 years.[55]

The British government has been blamed for its mismanagement and misrule during the years of the Famine and accused (at least by later nationalists) of indifference or even "actively pursuing a genocidal policy."[56] Among those responsible in the government for the administration of the crisis were chiefly Sir Charles Wood, Chancellor of the Exchequer, and Sir Charles Trevelyan, Chief Secretary to the Treasury and in charge of the government relief measures in Ireland. Particularly Trevelyan's belief in the economic *laissez faire* theories of Adam Smith and the population theories of Thomas Malthus made him see the Famine as a disaster which would in the long run shape the Irish economy for the better. "Many people in Ireland, including some highly respectable Tory landlords, called upon the British Government, [...] but Trevelyan, supported by the Chancellor, Sir Charles Wood, persisted in his policy of non-intervention."[57] Although people were starving to death, Irish food that was still available, for example on the better-off east coast, was being exported to the British market. When rioting endangered these shipments, they were put under armed guard. By June 1847, with the Famine at its height, the government decided that they had spent enough on famine relief[58] and, under The Poor Law Extension Act, Lord Russell's government transferred responsibility for feeding Ireland's starving onto the rate- (or tax) payers. Those were the landlords who had also been made responsible for paying the rates of all their tenants with landholdings worth less than four pounds a year. The effect was that landlords wanted to get rid of these smaller tenants and did so by evicting them.[59] Some landlords, especially in the poor west, were responsible for the rates of hundreds of literally penniless tenants and thus had little choice but to evict the tenants or lose everything they possessed. The government's long-range aims were to rid the country of inefficient and insolvent landlords, to modernise Irish agriculture and to make the poor peasantry become wage labourers working for cash on well-ordered farms. The immediate results of that policy, however, were the loss of small-income property, mass emigration, and death, either from starvation or on the 'coffin ships' to a better world.

The Text

In 1956 the first contemporary academic book on the Famine, *The Great Famine: Studies in Irish History*, 1845–52, ed. by R. Dudley Edwards and T. Desmond Williams[60], appeared but was very shortly after outshone by Cecil Woodham-Smith's *The Great Hunger: Ireland 1845–9*. This author's blaming of the British government, in particular Charles Trevelyan and Charles Wood, for the Famine "caused a furore [...]. Since then, the argument over British responsibility has gone back and

---

[53] Sinéad O'Connor, "Famine" from the album *Universal Mother* (London: Ensign, 1994).

[54] "A human balance sheet of the effects of the famine would suggest that after the famine there was a reduction of 2.5m in the population (Smith). Of this 2.5m it has been suggested by Smith that 1.5 m died and a further 1m emigrated." *Late Blight & the Potato in Ireland. A Short History of the Potato, the Famine, Late Blight and Irish Research on Phytophthora infestans,* compiled by Leslie J. Dowley and Eugene O'Sullivan (Carlow: Oak Park Research Centre: 1995).

[55] See Armin Ganser, "Der Fluch der Kartoffel", *Frankfurter Rundschau*, 11 March 1995.

[56] *The Oxford Companion to Irish Literature*, p. 180.

[57] John Percival, *The Great Famine* (London: BBC Books, 1995), p. 64.

[58] The government relief programme included public works such as the building of new roads, quays, etc., soup kitchens for free distribution to the poor and work in workhouses with an "atmosphere as chilling and humiliating as possible" (John Percival, p. 48).

[59] See extra information in the Study Aids, p. 26.

[60] *The Great Famine: Studies in Irish History*, 1845–52, ed. by R. Dudley Edwards and T. Desmond Williams (Dublin: The Lilliput Press, 1956).

forth especially among historians".[61] Woodham-Smith has also not been spared criticism for being too emotive in her presentation of the famine, yet, her book became a bestseller. It was newly reprinted as a Penguin paperback in 1991.

The extract chosen from the text gives the students a good idea of Woodham-Smith's technique of presenting the horrors of the Famine without a noticeable didactic purpose. In a seemingly detached, objective style she recounts the chronology of the events without ever pronouncing an open judgment on what she gives an account of. However, her choice of words discloses her sympathy for those suffering from the situation as it is. Thus she uses constructions like "unrelenting severity" (l. 2), "frantic appeals" (ll. 2f.) or "poured into Whitehall" (ll. 3f.). Twice in the extract she uses the word "horrified" (l. 91 and l. 154). In the last paragraph of the extract her tone becomes more appalled as is shown by the accumulation of words like "dead", "death", "died" or formulations like "derelict cabins" (l. 163) or "half-eaten by rats" (l. 163).

Nevertheless, it is by the use of the direct words of the contemporary witnesses that her record of the terrible events during the Famine is communicated to her readers with an incomparable immediacy and great emotional depth. The witnesses' letters are documents that tell the truth. And when one of the witnesses, Mr Cummins, writes that "the alarming prospect cannot be exaggerated" (ll. 12ff.), "the prospect is appalling" (ll. 19f.) or the Board of Works Relief Inspector at Sligo tells the government official in charge, Trevelyan, "that the people must die" (ll. 22f.) or "I cannot express their condition" (l. 27), then Woodham-Smith's readers cannot deny that they are being objectively informed about the situation even though they are, at the same time, aghast at what they read. The effect is heightened when the author confronts them with Mr Cummins' almost complete letter (ll. 96-151) and does not interrupt it with an author's comment but only adds laconically at the end of his letter: "These facts were confirmed by Government witnesses." (l. 152). Correspondingly, she does not judge James Trevelyan with her choice of words but simply quotes his own words. Thus the reader learns that there were "principles to be kept in view" (ll. 64f.), that orders should not "come into competition with our merchants and upset their calculations" (ll. 85ff.) or that purchasing more supplies of food for the Irish meant "a crying injustice to the rest of the country" (ll. 39f.), meaning the rest of the United Kingdom. Trevelyan is, indeed, not presented very favourably in this extract. Although there is no trace of direct personal fault-finding, Trevelyan is exposed in these quotations as the heartless representative of a far-away government of occupation. He not only follows the reasons of state in his decisions and looks at the Irish crisis as a minor problem but, as in the passage about the merchants' possible miscalculations quoted above, also appears to be a rigid follower of the economic theory of *laissez-faire*. At another place in the *The Great Hunger* Woodham-Smith argues:

> The influence of *laissez-faire* on the treatment of Ireland during the famine is impossible to exaggerate. Almost without exception the high officials and politicians responsible for Ireland were fervent believers in non-interference by Government, and the behaviour of the British authorities only becomes explicable when their fanatical belief in private enterprise and their suspicions of any action which might be considered Government intervention are borne in mind.[62]

This is why Trevelyan's main concern in this extract must be regarded as being to maintain an operative free market and "'political economy' rather than [...] simple compassion".[63] Even though Woodham-Smith may not always be fair to Charles Trevelyan historically, "what she told her English readers about the horrors of the Irish famine was what they needed to hear."[64]

At this point it might be useful to say that, in working on Project 14, Information Sheet 2 about the *laissez-faire* theory could be read by students before they are introduced to text 4. The same procedure is recommended when working on Opinion 12, since it should be made certain that students have solid background knowledge when dealing with this rather complex question and not simply remain at the surface or, even worse, fall back on simplistic views.[65]

---

[61] An Irish school of so-called 'revisionist historians', based mainly at University College Dublin, has dedicated their work to "demystifying" Irish history and also the Famine phenomenon by putting the 'scientific' approach against the more 'emotive' reading of the events particularly among Americo-Irish 'nationalists'. See Seamus Deane, "Muffling the Cry from a Hungry Past" and Terry Eagleton, "Die Geister der Toten".

[62] Woodham-Smith, p.54. For more information on the *laissez-faire* theory see Information Sheet 2. A more detailed characterisation of Charles Trevelyan is provided in Percival, p. 60.

[63] Percival, p. 179.

[64] Elizabeth Longford, "Woodham-Smith, Cecil Blanche", *The Dictionary of National Biography, 1971–1980*, ed. by Lord Blake and C. S. Nicholls (Oxford and New York: Oxford University Press, 1986), p. 925.

[65] For further information the following might be helpful: Austin Bourke, *The Visitation of God? The Potato and the Great Irish Famine*, ed. by Jacqueline Hill and Cormac O'Grada (Dublin: The Lilliput Press, 1993); Cormac O'Grada, *The Great Irish Famine* (Dublin: Gill and Macmillan, 1989); Stephen J. Campbell, *The Great Irish Famine: Words and Images from the Famine Museum, Strokestown Park, County Roscommon* (Strokestown: The Famine Museum, 1994); *The Great Irish Famine*, ed. by Cathal Póirtéir (Cork, RTÈ/Mercier Press, 1995); Christine Kinealy, *This Great Calamity: The Irish Famine 1845–52* (Dublin: Gill & Macmillan, 1994); Christopher Morash, *The Hungry Voice: The Poetry of the Irish Famine* (Dublin: Irish Academic Press, 1989); Helen Litton, *The Irish Famine: An Illustrated History* (Dublin: Wolfshound Press, 1995); Video *When Ireland Starved* (Dublin: Radharc Films, 1995) or the BBC television series *The Great Famine*, 1995.

5 | Cragie Hills

text type: (traditional) folk song
length: 286 words
degree of difficulty: *; 19 annotations and 6 explanations
theme: an Irish emigration song telling about the wishful thinking that accompanies such a decision

related visual material: photo of a Bodhran player; photo from an exhibition in the Cobh Heritage Centre emigration museum near Cork

for extra information about emigration and eviction see Study Aids p. 26; for additional background material see Information Sheet 3: "Irish Immigration to the United States by Decade, 1820–1970", Info Sheet 4: "The Great Ulster-Scots" and 5: "Folklore in Ireland"

On the occasion of the 1996 Frankfurt Book Fair, which had Ireland as its Focal Theme, 1995 Nobel Prize Laureate for Literature Seamus Heaney wrote in his introduction: "That the title '*Ireland and Its Diaspora*' should herald a celebration of the arts rather than look back at a calamity tells us much about the arts and about Ireland."[66] What is more, it also tells us much about that calamity.

Background to the Text: Irish Emigration

The outward movement has been a characteristic of Ireland ever since missionaries went across the water to preach the gospel and christianise the pagans of Europe. That was as early as the 5th century. But, in fact, it was the overthrow of the Gaelic system by the English in the 17th century that started what Seamus Heaney means by 'calamity': emigration. When Hugh O'Neill, the last leader of a united Gaelic resistance against the Tudor conquest of Ireland, was forced to sign the Treaty of Mellifont in 1603, this meant the end of the Gaelic world. Yet, instead of becoming landlords (rather than stay independent kings), O'Neill and ninety other Ulster chiefs escaped subjugation and went into voluntary exile in Europe. This decisive episode that has come down in history as the 'flight of the earls' is seen as archetypal of this Irish phenomenon since it started the first major Irish migration. Since then, emigration has virtually never ended. From the 16th century onwards the Irish, whether they were the Catholic nobility or Irish soldiers in the 18th century (the "Wild Geese" that served in many European armies), escaped social and primarily religious disadvantage through emigration. One of the distinguished groups of modern emigrants have been Irish writers who chose Britain, continental Europe or the United States as their homes. Among them are James Joyce, George Bernard Shaw and Samuel Beckett, but also modern authors such as Edna O'Brien or Rita Kelly.[67] They all contributed to what has come to be called the "Irish Diaspora,"[68] i.e. those Irish who chose to live outside their mother country. Their number has been estimated at 70 million. This drain on its population over the centuries resulted in Ireland's having the lowest population figures on record in the 1961 census (2.8 million compared to e.g. 6.5 million in 1841). Since then, increasing prosperity and better living conditions have resulted in a rise in population to an estimated 3.571 million in 1994 and an estimated 4,015,676 in July 2005, and increased inward migration over the last 30 or so years.[69]

However, if talk comes to Irish emigration, no other time will spring to mind more rapidly than that of the Great Irish Famine disaster of the 19th century (see text 4). In order to escape starvation more than one million people left Ireland for the "Promised Land", America. What is less known is that, in 1847 alone, probably 300,000 Irish also sought refuge in Britain and continued to do so in the following years, since Britain has always been the traditional destination of the Irish in their search for work and survival. Nearly every English city had its Irish quarter, which were often the hotbeds of disease and poverty. The most "Irish" city at that time was Liverpool, which had by far the biggest influx of all English cities as thousands of Irish people poured into its port, often diseased and feverish. The workhouses were overcrowded, begging was the paupers' usual means of breadwinning, and most of them were dependent on outdoor relief. Public opinion grew more and more unfavourable towards the Irish because of this, since the feeding of these masses was regarded as a growing burden imposed on the British taxpayers (see cartoon on p. 22, Study Texts). Finally the government intervened and Irish immigrants were returned to where they came from. This gradually stopped mass emigration to Britain which, however, resumed in the boom years of the 1950s. Even today there are an estimated one million people of Irish birth living in Great Britain.

Although North America had attracted many people of Irish origin as early as the beginning of the 18th century because of its better economic opportunities and religious

[66] Seamus Heaney, "Introduction", *Ireland and its Diaspora Festival* (Dublin: Ireland and its Diaspora 1996. The Arts Council, 1996), p. 3.

[67] On 2 October 1996, the national German television network ZDF broadcast a film by Jutta Szostak presenting Colum McCann, Dermot Bolger, Eoin McNamee and Joseph O'Connor, four young Irish writers who use the subject of emigration in their works. The film examined the tension these authors experience as they travel between Ireland and abroad.

[68] See the 1996 Frankfurt Book Fair Focal Theme.

[69] *Facts about Ireland* (Dublin: Government of Ireland: The Department of Foreign Affairs, 1995), p. 9 and *The CIA World Fact Book*: http://www.cia.gov/cia/publications/factbook/geos/ei.html#People.

tolerance, it was the Famine period in the 19th century that increased the numbers of emigrants to the United States[70] and Canada immensely. It is not widely known that Irish immigrants made up about 20% of the Canadian population in 1867 and formed the third-largest ethnic group in the country after those of British and French descent.[71] Most Irish emigrants, however, longed to go to the United States. Those who could pay for it, however, often enough found a place only on what came to be known as 'coffin ships' since unscrupulous operators frequently used vessels totally unfit for the passage across the Atlantic. Passengers were crammed into the ship's hold and for about three months had to suffer shortage of food, foul water, lice, typhus, fever and death.[72] It was reported that on board the *Virginius* from Liverpool 158 people had died before she landed.[73] Even after a safe arrival in either Grosse Ile in Canada or Ellis Island, New York, Irish suffering and hardships did not end. The proviso "No Irish need apply" was commonly attached to offers for jobs or accomodation as were other forms of discrimination and prejudice in those days.[74] Together with the blacks they formed the inhabitants of the New York or Boston ghettos. It was only very shortly that the Irish were able to make progress within American society. Today about 40 million people in the United States claim some Irish ancestry and many of them, such as Presidents John F. Kennedy, Richard M. Nixon and Ronald Reagan, have made it to the highest positions.[75]
Emigration has always been an option for the Irish and, despite opposite trends in recent years because of better conditions in Ireland, it still is.[76] All those emigrants contribute to the so-called Irish Diaspora of which Declan Kiberd, author of the book *Inventing Ireland: The Literature of the Modern Nation*, writes: "Exile has indeed been the cradle of Irish nationality. Since 1841 one in every two persons born in Ireland has emigrated, carrying a burden which few enough on native grounds still bothered to sustain – *an idea of Ireland*."[77] And in her criticism of Edna O'Brien's new novel *House of Splendid Isolation* Elisabeth Endres writes: "Irland ist ein Auswanderungsland. Not und Neugier treiben die Menschen in die Vereinigten Staaten und nach England. Irland, das Land an dem sie litten, lebt zärtlich weiter in ihren nostalgischen Herzen!"[78] Thus it is not surprising that in recent years so-called "Irish Homecoming Festivals" have attracted tens of thousands of overseas visitors of Irish origin to "come home" and celebrate their Irish heritage.

Irish Folk Music

Even in Germany Irish folk music has been very popular ever since *The Dubliners*, *The Wolfe Tones*, *The Clancy Brothers*, *Eddie and Finbar Furey* and other bands or singers brought Irish music over to the continent in the 1960s. Each year there is an Irish Folk Festival and folk groups or folk singers like *The Chieftains*, *Clannad*, *Christy Moore*, *Andy Irvine* or *Dolores Keane* are names every Irish folk fan knows. Particularly in the 1970s there was an Irish folk boom in Germany which has certainly faded out by now, but the spirit can easily be revived once the sounds of the fiddle, the tin whistle, the guitar, the Uillean Pipes (an Irish bagpipe) or the bodhrán (a round hand drum) fill the room or the Jig, the Reel or the Hornpipe dances make the audience tap their feet and clap their hands to their rousing rhythms. Some of the singers are even better known in Germany than in their own home country. Traditional music festivals, however, are also popular in Ireland. Many towns have their own festivals during the summer season such as, for example, *The Ballyshannon Music Festival* at the end of July or *The Sligo Irish Traditional Music Festival* in mid-August or the *All Ireland Fleadh* – each year in a different town – at the end of August. Of course, these are often enough just another tourist attraction and commercialisation of Irish folk music is fairly widespread but at these festivals, and most of all in the so-called Singing Pubs in nearly every village or town, genuine Irish music is played and many talents started their career there. The lyrics deal with Irish historical events, battles and rebellions and their heroes, but also with memorable events in social life or such personal strokes of fate such as tragic love affairs, unemployment or emigration. The songs alternate between moods of depression, sadness,

[70] See Information Sheet 3.

[71] Marianna O'Gallagher, *Grosse Ile. Gateway to Canada* (Quebec: Carraig Books, 1984; Michael Quigley, "Grosse Ile: An Argument and Some Modest Proposals", *The Canadian Journal of Irish Studies*, 20, 1 (July 1994), pp. 41-59.

[72] See Robert Whyte, 1847 *Famine Ship Diary. The Journey of An Irish Coffin Ship*, ed. by James Mangan (Dublin: Mercier Press, 1994), or James Mangan, *Gerald Keegan's Famine Diary: Journey to a New World* (Dublin: Wolfhound Press, 1994).

[73] See Percival, *The Great Famine*, p. 130.

[74] See *Irish History and Culture*, ed. by Harold Orel (Lawrence: University Press of Kansas, 1976), p. 355.

[75] See *Facts about Ireland*, p. 84. For more detailed information on Irish emigration to the United States see Kerby Miller and Paul Wagner, *Out of Ireland. The Story of Irish Emigration to America* (London: Aurum Press, 1994). Perhaps the most significant literary work on emigration to America is Liam O'Flaherty's novel from the 1920s, *Going Into Exile*.

[76] See, for example, Andy Pollak, "Studies to prepare for emigration advocated in commission's paper", in *The Irish Times*, 25 and 26 October 1993, in which he reports on a document commissioned by the Irish Catholic Bishops' Commission for Emigrants in 1993 that demands "that children must be prepared for emigration at school". In an article in *The Irish Times* of 16 October 1993 the Fine Gael party spokesman on finance, Mr Ivan Yates, was quoted to have said that government plans about the future of 25,000 school-leavers showed the government relied on emigration to keep unemployment down.

[77] Declan Kiberd, "Writing as Exile", in *Ireland and Its Diaspora Festival*, p. 6.

[78] Elisabeth Endres, "Die Dame und der Terrorist", in *Süddeutsche Zeitung*, 1 October 1996.

humour and a startling vitality that make Irish life 'visible' and lead to lively interaction between the artists and their audience.

The Irish have always had a great love of song. As Christopher John Farley writes in *Time* Magazine: "As a defining cultural activity, singing is for the Irish what baseball is for Americans or chess is for the Russians."[79] Yet one should not forget that Irish music is not only folk music. Irish bands and singers of other styles of music like U2, the Cranberries, Van Morrison, Katell Keineg, Mary Black or Sinéad O'Connor have carried this genuine Irish tradition into the world of pop and rock and have contributed many best-selling records to this field of music. And who has not heard of such internationally successful dance companies as *Riverdance* or *Lord of the Dance*?

Irish folk music must be seen in the broader context of Irish folklore. For further information see text 5.

The Text

Cragie Hills is a so-called 'traditional' song, i.e. it has been handed down from mid-nineteenth century emigration times through oral transmission, but no author has been identified. This is why it may happen that original words or even lines may have been lost and been replaced by others so that the text might sometimes have lost something of its logic. Dolores Keane, as many other singers do, has arranged the music as she learnt it from singer Bridget Tunney from Beleck, Co. Fermanagh. This might result in deviations from the original tune as each singer adds individual features to his or her way of singing a song.

Cragie Hills is one of the many emigration songs typical of the North. As most emigrants from this part of the island emigrated via Belfast harbour, it was the Cragie Hills (actually Cregeh Hills) south of Belfast Lough which they saw last when leaving Ireland. The song has a very simple story to tell: the singer overhears a young man and his sweetheart talking. He is about to emigrate to America but she does not want to let him go so soon – not before another season is over. While she is cautiously signalling to him that "if fortune does seem pleasing" (l. 6), she will go with him, he wants his love not to "annoy (his) patience" (l. 9) with her lamenting. In order to persuade her that he is doing the right thing he prophesies her a life as "happy as Queen Victoria all in her greatest glory" (l. 15) because he is going "to purchace a plantation" (l. 11) and they will be rich enough to drink "wine and porter" (l. 16). He has nothing to lose as everything he ever had was taken away by "the landlords and their agents" (l. 17), so "Amerikay" (l. 12) is his only hope. Since he is absolutely convinced of his success there, he assures her that there is no reason to be sad and "think on death" (l. 24) but that "pleasure" (l. 24) will surround her.

It is a striking feature of the lyrics of this song that the future tense predominates, either in its simple form (will + infinitive) as in "I'll" (l. 6), "We'll" (l. 15), "T'will" (l. 14) or in the present continuous as a future form as in "I'm going to a foreign nation" (l. 11) or "Now we're sailing on the ocean" (l. 19). Whereas will + infinitive is "used to express intention at the moment of decision", the present continuous is usually used to "express a definite arrangement in the near future". It may, however, be of interpretative relevance to know that "with verbs of movement from one place to another, e.g. "go" (l. 10) or "sail" (l. 19) [...] the present continuous [...] can express a decision without any definite arrangement in the near future."[80]

In contrast to the young man's seemingly definite announcements, the predominant use of the future tense reveals more of wishful thinking than solid knowledge or reliable information about their realisation. The use of the conditional in line 13 ("If fortune does seem pleasing") indicates some hidden uncertainty about what he pronounces and thus underlines this view. The girl, on the other hand, senses the uncertainty of the risky enterprise which will surely have only one consequence, namely that she will be alone and, thus intimidated, she uses the conditional "If fortune does seem pleasing, I'll...". There is an obvious purposive optimism in what the man says, as he seems to have no other chance because he was robbed of what belonged to his forefathers by "the landlords and their agents, their books and their bailifs" (l. 17). It is here that the issue of eviction is introduced and opens up the opportunity to deal with this widespread reason for emigration (see extra information on eviction on p. 26 in the Students' Book). Such self-motivation was necessary because often enough this optimism did not mirror the real feelings of the emigrants. Leaving their mother-country for an uncertain future somewhere in the world was a crucial decision and the departure to "Amerikay" was usually considered to be the same as dying. In the tradition of the Irish wake, a gathering to watch and grieve over a dead person on the night before the burial, there is, for example, an "American wake" in Liam O'Flaherty's *Going Into Exile* when the son and the daughter of an Irish family are about to move to Boston the following day. O'Flaherty describes this event as if it were the Last Supper, a sombre preparation for death.

Creative Poetry Writing

It is not only because the Irish are so creative in all kinds of art, especially with songs and poetry, that the members of a course on Ireland should try creative writing themselves. Another reason is that usually in the ELT

---

[79] Christopher John Farley, "Singing to a Silent Harp", in *Time*, 7 November 1994, p. 87.

[80] A.J. Thomson, A.V. Martinet, *A Practical English Grammar* (Oxford: Oxford University Press, rpt. 1993), pp. 180f.

classroom students are taught to read and analyse poetry but rarely taught to write a poem themselves. Of course, poetry is something very personal, it says more than anything else about the writer himself or herself; this is why the teacher as well as the students must make sure they accept the poem as it is and in whatever way it is presented. In order to avoid possible embarrassment it is suggested that the poems are written anonymously and then presented to the class on wall-posters for everybody to read silently and perhaps comment on them either by posting their opinion around the poem or in a group or plenary discussion. It may be a good idea to hand out the poems to others in the class and ask them to give their particular poems a special form, such as a decorative frame, or a book title according to how they understand the poems.

When approaching the text it may be profitable to watch the video *Out of Ireland. The Story of Irish Emigration to America* by Paul Wagner, Shanachie Entertainment, U.S.A. (111 minutes). And for a more modern version of an emigration song teachers and students should not miss The Wolf Tones' "The Flight of the Earls".

For further information on the topic of Irish emigration and the so-called Irish Diaspora (i.e. the Irish outside Ireland) that is available on the Internet, go to http://www.emigrant.ie or http://www.irishdiaspora.net/. It may also be profitable to work on Info Sheet 4, "The Great Ulster-Scots". The information provided there may help students to understand the background of the song better as it illustrates particularly the situation of emigrants from Northern Ireland at that time, just as the song "Cragie Hills" does.

6 W. B. Yeats "The Wanderings of Oisin"

text type: (excerpt from) long poem
length: 360 words
degree of difficulty:** ; 20 annotations and 8 explanations
theme: the clash between the wild, pagan world of the Celts and Christian Ireland at the time of St Patrick

related visual material: a photograph of a mural in Belfast depicting a Celtic warrior (Cúchulainn); photo of Grianán Ailigh, a ringfort in the area of Inisheoghan, near Derry.

for extra information about the Celts see Study Aids p. 29; for additional background material see Information Sheets 6: "Celtic Mythology" and 7 "A Province of Myth and Legend".

Background to the Text: Celtic Ireland

The special love of public singing of the Irish that students learnt about in the last unit, along with the rich fund of poetry and stories, not only points at a living tradition of folklore in Ireland but also at one of the most important and distinguishing features of the Irish: their Celtic origins.

From about 1000 to 100 BC the Celts, a grouping of diverse Indo-European peoples, spread out over Europe from their original central Euopean habitats and also settled in Ireland from about the 3rd century BC onwards. They shared a common culture that comprised a distinctive language similar to modern Irish, certain social and political institutions and religious beliefs and ceremonies. Celtic social structure was patriarchal with Celtic Ireland divided into about a hundred kingdoms each ruled by an independent king. Beneath the king, in rank, were the nobles, either warriors or owners of cattle, who were also significant as patrons of the learned class, i.e. the druids, judges, musicians, poets and other artists who enjoyed the highest social prestige. Freemen and other ranks of society were bound to a nobleman and by tilling the soil and tending the cattle provided for the nourishment and the wealth of that rural society. Pre-Christian Celtic religious life was dominated by the belief in deities of the rivers, the wells and the trees, especially the oak tree. (The name for a Celtic priest, Druid, by the way, means "knowing the oak tree"). But also animals were accorded divine significance, especially the stag. The Celts believed in an afterlife and an otherworld far across the ocean or even under it. Its inhabitants were believed to be eternally young and to celebrate continuously with feasts, music, and warrior-contests.[81] It was to a large extent the appearance of St Patrick on Irish soil and his teaching of Christian values in the 5th century that deeply influenced the Celtic socio-religious system.[82] The druids lost their authority, and enthusiasm for Christianity spread throughout the country. The most prominent manifestation of the new Christian movement was the blossoming of monasteries that grew into centres of learning and art which influenced all of Europe. Monks developed a written Irish language and, apart from their sacred objects of study, also described the old Gaelic world, its lore and traditions, and thus elaborated an extraordinary Irish Christian mythology and literature. Their illuminated manuscripts, such as the famous *Book of Kells*, are masterpieces of art. Gradually pagan and Christian elements merged and created a new Gaelic Ireland.

The monks' works are nowadays classified into three major groups, called cycles: the Mythological Cycle, the Ulster Cycle, and the Fenian or Fionn Cycle or Ossianic

[81] See "Celtic Religion" on *Britannica CD 2.0.*
[82] For a detailed study of how native beliefs about nature were rejected, transformed or restated as the peoples of early medieval Ireland made Christianity their own see Mary Low, *Celtic Christianity and Nature* (Belfast: Blackstaff Press, 1996).

Cycle. These records preserved many Celtic pre-Christian traditions in a Christian Ireland. For example, the Mythological Cycle, i.e. the twelfth-century *Lebor Gabála* or *Book of Invasions,* describes the invasion of Ireland by pre-historic supernatural races. According to these sources, the Celts were fierce fighters and reckless in battle. Many of their fighting customs can also be read about in the Ulster cycle, a group of Irish heroic tales about a pre-historic people in the north of Ireland, which reflect the culture of pre-Christian Celtic Ireland. Another of these cycles of tales that allows us an insight into Celtic customs and the life of the warriors is the so-called Fionn Cycle. This is "a body of stories centred on the exploits of the mythical hero Fionn mac Cumhaill, his son Oisin (whence 'Ossianic'), and other famous members of the fian (warrior-band) of Fionn, collectively known as the Fianna, who hunt, fight, conduct raids, and live an open-air nomadic life."[83] They are somehow outsiders of Celtic society but by retaining links with it also represent it as they are expected to "defend the country against natural and supernatural invasions."[84] The stories of the cycle are set in the 3rd century AD. It was James Macpherson (1736–96) who based his Ossianic tales on these stories, "thereby creating a European literary and dramatic vogue for Ossian and, at a remove, for Fionn lore itself."[85]

The Irish Literary Revival

In their studies of W. B. Yeats students cannot avoid dealing with the so-called 'Celtic Revival' or 'Irish Literary Revival' that, at least in its beginnings, inspired the humiliated Ireland of the 19th century through writings like "The Wanderings of Oisin", which drew on old Celtic materials and thus enlivened the memory of a uniquely Irish culture.[86]

Whereas Macpherson's romantic and rather amateurish approach to Celticism was finally superseded by more solid and scientifically orientated research, it was William Butler Yeats who initiated the new cultural movement at the end of the 19th century by combining both the Irish political struggle for national identity and the idealistic literary writings of the Young Ireland movement as well as the works of Samuel Ferguson (1810–86) and Standish O'Grady (1832–1915), for example the latter's translations of the old Celtic sagas and his *History of Ireland* (1878).

W. B. Yeats' connection with Irish nationalism had begun in 1885 with his introduction to John O'Leary, an active member of the Irish Republican Brotherhood, and a Gaelic writer himself, who encouraged Yeats and other young writers to adopt Irish subjects for their writing. Yeats, however, preferred to express his nationalism in cultural rather than directly political ways. Together with his strong interest in occultism and his growing attraction to the legends, folklore and songs of his country, Yeats, in his earlier years, created an immense interest in the old Celtic history of Ireland. It was Yeats, more than any other writer of the time, who shaped and inspired what came to be known as the movement of 'The Celtic Dawn', 'The Gaelic Revival', 'The Irish Renaissance' or 'The Irish Literary Revival'. In his writing he captured the mood of a troubled and divided nation as no other poet had done before him. In the end, although often restricted to the above mentioned terms, this new cultural movement should indeed, for the above mentioned reasons, be called the Irish Literary Revival. It roughly comprises the time of Yeats' early writings (1890) till the emergence of Joyce's *Ulysses* (1922). The Revival is an example of the enormous literary activity that included such illustrious writers as J. M. Synge, Sean O'Casey and James Joyce. Yeats's poetry lost more and more of its romanticism and grew bitter and satirical. His hope for a heroic Ireland only revived with the revolutionary events of 1916, which his famous poem "Easter 1916" is dedicated to. Yeats' heroism and nationalism, however, must not be reduced to that of the fanatics of his and later times. "By turning to the huge, pure myths of the Gaelic cycles [...] he fiercely attached himself to his country by discovering, in myth and symbol, an image which would free Ireland's identity in all its power and coherence [...]."[87]

The Text

"The Wanderings of Oisin" is Yeats' first long poem and, although full of lyrical passages and enlivened by dramatic dialogue, it is narrative in form. The whole poem consists of three parts, the extract being taken from Book I, which has free octosyllabics, as its metre, appropriate to the subject of narration as this is the traditional metre for epic stories.

"The Wanderings of Oisin" presents a world in the distant Celtic past. On the one hand it is the world of the pre-Christian warriors Fionn mac Cumhaill and his Fianna and on the other hand we are taken to the Otherworld, a magic land across the sea where the ever-young live a free and independent life full of earthly joys. Oisin is the warrior-bard of the Fenian cycle and son of Fionn mac Cumhaill, the hero of these tales. While they are hunting, they meet a beautiful woman, Niamh.

---

83 *The Oxford Companion to Irish Literature,* p. 193.

84 *The Oxford Companion to Irish Literature,* p. 193.

85 *The Oxford Companion to Irish Literature,* p. 194. See e.g. the enormous impact on the German "Sturm und Drang" movement with Wolfgang von Goethe and Friedrich Schiller as its most outstanding exponents. A discussion of the scientific controversy that Macpherson created by claiming to have 'discovered' the poems of Oisin, although no written Gaelic document could be dated back to the 3rd century, must be left out here for reasons of limited space.

86 For more details see Jeanne Sheehy, *The Rediscovery of Ireland's Past: The Celtic Revival 1830–1930* (London: Thames and Hudson, 1980).

87 *Encyclopaedia of Ireland,* ed. by Victor Meally (Dublin: Allen Figgis, 1968) p. 355.

As is very common in Celtic lore, Oisin is lured into following her to the Otherworld and despite the sadness of his Fenian companians he does so, bound by the spell of the beauty of this "pearl-pale, high-born lady." On her horse they ride across the sea and stay for 100 years each on the Island of the Young, the Island of the Living, and the Island of Victories. There he meets with a life of contest and hunting, singing and dancing, revelling and joy. Oisin, however, who is only a visitor to this place and time during his 300 years in the Otherworld, is troubled by memories of his Fianna friends and returns to Ireland where he realises the weakness of his old age, the fact that the Fianna no longer exists and that Ireland has changed into a Christian country with different people and values. Narrating his story to St Patrick he defiantly rejects the Christian Ireland of the present and praises the pagan Celtic Ireland of the Fianna.

In order not to get confused with the two worlds, that of the Fianna and that of the Otherworld (narrated time), and, in fact, the three worlds (i.e. the different temporal and spatials levels of the story), since we must not forget the Christian world of St Patrick (narrative time), it might be advisable to first disentangle the three settings.

In l. 1 Oisin is "sad to remember" and "sick with years", i.e. he is in the Christian Ireland of St Patrick. He tells St Patrick that "the tale [...] must live to be old like the wandering moon" (ll.7–9). What springs to his mind immediately when he remembers the Otherworld in ll. 2–6 are lasting impressions, but then he gives the tale a structure and starts it at the beginning. He talks about his memories of hunting in 3rd century Ireland together with his companions of the Fianna. The omission after line 16 comprises Oisin's ride to and stay in the Otherworld with Niamh. Then, from line 17-40, he recounts a significant event during his time in this Otherworld, while, from line 41 onwards, he generally glorifies his wonderful life there, repeatedly introducing each highlight with the sad exclamation "O Patrick!", thus indicating again that he is talking to St Patrick in the time of Christian Ireland. The last three lines ("But now [...] fasting and prayers") make this very obvious.

As to the description of the world and values of pagan Celtic Ireland it makes no difference whether Oisin is talking about the world of the Fianna or the Otherworld, since they are both part of the Celtic system. What we should focus our attention on is the contrast between the Gaelic and the Christian civilisation in Ireland that this extract points out.

There is no doubt that Oisin regrets his fate of having left Ireland in its heroic days of glorious paganism and coming back to find the Christians in possession with St Patrick and his priests praying and fasting (see line 55) and laying upon him the same procedures. He is all in favour of the old pre-Christian Ireland where "'God is joy and joy is God" (l. 17), where outdoor activities like hunting (l. 10, ll. 39f.) and fishing (ll. 47ff.), or human pleasures like singing (l. 17) and dancing (ll. 15ff.), fighting (l. 45) and loving (l. 52) make you feel and live free from limitations ("We mocked at Time and Fate and Chance", l. 16). His is not the colour 'grey', the "wandering osprey Sorrow" (l. 20) or "things that have grown sad" (l. 18). In his and his fellow-pagans' eyes "there flashed a glow" (l. 23), and they demand of the stars: "Shake the loose reins: you slaves of God, He rules you with an iron bond" (ll. 27f.), while they feel "unchainable as the dim tide, with hearts that know nor law nor rule" (ll. 33f.). But now, back in an Ireland that is unfamiliar to him, Christian Ireland, "two things devour my life; The things that most of all I hate: Fasting and prayers." (ll. 53ff.). The old pagan cannot accept the saintly and passive virtues of this new Ireland but advocates the heroic qualities of the old world. In vain does Patrick, later in the poem, seek to make him a Christian; on the contrary, Oisin holds fast to his pagan ways and at the end flings away his rosary and wishes from the depth of his heart, "be they in flames or at feast", i. e. in hell or in heaven, to be together with the pagan heroes of old.

Many interpretations have been offered as to what Yeats intended with this poem, and a short selection of them might help to spark a discussion about that question and, at the same time, see the work of an outstanding Irish writer unfold before the students in the light of criticism. Thus it has been said, for example, that the poem's mood hints at Yeats's "own longing for a life of the spirit, free from mortal limitations, from the chains of custom and convention, and from the hard tyranny of time, and change, and death",[88] whereas, for example, Daniel Hoffman denies that the poem presents a simple escape from reality and claims that

> [...] Yeats's theme of 'the flight into fairy-land from the real world' can become summons not merely to a nebulous escape from necessity but to the repossession of original energy, the powers of life and increase grasped by a mortal at their supernatural source.[89]

Nicholas Drake emphasises the nationalist point of view in his study *The Poetry of W. B. Yeats*:

> Yeats's ambition to create a new Irish poetry – nationalist but with occult perspectives, Celtic but written in English – reflect his need to root himself imaginatively in Ireland [...]. It also emphasized the contrast between the ugliness of modern English urban life and the simplicities of traditional peasant life. [...] In contrast England was seen as industrial, scientific,

[88] Horatio Sheafe Krans, *William Butler Yeats and the Irish Literary Revival* (New York: Haskell, 1966), p. 72.

[89] Daniel Hoffman, *Barbarous Knowledge. Myth in the Poetry of Yeats, Grave, and Muir* (New York: Oxford University Press, 1967), p. 75.

sceptical; railways, iron bridges, the Empire, religious doubts. The nationalist movement at this time was either inventing or rediscovering its 'Irish' nature, culture and mythology, specifically, if often simplistically, distinct from those imposed during the history of the English in Ireland.[90]

In a more general evaluation of a group of Irish writers around W. B. Yeats who all share the 'Irish experience' Hildegard L. C. Tristram writes:

> Diesen Werken ist das Konfliktpotential kolonialer und postkolonialer Empfindlichkeiten eingeprägt, d.h. das Konfliktpotential zwischen geschichtlichen Wunschbildern und gegenwärtigen Machtverhältnissen, ethnischen Selbstrealisierungsträumen und desillusionierter Resignation.[91]

Others simply praise the extraordinary poetic beauty of the poem, such as the following contemporary critic:

> It is easy to be fantastic, mystical, quaint, full of old-world delight in myths and legends, devoted to dreams and sentiments of a fairy antiquity; but [...] the distinction of Mr. Yeats, as an Irish poet, is his ability to write Celtic poetry, with all the Celtic notes of style and imagination, in a classical manner.[92]

If it comes to an evaluation of W. B. Yeats as a genuinely Irish writer, the following theory, with reference to "The Wanderings of Oisin", might perhaps make this phenomenon understandable:

> His poetry possessed charm, skill and brilliance [...]. Yet he felt a conflict within himself; he confronted a crossroads, and in his own fierce attempt to 'hammer his thoughts into unity' can be glimpsed the broader struggle of Ireland to realize her identity and solve her contradictions. Yeats's personality faltered between the worlds of action and ideal; between the harsh regulations of patriotism and the undefined vision of beauty. To heal his spirit and discipline his confusion, he adopted the integrity of heroism – an outcry against death and disintegration. In this personal crisis is summarized the greater historical crisis of Ireland. [...] He soothed his artistic conscience by turning to the huge, pure myths of the Gaelic cycles. In this way, he fiercely attached himself to his country by discovering, in myth and symbol, an image which would free Ireland's identity in all its power and coherence, not reduce it as the nationalism of fanatics had done.[93]

The Celtic Warrior

The mural painting, photographed in Belfast, not only gives the students a visual idea of how a Celtic warrior looked. It also conveys, in its Gaelic text, a meaningful message (see extra information "The Celts" in the Study Aids, p. 29). In fact, it is the emblematic poem of the nation of Ireland, the state of Ireland and the Republican movement. It was written by Patrick Pearse, a fervent nationalist and one of the leaders of the Easter Rising of 1916. The four two-liners summarize, somehow cryptically formulated, all Irish hardships and hopes: Ireland's Celtic past, its submission to foreign rule and the resurrection of a new Irish nation. The famous Irish composer, Seán Ó Ríada, wrote the music for the film *Mise Éire* which deals with this emergence of the Irish state. The tune he gave to this text and the poem have become inseparable to most Irish people.
The warrior in the picture is meant to be Cúchulainn, a legendary Irish figure and hero of the Ulster cycle of legends. He was of great size and beauty and was able to perform superhuman exploits and labours comparable to those of the Greek hero Achilles.[94]

Working on Project 20, students might start with http://www.authorama.com/god-idea-of-the-ancients-17.html which discusses the "male revolution" in religious worshipping when Christianity came to Ireland in the 5th century. On the website of The Printery House http://www.printeryhouse.org/mall/Icons/Saints/B01.asp an image of St Patrick is explained and more background information about the saint is provided. More information on Celtic Christianity and the early Celtic church as well as another Celtic saint, Saint Columba of Iona, is given on Karen Rall's Ancient Quest website http://www.ancientquest.com/deeper/2000-krm-celticchurch.html. There is a wealth of other internet material on this topic to be discovered by the students themselves.

One of the most comprehensive websites on Irish literature, mythology, folklore and drama is http://www.luminarium.org/mythology/ireland/.

[90] Nicholas Drake, *The Poetry of W. B. Yeats* (London: Penguin, 1991), p. 12.

[91] Hildegard L. C. Tristram, "Irland" in *Handbuch Englisch als Fremdsprache*, ed. by Rüdiger Ahrens, Wolf-Dietrich Bald and Werner Hüllen (Berlin: Erich Schmidt, 1995), p. 292.

[92] Lionel Johnson "'The Countess Kathleen' and Various Legends and Lyrics" in *The Academy*, July-December 1892; here quoted from *W. B. Yeats: The Critical Heritage*, p. 79.

[93] *Encyclopaedia of Ireland*, p. 355.

[94] See "Cúchulainn" on *Britannica CD 2.0*.

7 James F. Clarity "Gaelic Now Trips off Ireland's Silver Tongues"

text type: newspaper article
length: 702 words
degree of difficulty: *; 13 annotations and 5 explanations
theme: the revival of the Gaelic language in Ireland

related visual material: photographs of a Gaelic signpost, a road sign indicating you are entering the Ghaeltacht area (where Irish is spoken), a prohibition sign at the beach, another road sign which warns the driver he is approaching a school and a map of the Ghaeltacht areas

for extra information about An Ghaeltacht see Study Aids p. 32; for additional background material see Information Sheet 8: "Irish Bilingualism"

It is not only from literature that the students will learn about the Celtic roots of Ireland which contribute much to the specific character of Irish life and culture. Visitors to Ireland will immediately notice, for example, the many bilingual signs whether they be on Dublin litter boxes or on signposts along the countryroads. They are visible signs of Ireland's living Celtic heritage. In his 1994 article in the *New York Times*, James . Clarity points out the astonishing fact that the Irish language, which has only been preserved in some so-called Ghaeltacht-areas on the west coast and other pockets in Ireland, is gaining more and more popularity among the Irish.

Background to the Text: The Revival of the Irish Language

Learning and speaking Gaelic is 'in'. Irish universities and private institutions offer a great variety of courses which many attend even from abroad. As can be seen from the differentiated programmes of institutions advertising Irish language courses,[95] the learning of the Irish language meets the obvious needs of people on different levels, from carrying on simple conversations in Irish to reading and understanding poetry or the lyrics of old Gaelic songs.

There is, indeed, a revival of the Irish language taking place in Ireland, and obviously the efforts of Board na Gaelige, the government agency in charge of that process, are paying off.

Those efforts were absolutely necessary. At the end of the 16th century the destruction of Gaelic civilisation in the upper levels of society was complete (see background to text 2) and a new English-speaking landlord class had emerged. Only ordinary people who lived in the remote parts of the country, particularly along the coastline of the Atlantic Ocean, preserved the customs and the old Irish language to the present day. However, not only was speaking Irish forbidden and the reform of the national school system of 1831 carried through to further the superiority of the English language, but in many cases the Irish voluntarily turned to English simply in order to improve their socio-economic situation. Still, in 1835 the number of Irish speaking people was estimated at four million, but the great calamity of the mid-19th century famine and the emigration wave following it greatly diminished the number of Irish speakers and the official census of 1851 recorded that the native language was spoken by only one-quarter of the population; by 1891, the number of Irish speakers had been reduced to 680,000 and by 1911 this had fallen to one-eighth of the population.[96] The situation was alarming. A first initiative to change things had been taken by the poet Douglas Hyde in 1893 who founded the Gaelic League which worked to re-establish Gaelic as the national language and to advocate interest in Irish literature and culture. For this purpose the League inspired what later became known as The Irish Literary Revival (see text 6). After the establishment of the new Irish Free State in 1922 a Gaeltacht Commission was appointed in 1925 to save the Irish language, which by then only survived in some pockets of Ireland called Gaeltacht. These Gaeltacht areas, mainly located in Donegal, Mayo, Galway, Kerry, Cork and Waterford, have since been given a great deal of public support in order to safeguard Ireland's social, cultural and linguistic traditions since it had been understood that the survival of the Irish language and the old Irish traditions depended on the survival of the Gaeltacht. Today, the Irish Government Department of Arts, Culture and the Gaeltacht, together with its two statutory boards Údarás na Gaeltachta ('Gaeltacht Authority') and Bord na Gaeilge ('Irish Language Board') "has responsibility for promoting the cultural, social, and economic welfare of the Gaeltacht, and more generally for encouraging the use of Irish as a vernacular."[97] The Irish government therefore helps to fulfil Article 8 of the Irish Constitution which makes the following affirmation:

1. The Irish language as the national language is the first official language.
2. The English language is recognized as a second official language.

[95] See, for example, the Irish language organisations *Oideas Gael* or, specifically, *Gael-Linn* which offer Irish for Beginners, Irish for Post Beginners, Irish Conversation for Adults, Irish and Traditional Singing, and Irish Language and Heritage in *Cultural Programmes Ireland '97* (Cultural Ireland, September, 1996), pp. 2 and 9.

[96] See Information Sheet No. 02A "An Ghaeltacht" (Dublin: Bord Failte – Irish Tourist Board, 1990), p. 1, and *Facts about Ireland*, p. 13.

[97] *Facts about Ireland*, p. 15.

As a consequence of this article, Irish is an obligatory subject at primary and secondary schools for all the Republic of Ireland and among other government measures especially designed for the promotion of the native language in the Gaeltacht areas, are, for example, the maintenance of several Irish colleges, of Radio na Gaeltachta, an Irish-speaking radio station in the west (Teilifís na Gaeilge, an Irish-language TV station, has been on air since October 1996[98]), or an all-Irish theatre in Gweedore, Co. Donegal, as well as massive support for the tourism industry in these areas. County Donegal contains the largest native Irish-speaking population in Ireland.

Yet, although Irish is the spoken language, most of the people living in the Gaeltacht communities are bilingual, English being the second language.[99] What is more, one has to accept that "the number of Irish speakers is a decreasing proportion of the total because, for a variety of reasons, some of the indigenous population of the Gaeltacht continue to shift to English, and because new English-speaking households are settling there."[100]

Still, in 1991, as a consequence of the fostering of the Irish language by the Irish government, about 71% of the population of the officially-defined Gaeltacht areas and 32.5 % (about 1.1 million) of the total population of Ireland were registered as Irish-speaking and – as we can read in this text – the number of those interested in the language is growing.[101]

The Gaelic language belongs to the Celtic branch of the Indo-European family of languages. It was introduced by the Gaels when they moved from central Europe to, among other countries, Ireland in about 300 BC (see background to text 6). In the course of time spoken Irish began to split into various dialects, the main ones being spoken in Munster, Connacht, and County Donegal, but there are distinctive features of the original Gaelic still common to all of them. For an example, reference may be made to the article "Where the old ways survive" in which the visitor to Connemara is introduced to the peculiarities of the Irish of that area:

> The lilting, musical language is spoken rapidly and dramatically and there are words used in the Connemara Gaeltacht that are completely unique to the area. [...] Today, even the Galway people whose mother tongue isn't Irish, carry the sounds and qualities of the language into their speech. The distinctive pronunciation, dialect, the structure of their sentences and the rapid pace of their speech all reflect the Irish influence. [...]
> The very core of our culture and history of our people is contained in the language. The abundance of religious blessings and proverbs including such phrases as 'Dia Dhuit' (God be with you) reflect the Irish preoccupation with devotion and the abundance of adjectives in the language reflect the Irish people's love of dramatic descriptions. There are many words associated with the sea in the language and this is because the Irish language was strongest in coastal locations.[102]

According to Prionsias Mac Aonghusa, a member of the Irish Arts Council, "some 100 books are published in Irish each year including novels, biographies, poetry, drama, essays, and short stories and especially non-fiction works on politics, economics and history."[103] One of the most popular writers in Irish is Nuala NÌ Dhomhnaill whose publications include *Pharaoh's Daughter* and *The Astrakhan Cloak*. Dual language books in English and Irish, such as Padraic Pearse, *Short Stories* help to further establish the native language among the population. It should not be forgotten, however, that the main language spoken in Ireland today is Irish English, a variant of General English, with a certain degree of autonomy especially as to its pronunciation, but also to its vocabulary, grammar, and idiom.

Irish is not the only Gaelic language that has survived; there is also Scots Gaelic, Manx, Welsh and Breton in northern France.

The Text

The article describes a development in Ireland "that has not come overnight" (l. 6) but which seems to show signs of general acknowledgement among the Irish population: the growing active use of their own national language, Irish or Gaelic.

The report does not seek to provide an extensive description of this phenomenon or a comprehensive discussion of the socio-historical background but explains it to an international reading public by covering only certain aspects in a typically journalistic manner. In a combination

[98] For a more detailed discussion of the role of the media in the efforts to maintain a national identity see Luke Gibbons, "From Megalith to Megastore: Broadcasting and Irish Culture in *Irish Studies: A General Introduction*, ed. by Thomas Bartlett et. al. (Dublin: Gill and Macmillan, 1989).

[99] See "The Donegal Guide" (Dublin: Bord F·ilte - Irish Tourist Board, no year), p. 6. A fine illustrative overview of the development of the Irish language from 1851 until 1956 is provided in *Atlas of Ireland* (Dublin: Royal Irish Academy, 1979), p. 87.

[100] *Facts about Ireland*, p. 14.

[101] Further information on the Gaeltacht and its activities is available from: Údarás na Gaeltachta, Ardoifig na Forbacha, Gaillimh, Éire. One of the best books on self-instruction of Irish is Diarmuid Ó Sé/Joseph Sheils, *Teach Yourself Irish* (London: Hodder & Stoughton, 1993). It might also be helpful to have, for example, the following English-Irish, Irish-English pocket dictionary with key to pronunciation at hand: *Foclóir Póca* (Baile Átha Cliath: Oifig an tSoláthair/An Gúm) or the most up-to-date Irish-English dictionary *Folcóir Gaeilge/Béarla*, ed. by Niall Ó Dónaill (Baile Átha Cliath: Oifig an tSoláthair/An Gúm).

[102] *Western Tourism News, Galway '93, The County and the City of Galway* (Galway: Western Publications, 1993), p. 55. For an idea of the sound of Irish listen to an appropriate programme on Irish Radio RTE Cork or Irish Sat Radio (both via satellite), or to Michel Davitt reading his poetry on cassette: Michel Davitt, *Galar* Gan *Náire* (Indreabhán: Cló Iar-Chonnachta Teo, 1989).

[103] Prionsias Mac Aonghusa, "Publishing in the Irish Language" in *European Booksellers*, October 1996, No 17/18, p. 80.

of his own observations, objective information and expert contributions the author manages to cover the following aspects which, at the same time, serve as the structuring elements of the text: observation of the phenomenon, brief historical synopsis, statistical information, the phenomenon in everyday life, reasons for the interest in speaking the language, examples of measures for the revival of Irish, some linguistic information.

The author has deliberately chosen to take the outside view, supporting his observations with the expertise of more knowledgeable people from inside the country, in this case "Ms. Dierdre Davitt, the deputy chief executive of Board na Gaeilge, the Government agency" (ll. 8f.), and "Riobard MacGorain, a founder of Gael Linn, a private organisation that runs [Irish] language classes for adults" (ll. 69f.). The view from the outside allows the reader to follow the author in understanding the circumstance of the reawakening of the Irish language not only as an issue of domestic importance but of nternational relevance. Thus, for example, this approach shows the problems of Irish students (or Irish people in general) abroad who are mistaken for English people (ll. 56f.). This might prompt parallels from the students' own experience or it might call to their minds their own problems as speakers of a dialect or representatives of a special region. In general, the article might be a good starting-point for a discussion of the endangered idiosyncrasy of the various regions in a united Europe (see Opinion 11 and Project 12[104]). As is well known, e.g. from the case of Denmark's rejection of the Maastricht accord on European union in June 1992 or even Ireland's own rejection of the Nice Treaty in 2001 and its proposal to enlarge the European Union, reaching multinational consensus has proved to be extremely difficult. This has been especially the case with smaller countries which fear too much centralisation and the loss of national and regional identity. In general, Ireland is, indeed, regarded as part of the English-speaking world and correctly so since nearly all Irish use English as their main means of communication except perhaps those in the Ghaeltacht areas, and those former Ghealtacht inhabitants who have moved to other parts of the country or people who live in English-speaking parts but use Irish as their mother tongue. According to an interpretation of the relevant figures in the 1981 census, the Irish language is regarded by the majority of the Irish population as the traditional native language and a meaningful element of Irish culture. "Das Verhältnis von Irisch und Englisch ließe sich am besten als ein Nebeneinander zweier Sprachen charakterisieren: Die eine ist inoffiziell und bedroht, die andere offiziell und machtvoll."[105]

[104] Valuable addresses for the project might be The Council of Europe, and the embassies in Berlin of the countries chosen.

[105] Máirtin Ó Murchú, "Sprache als Symbol der nationalen Identität" in *EG Magazin*, 10, (Dezember 1984), pp. 23ff. See also here for more differentiated, particularly statistical, information.

Although the article quoted above is slightly dated, its findings nevertheless might warn us not to overestimate the author's observations on the rediscovery of their native tongue by the Irish. The article should therefore be regarded as a point of departure for more promising works on the Celtic heritage of the Irish (see text 6) and the impact of English domination of Irish culture during the course of Irish history (see text 2). The integration of the results of these studies into the examination of Riobard MacGorain's statement (ll. 70–81 and question 10) will make an enlightening experience for the students and give them a broader understanding of the point in question in this text.

8 | Richard Conniff "God Bless You, Father"*

text type: (excerpt from) travel report
length: 677 words
degree of difficulty: **; 24 annotations and 3 explanations
theme: an outsider's personal encounter with the influence of the Catholic Church in Ireland

related visual material: photograph of a bare-footed pilgrim at Croagh Patrick; photograph of the 40 shades of green in Ireland as background to one of the famous Irish blessings; cartoon about the problem of contraception in Ireland

for extra information about Saint Patrick see Study Aids p. 35

Background to the Text: The Role of the Church

When approaching the subject of religion in Ireland, it is necessary to avoid some of the stereotypes still current, one of the most frequently mentioned outside the country being that religion is the main contributory factor to the troubles in this country. Others include, for example, the uncritical attitude if not devotion of the Irish towards the Catholic Church and its dignitaries or its unquestioned control of public life. But, for good or ill, church and society have experienced considerable social and cultural change in recent years, and students need to be made aware of the difference between religion as spiritual instruction, as a social institution and as a means of moral or political power. Yet, again, it will soon be discovered that this is very difficult to do. An analysis of the role of Catholicism, and this is what religion means in Ireland, with the exception of Northern Ireland, will confront one with such different and difficult problems as the synonymity of Catholicism and Irish patriotism, the incorporation of Catholic principles into the Irish constitution, the perception of the clergy as authorities, and their massive influence on issues of public and private affairs. This is why any examination of religious matters in Ireland must reject speculative or suggestive comments and look for the facts.

One of the facts is, for example, "daß [noch in den 1980er Jahren] mehr als 85% der irischen Katholiken regelmäßig in die Kirche und zur Kommunion gehen, und zwar auch an Werktagen."[106] This is what Heinrich Böll, himself a Catholic, had already remarked on in the 1950s when he watched people leaving St Andrew's Church in Dublin after evening benediction: "[...] so viele Menschen würde man bei uns nur nach der Ostermesse oder nach dem Weihnachtsgottesdienst aus der Kirche kommen sehen."[107] This "overwhelming piety", as Böll put it, involved considerable support of the Church by the population. According to Jean Blanchard, who wrote about the Irish Catholic Church in the 1950s, it was mainly the local nature of the Irish Catholic Church that helped establish its strong position among the population. D. Keogh writes:

> There was a closeness between priest and people even if that relationship was unquestionably hierarchical and usually authoritarian. There were 1,141 parishes in Ireland administered, according to Blanchard, by 1,090 parish priests. In all, there were 3,798 secular priests for about 3.28m Catholics in Ireland. That was a ratio of one priest for about 860 laity. The ratio, was of course, much lower if priest members of religious orders were included.[108]

Thus, the Catholic Church in Ireland has always been the church of the ordinary people and has given them moral, social and political support, and relief, throughout centuries of national and private hardship.

It all began with the coming of St Patrick in 432 AD (for extra information see Study Aids, p. 35). Traditional knowledge has it that between 432 and 461 St Patrick was on a mission among the Celtic tribes of Ireland and finally became the *spiritus rector* of the complete transformation of the country towards Christianity. Naomh Pádraig, or St Patrick, became Ireland's patron saint. Many legends about his life are very popular in Ireland as are the famous pilgrimages to the holy places connected with his name, St Patrick's Purgatory on Station Island in Lough Derg and the rugged climb up Croagh Patrick. Each year his death is commemorated on 17 March, St Patrick's Day, which has become as popular in the United States as in Ireland itself due to the many Irish emigrants who introduced the custom there.

Irish monks from the monasteries that were founded all over the country in the wake of St Patrick's baptising activities followed his example and went to the continent as missionaries. In Ireland itself the struggle against political and religious domination by the powerful neighbour, England, started when Henry II of England set foot in Ireland in 1171. This struggle lasted for centuries and found its first real climax with the Tudor conquest of Ireland and Henry VIII's demand that he be recognised "rather than the pope as 'the only Supreme Head on Earth of the whole Church of Ireland'".[109] This made the Irish population, who were not willing to give up their faith, turn to their church, the Catholic Church, for protection and comfort. Especially after the Stuart Ulster Plantations of the early 17th century, which introduced into the country not only the beginning of political supremacy but also Protestantism, resistance to this Protestant religion became a factor of lasting hostility to those who had implanted it in this country. Ever since, the Irish Catholic Church has been more than an institution of the Christian religion.

> For much of Irish history, the sacred and the secular have been virtually indistinguishable. Catholicism in Ireland has long been a nationality as much as a religion. The words "Irish Catholic" do not denote merely a person of a specific faith born in a specific country. They have also come to stand for some third thing born out of the fusion of the other two – a country, a culture, a politics. Catholicism in Ireland has been a matter of public identity more than of private faith, and the struggle to disentangle the two is what defines the Irish Church now."[110]

However, the Catholic Church in modern Ireland is undergoing a great change, if not a crisis. The core of the problem can be found in the following:

> The range of human experience of the members of the Irish Catholic Church differed greatly and some members of the laity were fortunate to find that their encounters with clergy and religion could be life-enhancing and enriching. Unfortunately many had the more common experience of finding themselves the victims of authoritarianism – an authoritarianism which was also manifest in the institutions of the state.[111]

The result was not only a decline in the uncritical acceptance of Church policy and moral teaching among the population from the 1960s onwards[112] but also in the

[106] Erich Germer, "Ein Fachdidaktiker sieht Irland" *Englisch*, 19, 2 (1984), p. 45.

[107] Heinrich Böll, *Irisches Tagebuch*, (München: dtv, 1961), p. 19

[108] Dermot Keogh, "The Catholic Church and Politics in Ireland" in *Anglistik & Englischunterricht. Ireland: Literature, Culture, Politics.*, p. 148. Keogh refers to the figures given in Jean Blanchard, *The Church in Contemporary Ireland* (Dublin, 1963).

[109] Martin Wallace, *A Short History of Ireland*, p. 27.

[110] "The Role of the Church" in *Insight Guide: Ireland* (Hongkong: Apa Publications, 1995), p. 73.

[111] Dermot Keogh, "The Catholic Church and Politics in Ireland", p. 152.

[112] In a contribution to the book *Crime, Society and Conscience* former Taoiseach (Prime Minister) Garrett FitzGerald claims that especially "the attitude of young people to religion is most disturbing (...). They not only consider religion irrelevant, but actually see it as a hostile and negative force". See *Irish Independent*, 8 February 1997, p. 3.

philosophical consensus between church and state that had been the solid rockbed of the country's politics since the beginning of the modern Irish state in the 1920s. What brought about the split, something that also attracted international attention, were fundamental issues of sexual morality, predominantly contraception, divorce and abortion.[113] [The outcome of this long-standing and painful discussion was first of all the legalisation of the sale of contraceptives (which had been illegal under the Criminal Law Amendment Act of 1935) in 1979.] The case of a 14-year-old alleged rape victim in 1992 (the "X" case) aroused a heated controversy about abortion that was finally settled in the November 1992 referendum and made abortion legal in limited circumstances. The Irish divorce referendum of November 1995, however, which had been another major socio-moral issue in Ireland for decades, showed the surprising result of only 50.3 per cent in favour and 49.7 against. Even if the votes are relatively close, as was the case in the divorce referendum, for example, they still demonstrate that momentous changes are taking place in Irish society as a whole and not only in the middle class. Indeed, the crisis of Irish Catholicism is most dramatic in the poorer parts of the urban areas of Dublin and other Irish cities. A Catholic Church "which had failed to preserve dialogue and discussion" in the 1980s finally decided for

> [...] a Catholic integralist vision which sought to roll back the frontiers of the pluralist state and advance the protection of Catholic moral teaching by having it enshrined in the law and in the constitution. [...] That left many members of the laity outside the church.[114]

One does not gain the impression that the influence of the church is fading in the face of its omnipresent domination of schools, hospitals and other public services, or the high average level of attendance at mass (90% in 1974, 85% in 1984, 78% in 1992[115]), and one seems to be forced to come to the conclusion that "the Church cannot retain power without giving up power."[116]

The Text

Just like the previous text, Richard Conniff's article from the renowned American *National Geographic* magazine is another report on a specifically Irish topic, namely Irish preoccupation with religion, especially Catholicism, looked at from outside. For the advantages of taking such a perspective in a newspaper or magazine article see Resource Book, text 7. This article is written as a travel report and the extract chosen is divided into two parts. Whereas the first part takes a more personal and affective approach, the second part is more factual and informative about the topic in question.

The author presents his material in the first person, thus underlining the fact that he has indeed experienced what he is writing about. Again and again, he cites Irish 'experts' on the special aspect he is dealing with in order to give his report more authenticity.

In the first part of the extract, the reader is told about Conniff's climb up Croagh Patrick, Ireland's holy mountain, on Crom Dubh's Sunday together with thousands of other pilgrims. For reasons of atmosphere he describes in illustrative detail what he sees, most of all to make the reader feel the rigour and danger of that undertaking ("working their way up" [ll. 3f.], "penitentially steep and rocky" [ll. 5f.], "a rugged climb" [l. 10], "rescue teams edged down [...] bearing the injured, whose scalps were bloodied by falls; they used trailing ropes to brake the stretchers on their descent" [ll. 13ff.], "the rocks rumbled" [ll. 17f.]). All these formulations help the reader to understand Tom Collins's words and concern better when the author recounts his encounter with him. Collins walks "barefoot" (l. 31), leans "heavily on his cane to ease the burden on his unshoed feet, which were bruised and clammy with cold" (ll. 29ff.), talks of "penance" (l. 32) and "deep faith" (l. 33) and "Satan" (l. 36). He is on a pilgrimage, one of those severe pilgrimages that have been made in Ireland for centuries for self-punishment born from both a particularly sharpened Irish Celtic mysticism and Catholic consciousness of sinfulness.[117]

However, despite the fact that he "thought about Collins all the way back to level ground" (l. 44f.), the author already evaluates what he is witnessing by using such phrases as "we passed back into a former age" (l. 22), "a fierce clockwork of prayer" (ll. 26f.) or "Collins wanted the old Ireland back" (l. 33). On the one hand Collins's "words impressed on [him] how powerful the force of deep faith remains in Irish life" (ll. 45f.), on the other hand he already hints at the unrelenting conservatism that he exposes in part two of the extract when describing the Catholic Church and its impact on Irish society in the past and the present.

Part two shows that the writer is well-informed about the issue he has chosen to unfold to an interested non-Irish reading public, that is to say the situation of the Irish Catholic Church in the 1990s. Nevertheless he, again, gives his observations authenticity through the accounts of those who have experienced what he says and which underline them in an intense way.

---

113 For a more differentiated anlysis see D. Keogh, pp. 154ff.
114 D. Keogh, p. 165
115 Figures quoted from D. Keogh, p. 164.
116 "The Role of the Church", p. 79.

117 For more details see Siegfried Meier, *Das Wallfahrtswesen in Irland unter besonderer Berücksichtigung von 'Lough Derg'*, Europäische Hochschulschriften: Reihe 14, Angelsächsische Sprache und Literatur. Bd. 245 (Frankfurt/M.: Peter Lang, 1992), for Croagh Patrick especially pp. 50ff.

The basic structure and the main arguments of this second part, which provides a more cognitive and reflective approach to the subject, are these: Paragraph 1 (ll. 47–58) gives reasons why the "Catholic religion has long been the backbone of Irish Celtic identity" (ll. 47f.). Paragraphs 2 and 3 (ll. 59–73) point to the fact that the Church is undergoing a number of changes and identify as the most important one that "the use of religion as an instrument for counting the hairs on other people's heads" (ll. 59f.) "has disappeared, for the most part" (l. 59). Paragraph 4 (ll. 74–83) gives an impressive example of the particular "obsession with sex" (l. 74) and especially women's role in this, that has dominated the discussion about the need for reformation of the Catholic Church in Ireland. The final paragraph (ll. 88–93) puts this conservative and authoritarian world view of the Catholic Church that Tom Collins embodies so vividly, into striking contrast to the gradual emancipatory transformation of modern Irish society by pointing to one of its most prominent representatives: Mary Robinson, President of the Republic of Ireland until 12 September 1997.

The article can be discussed as a contribution to a very controversial current issue. Apart from the *intra*cultural dimension of the topic, an *inter*cultural relevance might also be established by developing arguments for and against church interference in private and public affairs. The questions and tasks in the Opinion section provide enough material for thought so that this controversial and basic question can be dealt with in more depth. The teacher should be well aware that the discussion might conflict with the students' very personal convictions and should avoid any form of one-sidedness. Students should be free to answer questions 12 and 14 as they wish, and should students interpret the article as being anti-clerical, the teacher should show by a careful study of the whole text that this is not the case. The tone of the article does not support such an interpretation as it is that of a detached observer from the outside, more descriptive and inquisitive than really critical.

The **cartoon** refers to the fierce controversy about contraception in Ireland some years ago, in which especially the ex-president of Ireland and former lawyer, Mary Robinson, played a hotly debated role, since she promoted contraception. The tragic-comic message of the cartoon is that the question of contraception is discussed as a step towards moral decline while the newsstand posters announce "murder", "support for Provos" (members of the the Provisional IRA, a militant breakaway group of the IRA), "robbery", "arms increase", "slums" and "tinkers" (Irish gipsies), which are reasons for real concern.

Finally, it might be advantageous for the teacher when planning the following lessons to know that the aspects dealt with at the end of the text already point to the topics of the next two texts (9 and 10), i.e. the role of women in Ireland and a portrait of modern Ireland and its president, Mary McAleese.

Irish Blessings

Irish Blessings are partly humorous, partly naïve, partly deeply felt religious little prayers, poems or proverbs. They are well-known and are attracting more and more attention even outside Ireland. Many of them have their origins in the early Celtic-Christian times. More Irish Blessings can be found under http://www.irishcultureandcustoms.com/Blessings/Bless.html or http://www.momwiz.com/porch/original.htm.

Websites to start research from in order to work on **Project 18** are The Catholic Encyclopaedia at http://www.newadvent.org/cathen/08098b.htm and a critical article about the crisis of the Catholic church in Ireland, http://www.highbeam.com/library/doc0.asp?DOCID=1G1:60648333&refid=ip_encyclopedia_hf. An article on the separation of church and state might lead to interesting discussions: http://separation-of-church-and-state.iqnaut.net/.

9 | Rita Kelly "The Cobweb Curtain"

text type: (excerpt from) short story
length: 2257 words
degree of difficulty: **; 57 annotations and 1 explanation
theme: a personal reunion with people from her past that forces the female protagonist to defend her life

related visual material: photograph of a dilapidated house in the country

for extra information about narrative techniques see Study Aids p. 40

Background to the Text: The Status of Women in Ireland

I'm only a housewife I'm afraid. I don't work at all. Well, yes I suppose you're right, I do work, but it's only housework, you know, very ordinary and dull. And the children they take over your life: there's the school and their friends, and worrying about them if they're not well. We're miles from the shops; I have the soles worn from my shoes pushing a pram up and down these roads. It's hard because he wanted the place to look nice so that he could bring people back from work. I think I didn't do too well on that front, he doesn't ask them back any more. I suppose our place wasn't smart like other people's. There's a lot of wear and tear on a house with children in it. Anyway I'm just as glad because, to be honest, I'm not up to conversation. I used to have plenty to say for myself when I was a young one, but the world moved on while I was trying to run the house [...]."

I suppose I was asking for it really. That's what they said; a woman on her own having a meal in a place like that. But I was tired after a long day, and I thought, why don't I treat myself to a drink and a meal out and a half-carafe of wine. I just didn't feel like going home and making something. But this crowd of men kept making remarks. They were all drunk, of course, coming from some reception. So I said to the manager that they were being offensive and he just shrugged and said that if you came into a bar by yourself men think you're a fair game. So I went home and they were all hooting and making remarks as I went out. I should have had more cop on, I suppose.[118]

Not only do these two quotations from the 1992 issue of *Status Journal*, edited by The Council for the Status of Women in Dublin, in an admittedly simplified way concisely depict the two opposing attitudes towards life of Mrs Scott and her daughter Julie in "The Cobweb Curtain" but they also point out the basic conflict faced by women in Ireland at the end of the twentieth century. At first sight it seems that their situation does not fundamentally differ from that of women in other countries. But as Ailbhe Smyth says in her acclaimed book *Wildish Things*: "The hard fact for Irish women is that our voices have been overwhelmed as much by the needs of the nation as by the dictates of the patriarchy."[119] Her bitter portrait of Irish women over the centuries culminates in the image, "Head down, feet together, mouth shut and whatever you say, say nothing."[120]

Smyth quotes in her last line the Seamus Heaney poem "Whatever You Say Say Nothing" from his cycle of poems, *North*. She equates the political situation in Northern Ireland that Heaney refers to with the situation that has been typical of women for so long: say nothing in times when words do not help or you might say the wrong thing. Characteristically, Smyth opens her anthology with a poem by Rita Kelly called "The Patriarch" in which Kelly compares the predicament and the feelings of women in Ireland with the sheep and the cattle that her father, a butcher, is slaughtering.

All this sounds dramatic and, indeed, the female voice comes out most resoundingly in the many examples of contemporary Irish *écriture feminine*. The most representative figure among contemporary Irish female writers, for example, Edna O'Brien, has certainly sharpened our consciousness of the specific situation of Irish women inside and outside Ireland with her famous trilogy from the 1960s, *The Country Girls, The Girl with Green Eyes* and *Girls in Their Married Bliss*, which combines both the exploration of young women's sexual and emotional needs with the rejection of the rural lifestyles of their parents. All three books were banned under the Censorship Act because O'Brien's novels speak candidly about personal relationships and sex, which was, certainly at that time, still a forbidden subject in many Irish families.

Liberation from male authority and attempts to gain independence and autonomy are not only Edna O'Brien's preferred topics but are the leading motifs in modern female Irish writing, as can be seen from the collection of stories in three representative anthologies: *Wildish Things. An Anthology of New Irish Women's Writing*, ed. by Ailbhe Smyth (Dublin: Attic Press, 1989), *Stories by Contemporary Irish Women*, ed. by Daniel J. Casey and Linda M. Casey (Syracuse, Syracuse University Press, 1990), and Katie Donovan, *Ireland's Women. Writings Past and Present* (London: Kyle Cathie, 1995).[121]

Often in Irish feminist writing, along with their rebellion against centuries-old patriarchal dominance, female authors choose rural Ireland as the most appropriate setting in which to describe the particular situation of many Irish women over the centuries. In the remote western parts of the country it was their fate to be dependent on men and to be excluded and isolated from the rest of the country. They were tied to long-established traditions and patterns of behaviour as well as closely defined roles in a tight-knit family and community. Their seeming backwardness was compared to the progress that women had made in the 'world outside'. The mostly young female protagonists of these writings leave their stifling environment to go east, first to Dublin, the "omphalos of the world" to the Irish (see text 1, p. 6, l. 37), and further to London, to find their own identities. Cait, Edna O'Brien's heroine (see above), does so and so do many others such as Julie in this text.

Compared to women living in the cities, rural women today still have to deal with some marked disadvantages. This is mainly due to "rural women's marginalisation and reduced access to essential services and resources,"[122] especially as far as "essential education, health, welfare, communication and childcare services"[123] are concerned. "These disadvantages prevent rural women from participating fully in community life and benefiting from

[118] *Status Journal*, ed. by The Council for the Status of Women (Dublin, 1992), quoted from Eckard Fiedler and Reimer Jansen, "Irish Studies" in *WIS-Materialien* 5/94 (Bremen: Wissenschaftliches Institut für Schulpraxis, 1994), p. 53.

[119] *Wildish Things. An Anthology of New Irish Women's Writing*, ed. by Ailbhe Smyth (Dublin: Attic Press, 1989), p. 8.

[120] *Wildish Things*, p. 9.

[121] Moreover, *Women Creating Women. Contemporary Irish Women Poets*, ed. by Patricia Boyle Haberstroh (Dublin: Attic Press, 1996) allows the reader to investigate modern Irish women's poetry (see here, most of all, the poems of Eavan Boland). Finally, *Unveiling Treaures. The Attic Guide to Irish Women Literary Writers*, ed. by Ann Owens Weekes (Dublin: Attic Press, 1993), *Irish Women's Studies Reader*, ed. by Ailbhe Smyth (Dublin: Attic Press, 1993) and Kit & Cyril Ó Céirín, *Women of Ireland. A Biographic Dictionary* (Newtownlynch: Tír Eolas, 1996) might serve to help the teacher and students alike in their closer analysis of Irish women's studies, as might the inclusion of such renowned films as Thaddeus O'Sullivan's *December Maid* or Stephen Frears's *The Snapper*.

[122] Anne Byrne, "Revealing Figures? Official Statistics and Rural Irish Women," in *Irish Women's Studies Reader*, ed. by Ailbhe Smyth (Dublin: Attic Press, 1993), p. 143.

[123] Anne Byrne, p. 141.

some of the changes in attitudes and improvements in services for women that have been achieved within the past ten years".[124]

This is why Ireland is facing the problem nowadays that more and more younger women are leaving the rural areas to try and find work in the urban centres. As a consequence of this, the number of women working in agriculture has decreased from 42,000 in 1961 to 12,300 in 1991.[125]

Yet, life in the city has its own problems. Accommodation is expensive, most women are in lower-paid jobs, and no childcare facilities are available for single mothers. An increasing unemployment rate will certainly raise the already high number of women not in the labour force (70%, compared to 30% men in 1991),[126] and those who give up the traditional role for a career are faced with the result of a 1992 poll that

> claims that the most important perceived role for modern Irish women is motherhood and providing for the family, with fulltime wives and mothers being held in the highest esteem by 70 per cent of respondents, compared to 5 percent who felt that a career was the most important role for women today.[127]

This overwhelming vote might find an explanation in Article 41 of the Constitution of Ireland which reads: "In particular, the State recognises that by her life within the home, woman gives to the State a support without which the common good cannot be achieved."

Nevertheless, in 1986, when still a senator, the later president of Ireland, Mary Robinson, demanded a change in the frame of mind, not only of Irish women, when she claimed:

> It is not simply a question of wanting more women *per se* involved in the various bodies [as lawmakers, as members of the government, as judges, etc.]. It is because the male domination at all levels affects the very ethos and culture of our society. It reinforces sex stereotyping and role conditioning. [...] At the moment it is male perceptions and male priorities that dominate. Are they necessarily the same as the perceptions and priorities of women?[128]

It might now be easier to explain why such issues as divorce, abortion, birth control, and women's rights in general are so fiercely fought over in Ireland (see text 8). At the beginning of 1997, however, a new equality bill was published by Equality and Law Reform Minister Mervyn Taylor that was designed to prohibit discrimination, among other things, on grounds of gender, marital and family status. The Minister described his Equal Status Bill as a "ground-breaking measure".[129] The Equal Status Act came into operation in 2000.

The Text

After everything that has been said above about patriarchal domination of women being the leading motif in modern Irish female writing, the absence of any male (except for the little son) in Rity Kelly's short story is the first remarkable thing about it. It turns out to be an interesting device as the reader is very effectively presented with the indirect effects of the patriarchal society on the three women.

"The Cobweb Curtain" is a story that introduces the students to the problem of the position of women in Ireland, particularly that of women in rural Ireland and to traditional and alternative forms of living as a woman in the Ireland of today. Whereas Mrs Scott represents the traditional role of the farmer's wife and their children's mother, her daughter Julie is clear-eyed, practical and is building up an existence in England. Kate, the protagonist of the story, is caught up in conflicting feelings as to whether she belongs to this or the other world - until she is finally forced to make a decision. The story affords a good opportunity for the students to discuss this issue on the premise of its intercultural relevance.

The extract has only left out marginal details so that it is complete in itself and represents the story very well. The text divides into 3 main sections:
Section 1 (ll. 1–152) describes the incidental meeting of Kate and Julie, which includes their conversation in the hotel and the drive home to Julie's mother,
Section 2 (ll. 153–259) takes the reader inside Mrs Scott's cabin,
Section 3 (ll. 261–286) shows Kate's reaction to what happened.

Many narrative devices employed in this short story are used to catch the reader's attention. There is no real traditional narrator but a mixture of traditional narration and interior monologue. Thus we find passages that very traditionally show the omniscient narrator at work when we read: "I'll keep the box, she thought" (l. 284), and then the use of interior monologue immediately after that when Kate thinks: "Nice child" about herself. Yet the traditional perspective is rare. We might therefore

---

124 Anne Byrne, pp. 141f.

125 Labour Force Survey, 1991; quoted in Anne Byrne, p. 142.

126 According to the National Women's Council of Ireland, Ireland had the highest rate of female unemployment in the EU in 1992; in 1993 women earned 61.3% of average gross male earning; 85% of low paid part-time workers and 53% of social welfare recipients are women; (...) in 1994 in excess of 60,000 women were in receipt of social welfare payments because they were rearing children alone. The 1995 payment of these women was £62.50 for themselves and £15.20 for each child. See *An Independent Report to the 4th UN World Conference on Women: "Beijing and Beyond"* (Dublin: National Women's Council of Ireland1995), p. 7.

127 Anne Byrne, p. 152. For a more detailed and critical discussion of this "culture of 'motherblame'" see Angela Long in *The Irish Times*, 11 February 1997.

128 Mary Robinson, "Women and the Law in Ireland," in *Irish Women's Studies Reader*, p.102f.

129 See Chris Glennon, "Equality bill covers pubs and night clubs," *Irish Independent*, 8 February 1997.

speak, in parts, of a selectively omniscient point of view with interior monologue and dialogue prevailing. This means that the impact of actions and emotions upon the inner self is shown without comment by the narrator, while it is at the same time expected that the reader will come to a clear understanding of the story and the attributes of the characters. For example in ll. 3–4, 48–55, 111–15, 129–38, 231–34, 275–76 Kate's interior monologues frequently make the reader actually understand what is really going on behind all the talking and acting. Kate judges Julie's outer appearance ("Still pretty, so casual, straight cords, always could wear anything" [ll. 3f.]); speculates on her marital status ("Married? Must be, and a family?" [l. 50f.]); comments on the actions and words of the other two ("Clipped and final, we mustn't detain. Dragging slattern heels across the concrete floor..." [ll. 231f.]); and talks to herself ("Go, or the moment will have spent itself" [l. 275f.]). While these interior monologues are still a device to intersperse the text with essential information necessary for understanding the interaction of the characters, the reader is completely left alone with his or her interpretation of the dialogues. Here the information is provided by the characters themselves, i.e. by their speech, the kind of language they use and by the thoughts revealed.

Since the narrator restrains him- or herself from giving any direct information or comment, characterisation is only possible through an analysis of the utterances and the way in which the characters act and react. We call this the dramatic point of view because we see the characters just as we see characters in a drama, where we also have to come to terms with what we understand ourselves about a special character.

"The Cobweb Curtain" presents three main characters: Julie, Kate and Mrs Scott. Julie is Mrs Scott's daughter but the two are 'worlds apart'. Whereas Mrs Scott is deeply rooted in the traditional way of living as a rural woman, Julie has totally broken with her past and lives the life of a modern, cosmopolitan, young woman. She still comes home, but more for rational reasons ("it would be less bother to write or telephone, nothing about the place draws me, [...] it keeps my mother in touch, [...] it seemed the most practical solution." [ll. 73–77]). She "nurtures no sentimental attachments" [l. 82f.] and "[...] a few years perhaps, and then I shan't ever come" [l. 79f.].

After twelve years Kate and Julie meet by chance at the place somewhere in the western part of Ireland where they spent their youth together. Kate, who has been living in the area since, immediately senses the difference between the two of them ("The coolness of it, clipped, London" [l. 3]; "alien almost", [ll. 18f.). Julie invites Kate for a drink to a pub, which might be something normal in London but is "so awkward, impossible almost" [l. 32] for women in the country. Kate is taken by surprise about Julie's independence, self-confidence and definiteness and starts feeling awkward in her presence because she herself has not changed, has never thought of changing, has just lived the life she was used to ("But Julie, all your past is there, locked within the landscape, the turns and bends of the road, the furzy hills, the..." [ll. 87–89]). But Julie has decided "to put the poverty and deprivation of rural Ireland behind her. She has resolved never to disturb the cobweb curtains of the past."[130]

Life behind the cobweb curtain is immobility, stagnation, decadence [ll. 129–138]. This is the life of Mrs Scott, an old farmer's wife, who lives in an old cabin that has not changed in years ("smell of sour milk and soap-powder" [ll. 166f.], "the same old dresser with the milk jugs, and cups on hooks" [ll. 181f.], "hen dung trodden into the pitted concrete floor" [ll. 240f]), nor have her habits or attitudes changed ("Then Mrs. Scott was at the door wiping her hands in her apron" [ll. 156f.], "'I was just going to make a cake when I heard the car.' 'But you know that there's plenty of bread in the house'." [ll. 194f.], "She has sat down too, in the armchair scratching the ashes with the tongs. Hushed intimate tone" [ll. 205f.], "Rub of a cloth, dab of breadsoda and a spit" [l. 239]). Perhaps the most significant passage is to be found in lines 250ff.: "You'd want to mind his eyes, Julia, too much of that reading altogether, now if I had a bit of straw for the bottom of the box."

Gradually, and this is what her encounter with Julie and her mother makes her become painfully aware of, this life behind the cobweb curtain is also becoming Kate's life ("She comes with an armful of turf and piles it on the fire. Kate's hand goes to take the tongs, so many times, the half-heard voice, the flapping flame" [ll. 183–85]). Kate, the protagonist of the story, has to accept that she is about to forfeit her life. Her reactions to cosmopolitan Julie waver between surprise ("The coolness of it, clipped, London [l. 3]), admiration ("Along the footpath, Julie's fashionable heels pricking the stone. Not a walk, an elegant glide, [...] now this suave young woman" [ll. 35–42]), self-protecting criticism ("The jacket is becoming, she can't wear it, but it's just a trifle common, superstore stuff, mustn't be a bitch, things at Scotts were never easy." [ll.53ff.]), curiosity ("Married? Must be, and a family? Strange she bothers to come home, [ll. 50f.]), shame ("Thought we could slip past it, keep talking, God, nothing, why won't she keep talking, anything" [ll. 106f.]), and alarm ("There all the time, shuttered, sealing something from the light. Undisturbed for years, but spiders tenuously tying things together" [ll. 129ff.]). Kate senses that Julie has alwas been her own woman during these twelve years whereas she must recognise herself to be convention-bound and steeped

130 Daniel J. Casey and Linda M. Casey, Introduction to *Stories by Contemporary Irish Women* (Syracuse: Syracuse University Press, 1990), p. 8.

in traditions ("'A pint, I, I didn't think-' 'Good for the blood, why not, besides I enjoy it.' 'Of course, I just thought-'" [ll. 64ff.]). She suddenly feels she is being forced to defend her life with so many questions arising from her encounter with Julie.

There is a certain tension between the two main characters – one still somewhat staid, a little romantic, a little nostalgic, the other clear-eyed, practical and getting on with things in England. The mother takes an extra dimension, fertility ('eggs'), motherhood combined with an acceptance of things, a little cruel sometimes, a little interfering. It is Kate's final awakening and the insight into the need to slough off the trappings of what society expects that give the story a surprising ending: Kate throws the eggs into the well, thus demonstrating her newly-found non-acceptance of the one-sidedness of the traditional role of a woman.

One really has to work at Rita Kelly's fiction and must know that much of it has an autobiographical background. When she lived in rural East Galway as a young girl, the landscape made her feel uneasy. In an interview she once said:

> The happenings of the world seemed to be happening miles away. I felt trapped in a place where nothing ever seemed to occur – in a place that was in a permanent state of stasis. Even the bogs made me feel as if I too was part of the rotting timber and the millions of fallen leaves; trapped in a slow process of physical, biological life.[131]

This explains the image of the cobweb in this story.

A final word on the author's language: Rita Kelly thinks of herself primarily as a poet and, in fact, her stories "also have the enigma of poetry."[132]. Her poetically impressionistic language is a fitting vehicle for expressing Julia's short, clipped sentences and Kate's nervous interior monologues, which give the whole story such a tense and irritable atmosphere.

10 | Mary McAleese "Hopes for the New Millennium"

text type: political speech
length: 514 words
degree of difficulty: *; 14 annotations and 4 explanations
theme: The second female Irish president's millennium address to the people of Ireland

related visual material: photo of the second female president of the Republic of Ireland, Mary McAleese

Background to the Text: Hopes for Ireland in a Changing World

Sequence Four ends with the second female Irish president's millennium address to the people of the Republic of Ireland. Whereas general information about the status of women in Ireland is not too positive, as the background to the previous text has made clear, the Republic of Ireland can claim to be one of the few countries in the world whose elected head of state is a woman. Apart from that she is the second woman president the Irish people elected. The first one was Mary Robinson who was declared elected on 9 November 1990. Although this came as a big surprise to most of the Irish themselves, Ms Robinson's victory has brought a change for the better – as far as women and their acceptance in public life are concerned. She was, indeed, elected by the women whose concerns she had fought for as a lawyer, who she promised would be heard and who, in the 1990 presidential elections "instead of rocking the cradle rocked the system."[133] But over the years of her presidency she gained general respect for her personal integrity and her personification of modern Ireland. Today she is still looked on as one of the most popular public persons in Ireland even after having resigned from office as President of the Republic of Ireland on 12 September 1997 to take up an appointment as United Nations High Commissioner for Human Rights, an office she held until 2002 when she became President of the Ethical Globalization Initiative (EGI).

Info-Box: Uachtarán na hÉireann, the President of Ireland, is the head of state of the Republic of Ireland. He or she is directly elected by the people for seven years and can be re-elected a second time. The president has limited powers and has mainly ceremonial tasks.

Mary McAleese became Robinson's successor in the presidential elections of 1997. Her nomination by Fianna Fáil caused much criticism among many commentators, because McAleese is a Catholic Northerner, born in Belfast and fears were expressed that relations with the United Kingdom and the Protestants in Northern Ireland could be strained. Her work as president, however, was excellent and she had no serious opponent in the 2004 presidential elections, in fact no other candidate had any hope of being elected. Prior to her presidency Mary McAleese had worked as lawyer, law professor in Trinity College, Dublin and journalist for the national television service RTÉ.
With her warm and informal ways she won the hearts of the people and respect amongst her critics. She even managed to bring Orangemen and former members of Northern Ireland Protestant paramilitary groups like the UDA (Ulster Defence Association) or the UVF (Ulster Volunteer Force) to the President's office. This made Jude Collins from the

[131] Caroline Walsh, "By the Lock", *The Irish Times*, 13 March 1986.
[132] C. Walsh, "By the Lock".
[133] Mary Robinson in her acceptance speech after she was declared elected on 9 November 1990.

Irish News call her "the soul of inclusiveness"[134] who is "far from fostering division."[135] On 12 July 2005 another example of her policy of "building bridges" could be witnessed when she, the President of the Republic of Ireland, also invited visitors from Northern Ireland to commemorate the 12th of July together when, at the Battle of the Boyne, Protestant William of Orange defeated Catholic King James II, a victory that is still today celebrated by Northern Ireland Protestants. The annual marches of the Orange Order (Orangemen) on 12th July are understood by many Catholics as a massive provocation and often enough outbursts of violence follow. In her speech McAleese, in an effort to point out that times have changed since then, tried to bridge the differences between Williamites and Jacobites:

> These centuries later we, their children, gather together acknowledging our very different debts to history but also our shared responsibility for the future. Williamite or Jacobite, we are each human beings who shine when we are befriended, respected and treated with kindness and compassion. It is to the goodness in all of us that we look with hope and confidence for a future where the unique heritage of each has a respected place in an island of good neighbours and good friends. This reception and the planned re-development of the site of the Battle of the Boyne are, I believe, positive signs of the spirit of inclusion and tolerance that characterise today's confident, successful Ireland. Today we showcase our differences, acknowledge them openly and colourfully and still offer each other a handshake, a smile and the offer of friendship.[136]

In text 10, the millennium speech, McAleese is also occupied with the past and again she tries to bridge it to the present in order "to liberate the present" (l. 43). She voices her belief that Ireland does "not have to accept the dead hand of fate", the paralysis of history" (l. 9f.) and points to the "unprecedented prosperity, peace and opportunity" (l. 5) that the country is experiencing today.

Ireland might, indeed, in the past have had the reputation of being on the periphery of Europe and backward when compared to other European countries. However, it would be a grievous error to hang on to this outdated stereotypical image. Since 1973, when the Republic of Ireland joined the EC, now the European Union, Ireland has changed rapidly. EU money has, over the years, helped to modernise the country's infrastructure, and changes in attitude especially among the well-educated younger population are turning Ireland into a modern, self-confident, open and pluralistic European country.

It all started in the seventies when tourists discovered the Emerald Isle. They were drawn by the natural beauty, the clean water, the unspoilt countryside, the clean air, the rich old and modern culture, and the friendliness of the people in the country. The tourist industry boomed during the eighties and nineties, massively supported by Bord Fáilte, the Irish Tourist Board, and still does. Ireland was the only European country that could boast of enormous growth rates in the field of tourism over the years. "In the first six months of 2003, the number of visitors from the United States grew more than 5 per cent, while the increase in European visitors amounted to almost 8 per cent."[137] In 2004, according to *The Irish Times*, "Tourism Ireland, which operates a joint marketing campaign for the Republic and Northern Ireland, has planned to increase tourist traffic by 4.4 per cent, bringing a total of 7.7 million visitors"[138] to the island.

In the early stages after the Republic of Ireland's entry into the EC it was especially Irish farmers who profited from that decision, as the Common Agriculture Policy brought money into the country to reshape the countryside. As a result, new houses replaced old cottages and living standards rose considerably. Central Statistics Office figures show even as early as 1994–95 that the centuries old gap in living standards between urban and rural Ireland has finally been closed.[139] Indeed, as modern technology advances more and more jobs are created in the so-called "techno cottages" in the country. Instead of commuting from their remote villages on traffic-clogged roads to their offices in the city and back home in the evenings, people work at home via the internet and other means of telecommunication. The "electronic cottage" may still be in its infancy, but "the age of the techno cottage dawns"[140] in Ireland.

Contemporary Ireland's economy is booming and today it is industry, particularly the new telecommunication, computer and software industries, that is contributing to this success. The Irish economy grew by 11 per cent in 1997, by about 9.9 per cent in 2000 and at an average rate of over 5 per cent for the last five years until 2005.[141] The Celtic Tiger's[142] GDP growth has soared above the

[134] Jude Collins, "Success a sign of the new reality," *The Irish News*, January 8, 2004, p. 2.
[135] Jude Collins, p. 2.
[136] www.president.ie/speeches/120705.html.

[137] *The Irish Times*, "Developing tourism", January 3, 2004.
[138] *The Irish Times*, "Developing tourism", January 3, 2004.
[139] See Sean D. Barrett, "Poor mouths becoming a thing of the past down on the farm", *Sunday Independent*, 9 February, 1997.
[140] Liz Morgan, "Age of the techno cottage dawns", *The Sunday Times*, January 4, 2004, p. 10.
[141] EU-Kommission/WKO, http://wko.at/statistik/eu/europa-wirtschaftswachstum.pdf.
[142] Ireland's nickname because of its economic success; adapted from the term "tiger states" for the economically booming East Asian states.

EU average[143] and by the year 2000, according to the report by the economic policy and statistics section of the House of Commons, the Irish were wealthier than the British with £12,811 GDP per capita compared to £12,623 in Britain.[144] This was not unexpected. "The country has been investing heavily in education, focusing on those so-needed high-tech skills."[145] And, indeed, its well-qualified young workforce and its specialisation in telecommunication and computer orientated industries are a great advantage to Ireland in times of the globalisation of markets. "Ireland's so-far disadvantageous out-of-the-way location is now irrelevant."[146] In 2005 Ireland was the second richest country after Luxemburg in the European Union and may, as Uwe Müller from *Die Welt* assumes, even serve as a role model for the new Bundesländer in Germany and their economic problems.[147]

Although like many other international economies at the beginning of the new millennium the Irish "engine of economy feels the pressure,"[148] and *The Irish Times* produced a headline entitled "Better outlook for the economy"[149] on January 2, 2004 which indicates that the Irish economy has seen some difficulties lately, the country seems to be on its way. Ireland's membership of the European Union aided its progress towards economic independence from the United Kingdom, which had, so far, been its only trading partner. And this also means that "Ireland is now a fully postcolonial country, no longer paralyzed by its ancient hatred of Britain. It sees itself as both Irish and European."[150] This is why Ireland voted for the Maastricht Treaty by a substantial majority of 69,05%. The Irish presidency of the EU in 1996 and 2004 gave Ireland another opportunity to demonstrate a new self-confidence and to present itself as an equal and accepted member of the European nations.

One other aspect of the many changes modern Ireland is undergoing which is often underestimated in its consequences for the country's future should be mentioned here: multiculturalism. Ireland is not Heinrich Böll's Ireland anymore or, as Conor O'Clery puts it, "Not my grandmother's Ireland."[151] Ireland is "inevitably becoming a multiracial society"[152] with new challenges for a society that always used to be an all-white, homogeneous one. As a result of Ireland's economic success and the good working opportunities in the country nowadays, it is not only the former Irish emigrants who are coming back home, but the country's opportunities are now also attracting people from all over the world. "Thanks to the roaring 'Celtic Tiger' economy, Ireland is now a place of immigration rather than emigration,"[153] and so Brazilians, Russians, Romanians, Portuguese, Chinese and many other nationalities now work and live in Ireland. This may have some exotic multicultural effects like the 2003 St. Patrick's Day Parade in Dublin which "was led by 20-year-old pop star Samantha Mumba, daughter of a Zambian refugee, who speaks English with a north Dublin accent...,"[154] but it also creates serious frictions and violent attacks against those foreigners not only in the Republic but also and mainly in Northern Ireland.[155]

The Text

The final text in this section is an excerpt from President McAleese's address "Hopes for the New Millennium" which she delivered on 11 June, 2000 in St. Patrick's Cathedral, Dublin. "Hopes for the New Millennium" was also the title of a monthly series of lectures that the Dean of St. Patrick's Cathedral had initiated and which many well-known speakers contributed to in the year 2000.

In this excerpt from the address[156], Mary McAleese talks about the changes that Ireland has undergone during the past few years and what they might imply. She also pins her high hopes on these changes and others that might be brought about in the future. Indeed, what stands out in this speech is the frequent use of the word "hope." In the text we can find the word six times and in her address as a whole she mentions the word "hope" twenty-nine times. Of course, the title of her address and the series of lectures in St. Patrick's Cathedral require her, from a rhetorical point of view, to use this prominent word often

143 "Consulting group PricewaterhouseCoopers says it expects Ireland's economic growth rate to be almost three times the euro zone average this year. Its European Economic Outlook predicts that Ireland's gross domestic product will expand by 5%, compared with an average 1.75% in the euro zone. For 2006, PwC forecasts Irish GDP growth of 4.75%, blaming the slight slowdown on an erosion of competitiveness which may dampen export growth." *RTÉ Business*, "Exports to keep Irish growth faster," February 07, 2005, www.rte.ie/business/2005/0207/economy.html.

144 Rory Carroll, "Irish 'wealthier than British in four years'" in The Irish News, http://www.irishnews.com, October 1996.

145 "Emerald Tiger", p.15.

146 "Emerald Tiger", p. 16.

147 Uwe Müller, "Von den Iren lernen," *Die Welt*, 12 März 2005, S. 12.

148 Damien Kiberd, "Engine of economy feels the pressure," *The Sunday Times*, 28 December, 2003.

149 *The Irish Times*, "Better outlook for the economy," January 2, 2004, p. 19.

150 John F. Stacks, "Irish Renaissance", *Time*, 11 December 1995, p. 24.

151 Conor O'Clery, "Not my grandmother's Ireland," *Newsweek*, 22 September, 2003, p. 13.

152 Kevin Myers, "An Irishman's Diary," *The Irish Times*, December 31, 2003, p. 13.

153 Conor O'Clery, "Not my grandmother's Ireland," *Newsweek*, 22 September, 2003, p. 13.

154 Conor O'Clery, p. 13.

155 See BBC News /Northern Ireland, "Racial attacks 'on increase'", 17 August, 2004.

156 The complete address can be found under www.ireland.com/newspaper/special/2000/mcaleease/.

enough, but it also demonstrates her deep commitment to what she has to say. The two words "change" and "hope" therefore dominate this passage in a way which is appropriate for a speech that welcomes a new millennium with all its implications for people's yearnings for a new beginning and a better life.
In the opening passage she first says how privileged she is to live in a country that enjoys "unprecedented prosperity, peace and opportunity" (l. 5), which, indeed, are the keywords of this great change that Ireland has undergone in recent years (see "Background to the Text"). By observing that the Irish people have been taught "that we can generate those changes" (l. 8), she makes an overt appeal to everybody to actively contribute to those changes and not to "accept the dead hand of fate, the paralysis of history" (l. 9f.). This refers to Ireland's tragic relationship to England that has, for centuries, left many Irish passively accept their fate or leave the country to live elsewhere. Today, after Ireland has become "the economic success story of Europe" (ll. 14f.) many former emigrants are now encouraged to return to their mother country. They are also being joined by many refugees and asylum seekers, who are a challenge that, as she admits later in her lecture, "we are struggling to deal with," full of hope, however, that "those who are today frightened of the stranger, tomorrow find the courage to become the stranger's friend and protector."[157] This is an obvious hint at the problems Ireland is facing with the many (often poor) people from countries other than Ireland pouring into the country (see "Background to the Text"). Two other factors which have contributed to a great change in Irish self-esteem and the international acknowledgement of Ireland, are the considerable impact of Irish culture on the world and the "seeds of peace" (l. 18) that can be seen sprouting in Northern Ireland. Irish culture, particularly Irish folk and rock music, with singers like Enya or bands like "U2" and Irish dancing like Michael Flatley's "Lord of the Dance" have, indeed, been highly successful over the years and raised great interest in Irish culture all over the world. And peace in Northern Ireland would certainly be a great relief to the world (see Text 16, "A farewell to arms?").

The President's main occupation in this excerpt, however, is Ireland's new and, above all, alternative look at its history and its relation to the present or, as McAleese formulates it, "between what has gone and what is" (ll. 24f.). These words are of particular importance as there is "impatience" (l. 26) prevailing among many who expect a change for the better and who want faster progress towards this modern Ireland. McAleese calls this impatience "hardly surprising (l. 28) since the Irish have too often been "prisoners of history" (ll. 28f.) History, and this must be understood as a serious criticism of her own countrymen, has been used too often by the Irish to "confirm our sense of victimhood and to identify the enemy" (ll. 30f.). And she is right: As becomes apparent in many Irish rebel songs the Irish have too willingly indulged themselves in this feeling of being the victims, with England being the all-powerful enemy and with themselves having no chance of ever being able to change this situation. Heroes were created and somehow this victimhood was romanticized and taken as an eternal well of self-pity. Of course, nobody wants to deny the injustice, the brutality, and the wounds that history has inflicted on Ireland. Those "wounds of history are still raw" (ll. 31f.). They are the "scars of emigration, discrimination and poverty" (ll. 32f.) which were the consequences of "centuries of colonization" by England. Another consequence of this infliction of heteronomy on Ireland that McAleese sees is the "low self-esteem" (l. 33) of the Irish learned from the cradle, generation by generation over the centuries. To support this statement she quotes Nobel-Laureat Seamus Heaney, who calls this phenomenon the "'high-banked clouds of resignation'" (ll. 34f.). The president admits that all these humiliations can still be touched and felt (l. 36). Nevertheless, in order to take up again what has been said above, Irish perceptions of history, of memories, have been "selective" (l. 39) and this has "served not to illuminate our present, but to disfigure it" (l. 39f). This is harsh criticism of her countrymen, but she calls the way the Irish remember their past "the core problem" (l. 37). A modern Ireland as she depicts it at the beginning of the extract, "today" (l. 40) has "an opportunity to remember it differently" (l. 41). Ireland is strong and self-confident enough now to be able to remember what has happened "with more generosity and forgiveness" (l. 41f.). Thus, a new and modern Ireland that has entered the 21st century can "create the future we hope and long for" (ll. 43f.). The president thinks positively and constructively when she hopes that many will follow her in her "attempt to build new friendships and partnerships" (ll. 46f.) between those who are still far apart at the moment, between "North and South, between unionist and nationalist, catholic and protestant, between Ireland and England, Scotland and Wales" (ll. 47ff.). Basing her hopes on the example of that little town of Greysteel in Northern Ireland, where cooperation between Catholics and Protestants has left former enmity behind, she conjures up a brighter future because "the past, even when it has brought us pain, can make us stronger, kinder, more sensitive to the pain of others" (ll. 54ff.).

[157] Mary McAleese, "Hopes for the New Millennium", *The Irish Times*, June 11, 2000, www.ireland.com/newspaper/special/2000/mcaleease/.

President McAleese's address is a fine example of a political speech which is intended to create vision, to open up new horizons, to demand positive thinking, express pride in what has been achieved so far and hope in what can be achieved. The core of her message (at least in this excerpt) is that a fundamental change in the approach towards Irish history, actually the dawning of a new historical consciousness will serve as a platform for a new outlook on Ireland's future.

As regards the style of the speech, one has to point out three aspects in particular: register, tone, and the use of some characteristic examples of rhetorical devices like metaphor, repetition, contrast, and rhetorical questions.

As to **register** students can easily recognize that the language is very formal since the serious, almost solemn topic, a speech in Dublin's most famous cathedral on the occasion of a celebration of the new millennium, demands a corresponding level of speech, namely a highly elaborate language.

The **tone** is one of pride and self-assertion at the beginning when she conjures up the achievements of modern Ireland but this becomes serious and insistent in the second part when she is talking about the new attitude towards Irish history that she advocates.

The **rhetorical devices** she employs underline this solemn tone. Some of them are, for example,
repetition: the word "hope" is repeated 6 times; *metaphor*: when she talks about the "seeds of peace" (l. 18) in Northern Ireland or quotes Seamus Heaney's metaphor " the high-banked clouds of resignation" (l. 34f.); *contrast*: when referring to "what has gone and what is" (ll. 24f.) or "North and South", "unionist and nationalist", "catholic and protestant" (l. 47f.).

For their work on Project 12, students could, in the case of Dr Martin Luther King's famous speech "I Have a Dream", refer to Peter Freese's *The American Dream* in *Viewfinder* (München: Langenscheidt, 2005) for the text of the original speech and to the accompanying Resource Book for a detailed analysis. Former President John F. Kennedy's 1961 inauguration speech can, for example, be found in *An English and American Reader*, ed. by Diether F. Simoneit (Paderborn: Ferdinand Schöningh, 1967, 4th ed.), pp. 127–129. Both speeches are also available from the nearest *Amerika Haus*. The former German president Richard von Weizsäcker's speech of 8 May 1985, which gained him much approval and respect, is contained in Richard von Weizsäcker, *Von Deutschland aus. Reden des Bundespräsidenten* (Berlin: Corso bei Siedeler, 1985). For Project 13 the two addresses are: The Government Supplies Agency, Publication Branch, 4/5 Harcourt Road, Dublin 2; Ireland and European Commission, Representation in Ireland, European Union House, 18 Dawson Street, Dublin 2, Ireland.

For further studies John Ardagh, *Ireland and the Irish. Portrait of a Changing Society* (London: Hamish Hamilton, 1995), is recommended.

11 | "No More Terror?"

text type: political commentary
length: 84 words
degree of difficulty: *; 4 annotations and 2 explanations
theme: a hopeful but pragmatic first evaluation of the IRA ceasefire announcement of 31 August 1994

related visual material: headline from *The Belfast Telegraph of Wednesday*, 31 August 1994 and two photos illustrating the situation in Northern Ireland before the ceasefire

for additional background material see Information Sheets 9: "The 1994 Ceasefire Statements", 10 "IRA Statement in Full" (28 July 2005), 11 "Independent International Commission on Decommissioning" (Chasterlein Report, 26 September 2005) and 12 "A Short History of the Conflict in Northern Ireland"

In a sensational statement on Thursday, July 28, 2005 the IRA formally proclaimed an end to its 35 years of armed struggle. Is this "farewell to arms" the beginning of the end, the fanfare to lasting peace in the troubled province? Or is there, as the leading article in Times Online of the same day puts it, "plenty of room left for disappointment" as with so many hailed new beginnings? Anyhow, it all began on 31 August 1994, when the IRA ceasefire statement opened the door to hope.

Text 11 marks the beginning of part II of this anthology, the study of the particular situation of Northern Ireland. Although Northern Ireland and the Republic of Ireland seem to the foreigner to be two different countries on the same island today, the students will by now have realised that the two parts are very tightly interwoven with each other in terms of history, culture, politics, and economy. But why then, the question might arise, has the name of Northern Ireland, at least until the events in former Yugoslavia, been synonymous for more than 35 years with Europe's most incomprehensible and most violent trouble spot? And why does it seem so extremely difficult to bring peace to this part of the island? The six texts in this section are an attempt to make students aware of various aspects of the problem and how difficult it is to create an atmosphere of mutual trust in and understanding of the other side that might form a basis for a lasting peace.[158]

The extensive introductory information to text 11 provides the general background against which the texts in the two remaining sequences can be approached. It traces the development of the conflict in Northern Ireland from the partition of Ireland in 1921 to the prospects of a possible peace today. As it serves as a reference section for texts 12 to 16 and contains facts or details central to all the issues presented in the second part of this Viewfinder volume, the background information to the remaining texts can be limited to their specific contexts.

Background to the Text: The Road to 'The Troubles' in Northern Ireland

In 1996/97 the Irish lined up in front of cinemas all over the country to see the Neil Jordan film *Michael Collins*, starring Liam Neeson. One can debate about how good *Michael Collins* is as a film[159] and it probably offended some people especially in the North, simply because it is about an IRA hero. But almost a century after the controversial life and death of Michael Collins, he remains one of the 20th century's most significant yet disregarded Irish political figures, and the film gives an easy-to-grasp key to the understanding of the roots of modern Ireland's tragic history. Michael Collins, companion to and rival of later Irish president Eamon de Valera in their common fight against British occupation after the events of 1916, is a rather disputed historical figure. Is he to be judged as a brutal terrorist who was responsible for the killing of many people[160] or will history in the end see him as dedicated to peace and freedom, since it was his guerilla warfare and his ingenious intelligence system which finally forced the British to the negotiating table in 1921? Collins's bravery, charismatic energy and political good luck resulted in both the triumph of an Irish Free State and the tragedy of continued violence in Northern Ireland, since the result of his and Arthur Griffith's negotiations with the British government was a divided country.[161] During the brutal civil war over this issue he was killed by his own side as a traitor. Michael Collins's tragic death at the age of 31 by his own people (the breakaway 'Irregulars' of the IRA) ended a life which contained countless contradictions and which can therefore be regarded as a symbol of the controversial and contradictory history of the Ireland that followed his death and which had already been foreseen in W. B. Yeats's famous poem "Easter 1916" (see Course Manager, "Getting the Course Started"). Thus, one can say, it all started with Michael Collins.

Of course, the history of the particular status of north-eastern Ireland did not begin in 1921, as the previous texts must have made clear (see also Information Sheet 8, "A Short History of the Conflict in Northern Ireland"). The Ulster Plantations of 1609, the victory of William of Orange ('King Billy') at the River Boyne in 1690 but especially Protestant reactions to the 19th-century Home Rule movement had already divided the Irish north-east from the rest of Ireland.

> Throughout the nineteenth century the Protestants of Ulster had become increasingly committed to the union with Great Britain. [...] Once Catholic emancipation had been granted, the Protestants realised they would be in a minority in any Irish parliament, and sectarian rioting became common as the Orange Order persuaded its followers that home rule meant Rome rule.[162]

This was the time when the slogan "Ulster Will Fight" originated. The various Home Rule debates in the British parliament finally pushed not only Arthur Griffith's new party Sinn Féin (1906) and the IRA (Irish Republican Army, 1919) to support the Republican side but also made the UVF (Ulster Volunteer Force, 1913), a Protestant loyalist organisation, ready to fight Home Rule. As the Third Home Rule Bill was stopped by World War I the Republicans finally took up arms and started the Easter Rising of 1916. The sixteen leaders were executed by the British authorities. "By these sixteen executions the British had accomplished what the rebellion itself had failed to do, and that was to arouse a lethargic Irish people into a rage that would ultimately

---

[158] A whole range of books gives detailed analyses of the situation and advice as to how to solve the dilemma. Among those which are easy to obtain and fairly up-to-date are: John McGarry and Brendan O'Leary, *Explaining Northern Ireland. Broken Images* (Oxford: Blackwell, 1995); Brendan O'Leary and John McGarry, The Politics of Antagonism. Understanding Northern Ireland (London & Atlantic Highlands, NJ: The Athlone Press, Second Edition, 1996); Sabine Wichert, *Northern Ireland since 1945* (London and New York: Longman, repr. 1992); J. B. Bell, *The Irish Troubles. A Generation of Violence, 1967-1992* (Dublin: Gill & Macmillan, repr. 1994); Tim Pat Coogan, *The Troubles: Ireland's Ordeal 1966-1995 and the Search for Peace* (London: Hutchinson, 1995); Dermot Keogh, *Twentieth-Century Ireland. Nation and State* (Dublin: Gill & Macmillan, 1994).

[159] But it did gain the Venice Film Festival's Golden Lion Award for Best Picture of 1996.

[160] Apart from many other atrocities, he was responsible for the November 1920 massacre of "Bloody Sunday" in which ten British officers were killed in front of their families, and his politics contributed to the outbreak of the Irish Civil War of 1922/23.

[161] Under the pressure of having to solve the long-lasting conflict over Home Rule, the British government under Lloyd George had a partition written into the Government of Ireland Act in 1920 in order to accommodate the dissenting Protestant majority in the North who feared they would be controlled by a Catholic government in Dublin. This partition was ratified in the Treaty negotiations. The Act, however, also included the later installation of a Council of Ireland that was intended to eventually lead to reunification.

[162] Martin Wallace, *A Short History of Ireland*, p. 64.

lead to nationhood and a new insurrection."[163] In the 1918 British General Election, Sinn Féin won 73 of the 105 Irish seats but they refused to take them up in Westminster. Instead, they met in Dublin and established the Dail Éireann, an Irish Parliament, on 21 January 1919, which declared the independence of Ireland from Britain. The British Army, among them the dreaded 'Blacks and Tans', marched in and a brutal War of Independence began in which Michael Collins as the leader of the IRA directed much of the resistance (see above). The 1920 Government of Ireland Act set up two subordinate parliaments in Ireland, one for the six counties of Ulster, which remained under direct British control, and the 26 counties of the rest of Ireland, which were given dominion status and became the Republic of Ireland. Although not even the North wanted it, the Unionists finally accepted partition while Michael Collins, as one of the representatives of the Irish parliament in their negotiations with London, signed the Treaty "under an ultimatum by Lloyd George to accept or to face an 'immediate and terrible war.'"[164]

The 1920 Government of Ireland Act and the 1921 treaty option of the partition of the island must therefore be considered the beginning of the problems that modern Ireland is facing today. "The roots of the division pre-dated partition; the constitutional, political and economic separation of Ireland ossified this division."[165]

After Collins, Griffith and the other delegates returned from London with the Anglo-Irish Treaty of 1921 in their hands, the Irish parliament was immediately divided over the terms of that treaty. The treaty

> provided that the new 'Irish Free State' should have dominion status, that members of its parliament should take an oath of allegiance to the crown, and that Britain should maintain naval bases in certain Irish ports. Northern Ireland was given the right to opt out of the Irish Free State, and the parliament in Belfast immediately took advantage of this.[166]

In particular, Collins's comrade-in-arms Eamon de Valera was unwilling to accept, above all, the oath of allegiance, but Collins was convinced they had achieved "'not the ultimate freedom that all nations aspire and develop to, but the freedom to achieve it.'"[167] The freedom the Irish had achieved, however, quickly developed into the first serious crisis after the Dail (the Irish parliament) ratified the treaty by a majority of only 64 to 57. In a general election in the South in June 1922, out of 128 seats 58 went to pro-treaty candidates, 36 to anti-treaty republicans led by de Valera, 17 to Labour, and 17 to other groups. After the IRA had already split into two factions, a civil war became unavoidable when de Valera became head of a republican-led rival government. In the end de Valera left the IRA and founded his own party, the Fianna Fail. In 1932 he won the elections and remained in power until his resignation in 1959.

While all this happened in the South, the North, under the Government of Ireland Act of 1920 and its right given in the Anglo-Irish Treaty of 1921 of opting out of the Irish Free State, was under a firm Unionist majority. In the 1921 elections for the first Northern Irish parliament, forty Unionists and only six Nationalists and six Sinn Féin representatives were elected. The cabinet was led by Sir James Craig. However, with a population of about 1.5 million of whom roughly one third were Catholics, the Northern Ireland government could always rely on the two thirds of the population who were Protestant.

> Since the constitutional compromise [of the Government of Ireland Act, P.R.] was accepted by only two-thirds of the population, but rejected and partly violently opposed by the rest, the government had to use force itself in order to stay in power. The resulting unrest amounted to something close to a civil war: between 1920 and 1922 almost 300 people were killed [...]. Violent republicanism aimed to destroy whatever and whomever could be said to represent the British administration, claimed to speak for the whole minority population and frequently used that civilian population as a shield. This reinforced the divide between the denominational communities and was thus socially much more destructive than the civil war in the South [...]. Religious identities more than ever before became national identities.[168]

And although Craig and Collins had suggested regular meetings at governmental level, the relations between the Irish Free State and Northern Ireland "deteriorated fast and contact ceased altogether."[169] A boundary commission was proposed to fix the border between Northern Ireland and the Irish Free State, an act that proved an abiding problem. Finally, an agreement was signed by the British, Irish and Northern Irish governments on 3 December 1925. Northern Ireland, i. e. the six counties of Antrim, Armagh, Down, Fermanagh, Londonderry and Tyrone, was now definitely separated from the rest of Ireland. What seemed to be a second state had been created on Irish soil with its own constitution, parliament and administration for local affairs and a separate political province of the United Kingdom with 17 MPs in Westminster.

The following fifty or so years were relatively quiet years, although the IRA continued its struggle to end the partition of Ireland. While in the Irish Free State (after

[163] Arbeitsgruppe Englisch Groß-Gerau, "Violence in Northern Ireland," *Englisch Amerikanische Studien*, 3 (September 1981), p. 398.

[164] Arbeitsgruppe Englisch Groß-Gerau, p. 398.

[165] Sabine Wichert, *Northern Ireland since 1945* (London and New York: Longman, 1992), p. 10.

[166] Martin Wallace, p. 72.

[167] Quoted from Martin Wallace, p. 72.

[168] Sabine Wichert, p. 15.

[169] Sabine Wichert, p. 13.

1949, the Republic of Ireland) continuity was secured through de Valera's long-lasting government, which favoured a Catholic conservatism, the predominance of the Unionist Party remained unbroken until 1972 when London assumed direct rule as a result of the escalating 'Troubles'.

'The Troubles' is a euphemistic understatement of one of modern European civilisation's darker chapters and must actually be called a 'war'.[170] It has cost more than 3,000 lives, injured and crippled ten of thousands and caused material damage of millions of pounds. And we cannot be certain that rioting, bombing or other types of violence will not break out at any time. Terrorism has been Northern Ireland's lot for over forty years since the IRA started a second campaign of terrorism for the reunification of the two Irelands in 1955, much more so since the Catholic Civil Rights movement appeared on the stage at the end of the 1960s.

From the beginning, the Catholic minority in Northern Ireland had to suffer from "Protestant control of local government and the favouring of Protestants in the distribution of jobs, public housing, education, and social services."[171] Its most obviously discriminatory form was gerrymandering, a form of "deliberate manipulation of local government electoral boundaries [...] in order to achieve and maintain Unionist control of local authorities and so to deny to Catholics influence in local government proportionate to their numbers."[172] What had kept the Catholics all these years from ignoring these disadvantages was Northern Ireland's relative economic security, especially the many jobs that Belfast's shipbuilding and textile industries could offer them.

In 1968, under the influence of the Black Civil Rights Movement in the U.S.A., this disadvantaged minority organised their own civil rights movement against the glaring inequities they were confronted with. The Protestant side reacted fiercely. Riots in Armagh, Enniskillen, Londonderry and other towns in Ulster, started by Catholics and Protestants alike, provoked violent reactions from the other side. The most serious riots of that time took place in Belfast and Londonderry (Derry). The great march of the Orange Order[173] and the following tumults of 12 August 1969 in Derry must be seen as the beginning of what is now almost 30 years of 'Troubles' in Northern Ireland. On that day the march ended with the Protestants' attack on the Bogside, a Catholic quarter in Londonderry (Derry), which raged for 48 hours.

The events of the summer of 1969 were reason enough for the IRA to re-emerge and support the cause of the Catholics with their own means. It was particularly the PIRA (Provisional Irish Republican Army) or Provos, who broke away from the 'official' IRA and turned to terror tactics. It cannot be denied, however, that those jointly responsible for the increasing terror in Northern Ireland were the Orange Order, the RUC (Royal Ulster Constabulary)[174], but especially the ultra-conservative right wing-faction of the Unionist Party. Among those to be particularly mentioned in this context is the militant Protestant clergyman Ian Paisley, co-founder of the DUP (Democratic Unionist Party),[175] who is fiercely opposed to any change in the status quo of Ulster. They were all, willingly or unwillingly, supported by paramilitary brigades like the UVF (Ulster Volunteer Force) or the UDA (Ulster Defence Association), the Protestant counterpart of the IRA. The militant wings of the two sides, Protestant and Catholic, are responsible for the extremely high death toll in this sectarian struggle.

The conflict, it seemed, could not be ended, although that was the hope of the authorities when the British Army was sent in in 1969. Their task was to help the local police, maintain British authority and keep Protestant reactions under control. The troops expected to be home in two weeks, but they are still there. They became more and more involved in this conflict, especially since the IRA focused their terrorist activities both on Loyalist targets and on a "Brits Out" campaign. With the arrival of the Army the number of deaths rose every month from 10 in August 1969 to nearly 100 in June 1972 with an increasing number of army deaths.[176]

One of the most atrocious events of the 'Troubles', which has come to be known as 'Bloody Sunday', happened on 30 January 1972 when British soldiers shot and killed 14 participants in a Catholic civil rights march in Londonderry (Derry). Almost 30 years after the event the wounds have not healed, since no official British apology has ever been made, although no weapons were found on the victims and a recently published book (*Eyewitness Bloody Sunday. The Truth*, ed. by Don Mullan [Dublin: Wolfhound Press, 1997]) aroused public attention by claiming that the British government has never told the whole truth. The answer in the years that

---

170 See Brendan O'Leary and John McGarry, *The Politics of Antagonism. Understanding Northern Ireland* (London & Atlantic Highlands, NJ: The Athlone Press, Second Edition, 1996), pp. 9ff.

171 "Northern Ireland since 1922", on *Britannica CD 2.0.*

172 *Disturbances in Northern Ireland Report of the Commission appointed by the Governor of Northern Ireland* (Belfast: HMSO, September 1969, Cmd. 532), p. 91.

174 The state police force of Northern Ireland that was responsible for the security, later together with the British Army and the UDR (Ulster Defence Regiment). It was then mainly recruited from Protestants and often accused of maltreatment of suspects and prisoners.

175 One of those many deviations from the old block of Unionism because of increasing diversity of political views that has left Unionism today with "a more petit-bourgeois and fragmented character." (Mark Ryan, *War and Peace in Ireland. Britain and the IRA in the New World Order* (London and Boulder, Colorado: Pluto Press, 1994), p. 131).

176 Figures taken from *The Sunday Times*, 11 January 1976.

followed was the terrorist bombings of the IRA, the counter terror of the various loyalist paramilitary organisations and again and again the deaths of hundreds of innocent victims.

Until 1972 all legislative power had been exercised through a governor of the British crown. On 24 March the growing violence led the British government to suspend Stormont, Northern Ireland's parliament, and Prime Minister Edward Heath imposed direct rule on the region. The administration became the responsibility of the Secretary of State for Northern Ireland. But civil disorder went on with increased intensity following a decision of the British government to allow internment without trial. Already in 1971 Edward Heath's government had given way to the demand of the UUP (Ulster Unionist Party) for the government to use this mode of repression against nationalist insurrection.

> By authority of the the Special Powers Act the Internment Policy was started. Searching for IRA people doors were kicked in by boot or gun butt in the traditional middle-of-the-night strikes, men were beaten and dragged half naked before the eyes of their children and hysterical wives, furniture was smashed up and windows broken. By the end of 1971 nearly one thousand men were interned for indefinite terms without charges against them and without legal rights. Among them were some IRA people, but the majority were sympathizers, Civil Righters and old Republicans. Moderate Catholics now flocked to the IRA, and hatred of the British became as intense as at any time in their centuries of occupation.[177]

Nevertheless, all through the 1970s steady terrorist pressure was maintained by the Provisional IRA and the Loyalist extremists. Viewed historically,

> internment [...] proved to be a political and military disaster. It unified most Catholics, prompted civil and armed disobedience, brought a propaganda coup for the Provisional IRA, international embarrassment for the British, and was the catalyst for even greater violence.[178]

At the beginning of the 1980s a new tactic was employed by the IRA to win sympathy among the population: hunger strikes by IRA members confined in British prisons to demand political status for IRA prisoners. The most popular hunger striker was Bobby Sands, who even won a seat in the British Parliament and whose death on 4 May 1981 set off a wave of support for Sinn Féin, the political wing of the IRA.

All through the 1970s, with an average of 275 deaths per year from 1971–76, and the first part of the 1980s, with 50 to 100 political murders each year,[179] the antagonism between the two communities remained as sharp as ever. British efforts at arbitration were in vain. Sectarian conflict between the two communities prevented any form of cooperation such as power-sharing or common assemblies. Northern Ireland had reached a deadlock.

It was only with the *Anglo-Irish Agreement* of 1985 that hopes were raised that cooperation was possible – at least between London and Dublin. The two Prime Ministers, Margaret Thatcher and Garret FitzGerald, signed the Agreement that established an "Intergovernmental Conference in which the Irish Government will put forward views and proposals on certain aspects of Northern Ireland affairs."[180] This meant that the Republic of Ireland was given a say in Northern Ireland. On the other hand the two governments affirmed "that the status of Northern Ireland would remain unchanged so long as that was the wish of the majority of its people" and they recognised that it was "the present wish of a majority [...] to remain part of the United Kingdom."[181] The Agreement was strongly opposed by both Unionists and the IRA. By the early 1990s according to rival interpretations "the emergent consensus of commentators was that the AIA had merely created a new stalemate; coercive consociationalism had run up against the limits of entrenched antagonisms."[182] In the meantime, despite these endeavours for a possible peace, the IRA had intensified its bombing terror and even spread it to mainland Britain and the continent where British military personnel were the main targets. Again, Loyalist terrorist groups responded violently with increasing numbers of sectarian murders. How was the antagonism to be transcended?

Apart from the Intergovernmental Conference that was established under the AIA and that met on a regular basis, other peace initiatives were taken in the 1990s, private ones as well as official ones. Peace rallies brought thousands onto the streets; after his daughter's death in the IRA bombing at Enniskillen in 1987 Protestant Gordon Wilson caught public attention when he met with the IRA in April 1993 to persuade it to give up violence; John Hume, leader of Northern Ireland's Catholic-based Social Democratic and Labour Party secretly met Sinn Féin leader Gerry Adams to find ways for a peace settlement. Among the more prominent were the so-called Brooke initiative from 1990 onwards, named after Peter Brooke who was appointed Secretary of State for Northern Ireland in 1989, the *Joint Declaration* (Downing Street Declaration) of British and Irish Prime Ministers John Major and Albert Reynolds (1993), the Forum for Peace and Reconciliation established by the Irish government in October 1994 to bring together representatives of most political parties (including Sinn Féin) and examine ways in which lasting

[177] Arbeitsgruppe Englisch Groß-Gerau, p. 399.
[178] Brendan O'Leary and John McGarry, p. 176.
[179] Figures taken from "United Kingdom: Northern Ireland since 1922" on *Encyclopaedia Britannica CD 2.0.*
[180] "Northern Ireland: Agreement between the United Kingdom and the Republic of Ireland" (London: Reference Services, Central Office of Information, No 273/85, 1985) p. 1.
[181] "Northern Ireland: Agreement", p. 1.
[182] Brendan O'Leary and John McGarry, pp. 273f.

peace, stability and reconciliation could be established,[183] and the *Frameworks for the Future* signed by John Major and Irish Taoiseach (Prime Minister) John Bruton (1995). In particular, Albert Reynold's work during his years as Irish Prime Minister should not be underestimated.

In 1993 the *Joint Declaration for Peace* of the British and the Irish Prime Ministers, named the Downing Street Declaration after the place where it was announced, set out a framework for peace. It underlined the self-determination of the people of Ireland "to bring about a united Ireland, if that is their wish." But it also recognised that this right "must be achieved and exercised with and subject to the agreement and consent of a majority of the people in Northern Ireland." This Declaration mainly defined the British position in this conflict and made clear that Britain was neither opposed to Irish unity in principle nor had it any selfish interest in Northern Ireland. Its final aim was to see "peace, stability and reconciliation established by agreement among all the people who inhabit the island." The Republic of Ireland, on the other hand, was willing, if necessary, to make changes to its Constitution of 1937, which claims in its Article 2: "The national territory consists of the whole island of Ireland."

This Declaration marked a significant shift in British policy and despite simplifications in its evaluation like

> [the] British government certainly derives no pleasure from its continuing occupation of Northern Ireland. Every British politician would dearly wish to be rid of the place, allowing the government to run Britain proper without the trouble of a colonial war,[184]

its message was understood by those it was aimed at. On 31 August 1994 the IRA announced an unconditional and open-ended cessation of all military activities which was followed by a similar declaration of the Combined Loyalist Military Command on 13 October 1994 (see Information Sheet 9). For the first time in a quarter of a century there was solid hope for an end to the terror in Northern Ireland.

According to O'Leary and McGarry,[185] four reasons accounted for the fact that the guns were silenced:

- a strengthening of the political (compared to the military) option on the Republican and the Loyalist side (in particular Sinn Féin under Gerry Adams wanted to get rid of its image as the party of war)
- unofficial diplomatic activities of Northern Irish parliamentarian John Hume (SDLP) and Gerry Adams (Sinn Féin) supported by an Irish-American peace delegation (1993) "helped persuade the republican leadership [...] that a switch to a purely political strategy, 'unarmed struggle', could pay dividends"
- clandestine negotiations, although officially denied, between the British government and the IRA from October 1990 until the winter of 1993. Republicans could not propagate any more "that the British state was the central obstacle to Irish unification"
- the long-term co-operative diplomacy of the British and the Irish governments.

As usual, interpretations of the wording (was a 'complete' cessation of violence the same as a 'permanent' cessation?) and incidents like the shooting of a postal worker during an armed IRA robbery hampered full confidence in the ceasefire. But gradually it became obvious that the Republicans were committed to the ceasefire. Meanwhile John Bruton was elected Taoiseach and made clear his determination to continue the work of Albert Reynolds. On 22 February 1995 Bruton and John Major released the *Frameworks for the Future* which comprised the jointly published "A New Framework for Agreement" and a separate British paper "A Framework for Accountable Government in Northern Ireland". This Joint Framework Document was designed to consolidate the peace process and laid out the two governments' programme for a comprehensive political settlement.

Some of the more practical steps to follow the ceasefire of 1994 were listed in *Newsweek* of 12 September 1994: Opening roads, release or transfer of some political prisoners, reduction of the military presence, investment in Northern Ireland, handing over weapons, making constitutional revisions.[186]

Yet political talks about the future of Northern Ireland only moved forward slowly. The most important problem turned out to be Britain's insistence on the 'decommissioning' of IRA weapons before Sinn Féin, their political representatives, could take part in the talks. The IRA rejected this and Sinn Féin insisted that no pre-conditions be demanded. The political representatives of the Republicans were therefore never allowed into the talks. Thus, a year after the announcement of the ceasefire the real dialogue had not even begun.

On the contrary, on 9 February 1996 an IRA bomb detonated in London's Docklands that killed two and injured 100. The end of the ceasefire seemed to end hopes of a settlement. More bombs have exploded since and senseless deaths and injuries have been caused. The reason, it was speculated,[187] was that the militants of the IRA lost patience with the political approach. Early in 1996 President Clinton's delegate to the Irish peace process, George Mitchell, in the so-called Mitchell Report had offered the compromise under which some decommissioning would take place during the process of all-party negotiations rather than before or after.

183 The regular sessions of the Forum were suspended after the ending of the IRA ceasefire.

184 Mark Ryan, *War & Peace in Ireland*, pp. 148f.

185 Brendan O'Leary and John McGarry, pp. 329ff.

186 See Daniel Pedersen, "Slouching toward Peace", *Newsweek*, 12 September 1994, pp. 8–14.

187 See "Terrorism and Ireland", *The New York Times*, 22 February 1996.

Instead, John Major suggested that before all-party talks, elections be held to choose participants in all-party talks. Republicans regarded this as a delaying tactic, because Major needed the nine Ulster Unionists in the British parliament to save his power and could therefore not antagonise them. It seemed the many reasonable concessions he had made in the years before that had furthered the peace-making in Northern Ireland were in jeopardy and war would be back in the streets of Belfast. The renewal of the IRA bombing campaign had continued to reduce Gerry Adams' authority as the spokesman for the republican side. Yet he was needed. Without the republicans at the negotiating table there would be no peace in Northern Ireland. And that is what the British, the Irish and the American governments knew just as well as the Unionists and the Catholics in Northern Ireland.

On 30 May 1996 out of a total electorate of about 1.2 million people 64% took part in the election for the Northern Ireland Forum. The "top 10", it had been decided, would take part in the all-party negotiations which had been fixed to begin on 10 June. The results signalled the people's yearning for peace or as *The Irish Times* wrote: "The people turned out to back the ballot over the bullet."[188] Of course, as was expected, the Ulster Unionist Party won the largest number (30) of the 110 seats for the Northern Ireland Forum. But what was surprising was how well Sinn Féin did, with 17 seats (15.5 per cent of the overall vote), especially Gerry Adams, who won four out of five votes in his West Belfast constituency. This also sent a message to the IRA to stop their policy of confrontation and give compromise a chance. The strong gains in the election were a clear verdict that Sinn Féin must join the all-party negotiations as Gerry Adams underlined, but the British and the Irish governments made Sinn Féin's entry to the talks dependent on another IRA ceasefire. And there was no prospect of that. On 22 June 1996 another bomb went off in Manchester during the European Soccer Championship. When even the Unionists and the IRA objected to former U.S. senator George Mitchell as neutral chairperson and the leader of the DUP (Democratic Unionist Party), Ian Paisley, said his party would not be at the talks if Sinn Féin was there, the situation at the beginning of the all-party talks for a peaceful future of Northern Ireland in mid-June 1996 was aptly described as follows:

> [...] whether or not the parties can agree on what to talk about, where and with whom, the fact is that they count for little if they do not in the end deliver a settlement with which Sinn Féin is happy. Sinn Féin will not be happy with any settlement to which it is not a party; and Sinn Féin will not be allowed into any talks unless the IRA disavows violence. And if the Manchester bomb is what it looks like, the IRA hasn't. Here, in other words, is the definition of deadlock.[189]

Thus, it seemed, prospects of peace remained slim as long as people stuck to their principles. And that is what they did. The peace talks were lingering on with Senator Mitchell finally accepted as talks chairman and American influence defined as "helpful, supportive, encouraging, (although) the decisions will be made by the parties themselves, by the governments themselves."[190]

Yet, on Friday 10 April 1998 the parties approved the Good Friday (or Belfast) Agreement (see text 12) which aimed at restoring self-government in Northern Ireland. Among other major aspects it also included the demand for a cross-community coalition government in Northern Ireland and the recognition that Northern Ireland remain part of the United Kingdom for as long as a majority of the population so desired. Likewise, Articles 2 and 3 of the constitution of the Republic of Ireland were changed and replaced the Republic's former territorial claim to Northern Ireland by an aspiration to a united Ireland. In May 1998 two referenda were held, one in Northern Ireland and one in the Republic, to let the population vote on this agreement. An overwhelming majority of 94 per cent of the votes cast in the Republic endorsed the agreement and more than 71 per cent of the votes cast in Northern Ireland were in favour with a clear majority among unionists and complete agreement among nationalists. The new power-sharing Northern Ireland Assembly gathered in mid-1998 for the first time after 1974 and the SDLP, the Ulster Unionist Party (UUP), the DUP, and Sinn Féin became partners in a new coalition government. David Trimble, leader of the Ulster Unionist Party (UUP), was elected as Northern Ireland's First Minister. Hopes for the future were high.

Yet, it was a fragile situation. On 15 August 1998 the Real IRA, a splinter group of the official IRA, laid another bomb which killed 29 people in Omagh/Northern Ireland. It came as a shock and seemed to damage confidence in the development of the peace process. The same year David Trimble and John Hume, leader of the SDLP, were awarded the Nobel Peace Prize for their work in bringing peace to Ireland. Sinn Féin, the political wing of the Irish Republican Army (IRA), had gained political respectability through its participation in the peace process. Especially Gerry Adams, president of Sinn Féin, was considered one of the main designers of Sinn Féin's shift to a policy of seeking a peaceful settlement to sectarian violence in Northern Ireland. Nevertheless, it was the IRA's reluctant agreement to decommission weapons which was a decisive

---

188 Denis Coghlan, "The people turned out to back the ballot over the bullet", *The Irish Times*, 1 June 1996.

189 Michael Elliott and Daniel Pedersen, "Instead of Talk", *Newsweek*, 24 June 1996, p. 22.

190 Mary Carolan, "Mitchell is 'committed to the talks'", *Irish News*, 8 November 1996.

part of the Belfast Agreement. Despite former U.S. senator George Mitchell's "confidence" statement in his renowned Mitchell Review at the end of 1999, the peace process was running into a deadlock. Problems amounted to a degree that devolution, i.e. the self-government of Northern Ireland within the UK, was suspended several times – and still is. When in the 2003 elections and the European elections of June 2004 Gerry Adams's Sinn Féin and Ian Paisley's DUP turned out to be the two major players in Stormont, the Northern Ireland parliament, the question was raised: "Can polar extremes do business"?[191] These difficulties have dogged the Northern Ireland peace process and the good intentions of the Good Friday Agreement. But although progress has been frustratingly slow over the years and there have been major setbacks, demilitarisation has brought something like normality back to the streets of Belfast and other places in Northern Ireland and what seems to be certain is that after nearly forty years, few wish to see the violence continue. All this hope started with the IRA's first ceasefire statement on 31 August 1994.

The Text

It can hardly be claimed that text 11 is as full a text as all the others. It would be a good idea to use it only to create a general awareness of sequence five: Northern Ireland and the story behind it. Its content helps to lead the students right into the heart of ambivalence that is so typical of Northern Ireland, since the text has both an emotional and a rational appeal.

The Belfast Telegraph is Northern Ireland's biggest-selling newspaper. Its large headline "It's Over!" probably expresses what the majority in this region blighted by terrorism felt when they read it: a great relief at a possible end of 'the long war'. Of course, the terror is not really over, the IRA has 'only' announced a ceasefire, but even this arouses intense excitement "after 3,168 deaths and 25 years of terror". The citizens of Belfast, Londonderry and elsewhere in the province hope for a normal life, for reconciliation, and for progress, after a life of permanent tension and fear. The photos that show us what used to be everyday life in Ulster make us aware of this: the omnipresence of the security forces in their armoured vehicles looking for snipers or checking your bags, and in spite of all precautions, the sudden blast of another bomb that brings death, injury and destruction of property.

It is this reality of 25 years that, despite all the joy and the longing for possible peace, causes the author of the commentary to remain rather sceptical. A couple of indicators in this short extract reveal his obvious distrust of the good news. First, he puts a question mark at the end of "No more terror?" This question simultaneously sums up the whole article and is the title of the commentary. Second, he states that "today *could* be one of the most significant days [...]" (l. 3). This is repeated in l. 5. His distrust comes out very clearly in the last sentence: "Or it could be another false dawn, to add to all the rest." (ll. 8f.)

In order to work on Analysis 4 in a productive way, students should be given a copy of Information Sheet 12 ("A Short History of the Conflict in Northern Ireland"). They might also read text 2 again to make sure they realise the all-Irish impact of the event. The two statements by the IRA and the Combined Loyalist Military Command are also available as Information Sheet 9 and 10; it might be interesting to study the tone of such documents.

To work on the **project task** successfully some preparation is necessary as is the case, of course, with any of the project tasks. In this case the students are required to enter into a concrete intercultural relationship and this might involve some risks like causing embarrassment because they might ask the wrong questions or they simply might not know what to do after the initial two or three contacts have been made. This is why the task offers some clues as to how to start. It might be a good idea to read Christian Alix's and Christoph Kondron's article "Deutsch-Französische Schulkooperation: Lernen im Dialog,"[192] which provides some helpful suggestions as to how to manage such a project, even though it has to be adapted to a more advanced level. For a more comprehensive approach towards project learning, in which some interesting examples are given, Michael Legutke's and Howard Thomas's book *Process and Experience in the Language Classroom*[193] is highly recommended. If the group wants to exchange their questions and answers and other project ideas via e-mail or wants to try the Internet to establish contact, Reinhard Donath's little brochures *E-Mail-Projekte im Englischunterricht* and *Internet und Englischunterricht*[194] can be very useful.

The following addresses might provide help in finding a school in Northern Ireland which is interested in co-operating in a project of this type: Belfast Education and Library Board, 40 Academy St Belfast BT1 2 NQ; North Eastern Education and Library Board, County Hall, 182 Galgorm Rd., Ballymena, Co. Antrim BT42 1HN; South Eastern Education and Library Board, 18 Windsor Ave, Belfast BT9 6EF; Southern Education and Library Board, 3 Charlemont Pl, The Mall, Armagh. Co. Armagh;

[191] BBC News, 14 June 2004.

[192] Christian Alix, Christoph Kodron, "Deutsch-Französische Schulkooperation: Lernen im Dialog," in *Über die Grenze. Praktisches Lernen im fremdsprachlichen Unterricht*, ed. by Christoph Edelhoff and Eckart Liebau (Weinheim und Basel: Beltz Grüne Reihe, 1988), pp. 176-191.

[193] Michael Legutke and Howard Thomas, *Process and Experience in the Language Classroom* (London and New York: Longman, 1991), especially pp. 157-256.

[194] Reinhard Donath, *E-Mail-Projekte im Englischunterricht* (Stuttgart: Klett, 1996), and *Internet und Englischunterricht* (Stuttgart: Klett, 1997).

Western Education and Library Board, 1 Hospital Rd, Omagh, Tyrone BT79 0AW.

Regarding the **internet project** one possible first good source is CAIN Web Service (Conflict Archive on the Internet); see www.cain.ulst.ac.uk/index.html.
For a detailed year-by-year chronology of the events of the troubles and the path to peace see http://www.cain.ulst.ac.uk/othelem/chron/ch02.htm.

12 | The Good Friday Agreement

text type: (excerpt from) legal document
length: 1091 words
degree of difficulty: ***; 39 annotations and 8 explanations
theme: key points of the Good Friday Agreement

additional text: editorial from *The Derry Journal*, Friday 2 January, 2004

related visual material: the official government referendum brochure; a graph of The Good Friday Agreement Latest Public Opinion survey by Millward Brown Ulster (formerly *Ulster Marketing Surveys*) Northern Ireland's premier market and social research agency (first published in *The Belfast Telegraph*, 25/26 October 2000)

Background to the Text: The Most Decisive Document for Peace in Northern Ireland

Based on the general information given in the introduction to this chapter in the Students' Book, (p. 46) the elaborations here will focus on a short analysis of the Agreement in general and a rather personal evaluation after a couple of years since its implementation.

The Good Friday Agreement, also called Belfast Agreement, as it was signed by all the participating parties in Belfast on Good Friday, 10 April 1998, is a political agreement of paramount importance for the Irish peace process. Its promise is nothing less than Northern Ireland's change from war to peace. The multi-party agreement is divided into eleven sections and provides for constitutional and institutional aspects, but also covers civil rights issues and relationships between the different parties. The so-called three strands of the settlement address relationships within Northern Ireland (most of all a Northern Ireland Assembly (or parliament) to exercise devolved legislative powers); between Northern Ireland and the Republic of Ireland (a so-called North/South Ministerial Council to develop forms of cooperation between ministers from the North and the Republic) and between the British and Irish governments (to reach agreement on matters of mutual interest). Apart from that the Agreement also contains measures on human and civil rights, policing, prisoners, decommissioning, and other aspects.

Multi-party talks which involved the two governments and the main Northern Ireland parties, but excluded Sinn Féin because of its indecisiveness on the issue of a ceasefire, started on 10 June 1996. On 20 July 1997, the IRA announced a resumption of its ceasefire and was then able to join the talks which made two unionist parties leave the negotiating table. However, negotiations under the chairmanship of U.S. Senator George Mitchell continued and gradually became substantive. Areas of agreement were outlined and potentials of remaining conflict were set apart. In the final round Irish Taoiseach, Bertie Ahern, and the British Prime Minister, Tony Blair, headed their two governments' delegations. On Good Friday 10 April 1998 a comprehensive political agreement was approved by all parties and the Good Friday or Belfast or Stormont Agreement was signed.

The overwhelming support of the Agreement on both sides of the border on the island gave hope for a chance for lasting peace; at the very least, it signalled a profound transformation in the politics of Northern Ireland.

One of the crucial points of the Agreement was the amendment of Articles 2 and 3 of the Republic's constitution, which claimed the territory of Northern Ireland to be part of a united Ireland. Its wording was as follows:

> "Article 2: The national territory consists of the whole island of Ireland, its islands and the territorial seas.
> Article 3: Pending the re-integration of the national territory, and without prejudice to the right of the Parliament and Government established by this Constitution to exercise jurisdiction over the whole of that territory, the laws enacted by that Parliament shall have the like area and extent of application as the laws of Saorstát Éireann (the Irish Free State established in December 1921 by the Anglo-Irish Treaty, P.R.) and the like extra-territorial effect."[195]

The new version of Article 3 includes the following words:

> "It is the firm will of the Irish nation, in harmony and friendship, to unite all the people who share the territory of the island of Ireland, in all the diversity of their identities and traditions, recognising that a united Ireland shall be brought about only by peaceful means with the consent of a majority of the people, democratically expressed, in both jurisdictions in the island."[196]

---

[195] *Bunreacht Na hÉireann (Constitution of Ireland), 29th December, 1937*, Government Publications Sale Office, Sun Alliance House, Molesworth Street, Dublin 2, p.4.
[196] Northern Ireland Office Online, *The Agreement*, www.nio.gov.uk/agreement.pdf, p.6.

Thus, the former territorial claim of the Republic has been substituted by an aspiration to a united Ireland. Change in the status of Northern Ireland can thereby only be achieved with the consent of a majority of its people. Until then Northern Ireland remains part of the United Kingdom. Only if the situation changes are the two governments bound to give effect to whatever the wish of the people of the North may be.

Another and probably the most hotly discussed problem was the issue of decommissioning, which also cost years of delay in the implementation of the Agreement. Decommissioning was understood in the Agreement to be the total disarmament of the paramilitary organisations but it was exactly this rather general wording that led to hair-splitting interpretations on both the Unionist and the nationalist side. The peace talks ended up in a deadlock. Finally, on 11 February, 2000 and again, after a new attempt of constructive talks, on 14 October 2002 the British Secretary of State for Northern Ireland suspended the Northern Ireland Assembly and Northern Ireland has been returned to direct rule from London. Elections were held on 26 November 2003, but the Assembly has remained suspended since. The Assembly will come back into force if and when the Assembly's current suspension is lifted. For further details on the decommissioning issue see Information Sheet 11.

It seems at the time being (October 2005) that the Agreement pursued too high-flying aims and the November 2003 elections practically produced a stalemate, at least a polarisation with its outcome of a strengthened unionist DUP and nationalist Sinn Féin (DUP 177,470 25.6% +7.5% 30 seats +10; SF 162,758 23.5% +5.9% 24 seats +6)[197], but the results of the two 1998 referenda on both sides of the border signalled, as the Irish Times of May 25, 1998 put it, "An Imperative From The People."[198] "The two great cultures of nationalism and unionism have committed themselves to a new accommodation with each other and that commitment has been solemnised by the votes of a majority of both traditions."[199] The latest sensational news about the IRA's July 28, 2005 statement on laying down its arms indicates: the Good Friday Agreement is a point of no return. But see also Information Sheet 18 "Opinion Poll March 2005" which shows some disappointment after the "hype" about the Agreement in 1998.

The Text

The text comprises five excerpts from the original Belfast Agreement: its preamble, called "Declaration of Support", and four of the more important sections of the complete text which may expose more generally understandable aspects except for the very detailed and sophisticated wording of this rather complex document. The texts will probably need word-by-word analysis as is usual with law texts to get their full meaning, yet, it may be the teacher's choice to have his or her students only understand the gist of the various paragraphs of the extracts to uncover their general meaning.

Basically the five extracts offer the following ideas:

Declaration of Support: the signatories of the Agreement testify their commitment to a range of basic principles, among them partnership, non-violence, equality and mutual respect. They also express their willingness to work in good faith and thus guarantee the success of the agreed arrangements. The participants recognise the interdependence of the various institutions and state "that the success of each depends on that of the other." This *Declaration of Support* demonstrates the spirit of consent and cooperation.

Constitutional Issues: Both the governments of Great Britain and the Republic of Ireland share the position, based on the principles of self-determination and consent, that Northern Ireland remains a part of the United Kingdom as long as the majority of the people of Northern Ireland wishes so but also that if a majority of the population of both parts of Ireland will one day want a united Ireland, both Governments will be bound to find ways of achieving a united Ireland.

Human Rights: This part of the Agreement also includes equality issues. All those rights that may be taken for granted by the students must be considered against the background of the particular Irish Question, i.e. the conflict of two cultures, societies and religions. The establishment of a special Human Rights Commission both in the South and in Northern Ireland was meant to ensure the realization of the obligations from this section of the Agreement.

Economic, Social and Cultural Issues: the British Government commits itself to contributing massively to economic growth and security in Northern Ireland by a new economic development strategy for Northern Ireland which also includes measures on employment equality.

Decommissioning: The participants confirm their intention to work with the Independent Commission on Decommissioning. Their common aim must be the total disarmament of all paramilitary groups on both sides.

197 Nicholas Whyte, *Northern Ireland Assembly Elections 2003*, www.ark.ac.uk/elections/fa03.htm, December 2005.
198 The Irish Times, *An Imperative From The People*, May 25, 1998.
199 The Irish Times, May 25, 1998

As has been said above in "Background to the Text" the controversies over the issue of decommissioning have delayed the process for years, yet, a return to normal peacetime security arrangements to replace the presence of the British military forces is part of this section of the Agreement.

A longer assessment of the Belfast Agreement by Dermot Nesbitt, who was a senior negotiator in the negotiations leading to the Good Friday Agreement on the Unionist side, may be interesting as a supplementary text – in spite of representing only one side of the argument.
See www.c-r.org/accord/ireland/accord8/assess.shtml.

Confidence Essential

This editorial from *The Derry Journal* dated Friday 2 January, 2004 is an ardent plea for the continuation of the implementation process of the Belfast Agreement. The author wrote the article on 2 January, which might be an indication that it is a kind of New Year's message from the *Derry Journal*. He may also still be influenced by the outcome of the Northern Ireland Assembly elections of November 2003 which brought about a radicalization of the situation by making Ian Paisley's Democratic Unionist Party (DUP) the strongest (25.6%) and Sinn Féin second strongest party (23.5%). He is very much in favour of an end of the suspension of the Assembly and wishes its restoration. However, this will essentially be dependent on the delivering of all the points of the Belfast Agreement, first and foremost of the end of any kind of paramilitary activity. There cannot be any ambivalence that the Agreement's main demand – a peaceful and totally democratic society – must become reality. The author appeals to all the political leaders in this process to make a full commitment to this task. There should be no uncertainty about this. The peace process is in full swing and cannot be reversed, not even be dismantled or end in a stalemate. The Agreement's requirements must be met as they are fair and thus acceptable to both nationalists and unionists. Every politician should be aware of that and return to work on the implementation of the Agreement.

The Graph

This survey by the Millward Brown Ulster market and social research agency from the year 2000 shows a small decline in support for the Agreement as compared to 1998 when 71% of the people in Northern Ireland voted "Yes" and in 2000 only 69%. The figures show a sharper loss of confidence among Catholics than Protestants, but in general terms the original narrow majority support of 51% amongst Protestants has changed to a narrow majority opposition (53%).[200]

[200] Millward Brown Ulster, 115 University Street, Belfast BT7 1HP; www.ums-research.com/reports/2000/good friday agreement/.

Literature on The Good Friday Agreement

- Mike Morrissey, Mary Smyth, *Northern Ireland after the Good Friday Agreement: Victims, Grievance and Blame*, UNIpresses, Georgetown ON, 2002
- Jorg Neuheiser, Stefan Wolff (eds.), *Peace at Last: The Impact of the Good Friday Agreement on Northern Ireland*, Berghahn Books, 2004

Literature as provided by CAIN: http://www.cain.ulst.ac.uk/events/peace/index.html:

- Birney, Trevor, and O'Neill, Julian (1997), 'Nailing the Balance' in, *When the President Calls*. Derry: Guildhall Press.
- Farren, Sean, and Mulvihill, Robert F. (2000), 'Transforming the Conflict,' in, *Paths to a Settlement in Northern Ireland*. Gerrards Cross: Colin Smythe.
- Gilligan, Chris (1997), 'Peace or pacification process? A brief critique of the peace process,' in, Gilligan, Chris, and Tonge, Jon (1997) (eds), *Peace or War?: Understanding the Peace Process in Northern Ireland.* Aldershot: Ashgate.
- Ingraham, Jeson (1998), 'The Irish Peace Process'. CAIN: http://cain.ulst.ac.uk/events/peace/talks.htm.
- McCartney, Clem (1999), 'The Role of Civil Society' in, McCartney, Clem (ed) (1999), *Accord – Striking a balance: The Northern Ireland peace process,* (No.89). London: Conciliation Resources.
- Morgan, Austen (2000), 'What is the Belfast Agreement?' in, *The Belfast Agreement: a practical legal analysis*. London: The Belfast Press.
- Murray, Dominic (ed.) (2000), *Protestant Perceptions of the Peace Process in Northern Ireland,* [contributors: Duncan Morrow, Chris Gibson, May Blood, Robin Eames, Gregory Campbell, Barry White]. Limerick: University of Limerick.
- Murray, Gerard (1998), 'Towards a Permanent Settlement', in, *John Hume and the SDLP: Impact and Survival in Northern Ireland.* Dublin: Irish Academic Press.
- Rowan, Brian (1995), 'Going to the Edge' in, *Behind the Lines: the Story of the IRA and Loyalist Ceasefires.* Belfast: Blackstaff Press.
- Stewart, Paul, and Shirlow, Peter (eds.) (1999), *Northern Ireland between peace and war?,* [special issue of Capital and Class, Autumn, no. 69]. Capital and Class, No. 69, Autumn 1999. London: Capital and Class Editorial Committee.
- text of The Agreement, reached in the multi-party negotiations, 10 April 1998
- newspaper headlines, 11 April 1998
- the referendum on 'The Agreement', 22 May 1998
- summary of the position of the political parties and campaign leaflets
- the result of the referendum, Friday 22 May 1988

- article on 'Education and the Peace Process in Northern Ireland' by Alan Smith (1999)
- a brief note on decommissioning
- list of source documents – these documents include all the major reports, statements, and press releases of the various parties

The former very informative free service of *The Irish Times,* "The Path to Peace", which accompanied the development of the implementation of the Good Friday Agreement, is now a premium service which, however, must be subscribed to.

13 | Bernard MacLaverty *Cal*

text type: (excerpt from) novel
length: 1172 words
degree of difficulty: **; 55 annotations and 7 explanations
theme: a young boy's nervous wait for an imminent terrorist attack on him

related visual material: chart "The Christian Churches in Northern Ireland" showing the distribution of religious groups in 2001; photograph of an unusual warning in Northern Ireland; detail of a memorial in Catholic Falls Road, Belfast; mural in Protestant Shankill Road, Belfast.

additional extra information: the IRA, the Fenians and the Twelfth of July.

Background to the Text: Life in a Divided Society

To the outsider the situation in Northern Ireland is often very inadequately reduced to sensational news of just another bombing, well-worded official statements or dry statistics about the number of deaths and which paramilitary group of which side has killed more people than the other. Northern Irish experiences, however, are not statistics and analysis. They are fears, strain, confusion, distress, pain, horror, death. Just as text 11 caught something of the emotional response of Northern Ireland after the IRA ceasefire announcement, this extract from Bernard MacLaverty's well-known novel *Cal* is intended to convey something of the atmosphere in an area of this world that has learned to live between hate and hope, trust and suspicion. It offers the students an opportunity to sharpen their sensibility for and to promote their understanding of what everyday life might be like if one's life is exposed to permanent danger.

Cal takes place somewhere in Ulster, as Northern Ireland is often called.[201] According to the 2001 Census[202] 43.76% of the roughly 1.685 million of the population of Northern Ireland are Catholic, 53.13% are Protestants with strong historical, political, social and cultural ties to Britain. (One should not, however, forget that 'the Protestants', as they are commonly called, have to be broken down into various groups as can be seen from the chart in the Student's Book on p. 51). Two of the six counties – Fermanagh and Tyrone – have Catholic majorities as has the town of Londonderry. Most towns in Northern Ireland, among them Belfast, have a Protestant majority with Roman Catholics, however, heading for 50%. It is, indeed, religion, by definition, that has divided the people of Northern Ireland into rival groups. Yet,

> no social scientist has satisfactorily demonstrated that theological beliefs are particularly important either individually or in aggregate in explaining political violence in the region. Although we share the liberal prejudice that religious fanaticism and dogma are likely to be productive of violence, we are not persuaded that they are the keys to understanding violence in Northern Ireland.[203]

The continuing dispute between the two communities that has turned into sectarian war is as much due to a political system that is designed to disadvantage the Catholic minority through British and Unionist governments as a historical experience, differences in national political identity (Nationalism vs Unionism or, in its extreme form, Republicanism vs Loyalism), socio-economic dissimilarities,[204] or simply long-cherished myths, prejudices and ancient hatred. Whatever the reason, the two communities have long since lost the ability to communicate with each other, and their living together has been dominated by fear, distrust, fights, killings, burning streets, barricades and finally 'peace' walls put up by the British army. As a consequence, Belfast is divided into exclusively Catholic parts, for example Falls Road, and Protestant parts, for example Shankill Road. Even if segregation seems to be dominant, there are mixed communities, mainly in the middle-class suburbs. Segregation correlates with lower socio-economic status and contributes significantly to the outburst of civil disturbances.[205]

[201] For detailed background information about the Northern Ireland situation see background to text 11.
[202] CAIN Web Service, Background Information on Northern Ireland Society - Population and Vital Statistics, http://cain.ulst.ac.uk/ni/popul.htm.
[203] John McGarry and Brendan O'Leary, *Explaining Northern Ireland. Broken Images* (Oxford: Blackwell, 1995), p. 212.
[204] "The Catholic community continues to suffer from a level of unemployment which is significantly higher than the average," *Facts about Ireland,* p. 72.
[205] See "United Kingdom. The People" on *Encyclopaedia Britannica CD 2.0.*

All these specific features of the Northern Irish scene are an ideal hotbed for more violently orientated forces. Apart from the IRA (see extra information on p. 52 of the Study Aids), who back the so-called Catholic side (in order to create a re-united Ireland), there are the less well-known but no less extreme Protestant or Loyalist paramilitary organisations, among them mainly the UVF (Ulster Freedom Fighters), the UFF (Ulster Freedom Fighters) and the UDA (Ulster Defence Association). All these organisations oppose a possible reunification with the Republic and fight for Ulster's status as part of the UK. Whereas the UDA sees itself more as defensive but is also responsible for sectarian killing, the UVF, with up to 500 members, is fiercely and militantly opposed to the IRA. The number of Loyalist killings surpassed that of the IRA in the 1990s.[206] They often choose their victims at random, mostly in revenge for IRA attacks.

It should not go unmentioned at this point that again and again there have been attempts to bridge Northern Ireland's divisions, for example through the Peace People organisation, which was able to attract 20,000 Catholics *and* Protestants for a peace rally in 1976,[207] through community relations projects (see Information Sheet 16) or often through private efforts – such as cross-religious marriages. Yet nothing has proved strong enough to create a lasting reconciliation.

It might be advisable to include Information Sheet 13 ("Who is Who? The Major Players") in a reading of this excerpt from MacLaverty's novel.

The Text

Ireland has been famous for its rich literary culture and wide range of quality authors. One among them is certainly the noted author Bernard MacLaverty whose second novel *Cal* has already become a classic because MacLaverty's art of storytelling conveys the tragic conflict between Catholics and Protestants in the north of the island, especially to the young reader from outside Northern Ireland, in a remarkable way. He looks beyond the sensational news headlines and tries to deal with the human story behind them. The sectarian conflict is given a personal face.

The theme of *Cal* is a study of guilt, expressed through the wonderfully drawn central character. 19-year-old Cal Mc Crystal is a Catholic who lives together with his father in a Protestant area of a place somewhere in Ulster. He is under Loyalist pressure and has been talked into paramilitary activities by some IRA friends and actually been involved in the murder of a Protestant policeman. Paradoxically, he falls in love with the dead man's widow. His IRA friends urge him to "steel himself" and to think of the issues rather than the people, but Cal runs away from his "friends". He finds a way to get closer to Marcella, the victim's wife, and the story develops into a moving love story, but Cal knows that love must be built on honesty and truth. In the end, when he is eventually arrested after being betrayed, he is grateful that he can atone for his crime. The story leaves the reader with the feeling that Cal is as much a victim as a perpetrator because of extraordinary circumstances in an extraordinary environment. This excerpt was chosen because it is a subtly accomplished dramatic depiction of the stifling atmosphere of fear and omnipresent danger which prevails in parts of Northern Ireland.

MacLaverty's language is vivid, precise and clear in its description of a situation of extreme tension. The author examines the seemingly unimportant, limited world of a young man who just has the bad luck to live in an area that is 'not his'. The clear division between 'us', the Protestants, and 'them', the Catholics, becomes obvious very distinctly in passages like the following: "He could not bear to look up and see the flutter of Union Jacks, and now the red and white cross of the Ulster flag with its red hand. Of late there were more and more of these appearing in the estate. It was a dangerous sign that the Loyalists were getting angry" (ll. 4–9) or "'A good man, Shamie.' And implied in everything they were saying was 'for a Catholic'" (ll. 33–35). The flags are a sign of identity and unity that repel anyone who does not belong. As do the eyes he feels on him which "would be at the curtains or behind a hedge as a man paused in his digging" (ll. 3f.). The only thing that is left for Cal to do is to look "at the ground in front of him" (l. 2), just as somebody does who is doing something wrong. His being an outsider in this neighbourhood is dramatically underlined by the UVF warning that makes it quite clear to him that he is a *persona non grata*, that he has to "get out". The language that his father uses reveals the same non-acceptance of the other side: "'No Loyalist bastard is going to force me out of my home. They can kill me first.'" (ll. 20f.) It is not just an everyday quarrel with some neighbours, it is a question of death, as his words make quite clear.

Death, then, is what the UVF warning contains and death is what is meant when Shamie gets out the 38. The danger of sudden death, most probably through an explosion, lingers in the room:

> He kept expecting the window to burst into a shower of glass and flame [...]. The panic of jumping from his window. He saw the ungainliness of his father's bulk crashing through the asbestos material of the shed roof. Would they be waiting outside to take pot-shots at the Fenians they had smoked out? (ll. 57–64)

It is also the blanket drained with water from the bath-tub to quench the flames (ll. 94–101) if they come or the

---

[206] See chart in Daniel Pedersen, "Their Move Now", *Newsweek*, 19 September 1994, p. 21.

[207] Its founders, Betty Williams and Mairead Corrigan, were awarded the Nobel Peace Prize in 1977.

glow of the cigarette ("It was strange how much the room glowed red each time he took a draw", ll. 115ff.) that point at this possible event.

The expectation that an explosion will happen is sharply contrasted with a silence that is just as unbearable. The author communicates this to the reader by the frequent use of passages and words that indicate this, such as in: "The street was empty" (l. 54), "As quietly as he could, he opened the window and listened" (ll. 53f.), "he whispered" (l. 71; see also l. 108), "It was so quiet that he heard the faint hiss of burning tobacco" (ll. 117ff.), "But it was too quiet" (ll. 122f.), "the silence returned" (ll. 127f.).

The tension is underlined by the many references to darkness: "Cal switched out the light and tiptoed into the darkness" (l. 47), "He peered between the slats of the blind" (ll. 48f.), "At the back everything was dark" (ll. 51f.), "pinpoints of light" (l. 52), "using only the light from the curtained landing (ll. 66f.), "then in the dark he undressed [...] (l. 113).

Alarm and tension prevail as can be seen from expressions like "threatening" (l. 28), "panic" (l. 60), "made his skin crawl" (l. 68); "He asked, 'Should we fill the bath?'", "Shamie was putting the gun beneath his pillow" (l. 102), "'Are the doors all locked?'" (l. 105), "Cal thought about sleeping with his shoes" (l. 109), "He checked by touch that his stick was beneath the bed" (ll. 111f.), "then in the dark he undressed to his jeans. Normally he slept in his underpants" (ll. 113ff.), "He stubbed his cigarette out with more pressure than was required" (ll. 120f.), "Now and again he raised his head off the pillow and listened" (ll. 123f.), "He listened so hard there was a kind of static in his ears" (ll. 128f.).

Towards the end of the passage the tension reaches a climax. Cal's nerves are as taut as a bowstring; he anticipates the detonation ("an unimaginable explosion", l. 134) and is only "waiting for his window to explode" (l. 136).

The limited third person narrator is a device to enhance this extraordinary situation. It enables us to experience the whole scene only through the eyes of Cal, so that we, the readers, only see what Cal sees and the way that he sees it; we immediately participate in his fears and perplexity since we have access to his thoughts and feelings. Yet we are not completely dependent on his point of view as there is a greater degree of objectivity than if the author had employed a first person narrator because we get additional information that Cal cannot know of.

Setting and atmosphere contribute to the intense impact this extract has on the reader. Cal and his father are the only Catholics left in the area. When outside in the streets, the hostility of the Protestants is being displayed by their flags, they are "a dangerous sign" (l. 8). Apart from their near neighbours "everyone else in the estate seemed threatening." (ll. 27f.). Cal's father Shamie is a stubborn man who does not want to leave because of the pressure of the Protestants, and so the house of the Mc Crystals becomes a refuge, a fort even in which they live in permanent fear of being evicted (l. 30) or "smoked out" (l. 64). Indeed, their house is in danger of being blown up. This setting and MacLaverty's language create a threatening, depressing atmosphere that becomes more and more oppressive and feverish towards the end of the scene.

The photo "Sniper at Work" expresses visually what the text imparts to the reader in a more differentiated way and what the reality of life is like in Northern Ireland: the permanent unease, the sense of danger, sudden death.

Bernard MacLaverty's new collection of short stories, *Walking the Dog*, follows up the theme of worlds in collision and of innocence coming face to face with death.

The Visual Material

This chapter contains two photos, one illustrating a detail of a massive memorial in Catholic Falls Road, Belfast, and the other one a mural in Protestant Lower Shankill, Belfast. Actually one should call them Nationalist or Republican, Unionist or Loyalist demonstrations of presence as they are meant to draw the visitor's attention to the political messages they convey. Murals are another kind of warfare; they are trying to get messages across, either to support one side, Protestant or Catholic, in their attitudes, or to provoke the other side. Today they are also very sought-after sights by tourists who are taken around on a tour in the so-called Black Taxis to photograph the murals in the Protestant or Catholic areas of Belfast. The murals have been important message boards all through the 35 or so years of the sectarian conflict in Northern Ireland.

The monument in Falls Road is set back from the road, in a garden-like area and commemorates IRA volunteers and Sinn Féin members who were killed in the violent conflicts in former years. It shows a female figure (probably a symbolic representation of Ireland) who is carrying a corpse, obviously a Republican, as the words engraved below read: "The fools, the fools, the fools! They have left us our Fenian dead and while Ireland holds these graves, Ireland unfree shall never be at peace". Further on one can read the names of the victims and the words: "This monument was erected by the Falls Cultural Society on behalf of the residents of the Falls Road, dedicated to those brave and gallant Vols of 'D' Company, 2nd Batt Irish Republican Army who made the supreme sacrifice in their quest for Irish Freedom." This emotional depiction of suffering and sadness contrasts sharply with the victorious pride that **the Loyalist mural** in Shankill Parade, near Shankill Road in the Protestant area of Belfast reveals. It shows King William of Orange

(William III, 1650–1705), a Dutch aristocrat and the Protestant King of England, riding across the River Boyne where he defeated the Catholic King James II of England, his uncle and father-in-law, on 1 July 1690. King James is seated in the foreground, mortally wounded and comforted by another soldier. The Battle of the Boyne is now celebrated by the Protestants of Northern Ireland, especially the so-called Orangemen or Orange Orders, in marches through the towns on 12 July each year. These marches have caused great troubles at times as they often take their routes through Catholic areas or streets.

Information sheet 14: "Jet Log: Irish murals illustrate history and tension" recounts a very personal confrontation with these murals.

14 | Michael Elliott "Overburdened with History"

text type: monograph
length: 796 words
degree of difficulty: ***; 23 annotations and 25 explanations
theme: a critical comment on the over-emphasis on historic events and their significance for life today in Northern Ireland

related visual material: photograph of a mural depicting Oliver Cromwell in the Loyalist Shankill Road area, Belfast; a political cartoon about the almost insoluble problem of Northern Ireland;

Background to the Text: The Prospects of Reconciliation

More than 40 years after the first outbreak of 'The Troubles' in Northern Ireland, 85 years after the partition of the island and more than 800 years after its occupation, there is, it seems, no end in sight to one of Europe's longest-lasting political problems. After the announcement of the IRA ceasefire in August 1994 hopes were inspired that peace talks could begin with the final aim of reconciliation and end the century-old antagonism. But the resumption of IRA bombing in February 1996 shattered these hopes and has brought back tension and uncertainty. Nevertheless, on 10 June 1996 all-party peace negotiations began, but they were again endangered over the question whether Sinn Féin should sit at the table without the IRA turning in their arms. Later this demand was replaced by the requirement of the British and the Irish governments that there should be another credible ceasefire. As long as this did not happen, Sinn Féin would not be involved in inclusive talks. But there will never be a political settlement in Northern Ireland without Sinn Féin or its military wing, the IRA.

However, the prospects for a durable settlement "have improved significantly."[208] The two governments of Britain and the Republic of Ireland have shown, over the last few years, much better conflict management than ever before. "The Framework documents have accurately analysed the conflict as nationally-driven"[209] and not, as is often misunderstood outside Ireland, as primarily a religious issue (see background to text 13). Of course, the economy is another important point. Northern Ireland is one of the poorest regions in the UK; in 1994/95 the British government supported it with £7.4 billion. The continuing terror has brought enormous economic damage to the region. In 1994, 13.4 per cent of the workforce were unemployed, with Catholics affected 70 per cent more than Protestants. If peace came, this would mean, for example, 3,000 new jobs in the tourism industry alone.[210] Nevertheless, McGarry and O'Leary feel that

> affirmative action, economic growth, anti-racketeering offensives, cross-border economic co-operation, the promotion of more competitive enterprises, and European economic integration, while welcome for a host of plausible reasons, must be welcomed for their own sake, but it must always be remembered that at best they will fall short of what is required to resolve the conflict [...].[211]

The root of the problem remains the national aspirations of the two communities. Yet they are so divergent that no compromise seems feasible. Possible options for Northern Ireland have been put up for discussion in project 18. Along with those, other catchwords have been put up for discussion like 'demilitarisation', 'power sharing', 'equal citizenship', 'Europeanisation', 'Internationalisation', etc. Even in 2005, with the peace process still in disarray, Ireland stands at the turning point between a democratic way of inclusive all-party peace negotiations or, as so often, the nihilistic return to violence. The peace has yet to be built. Another of the many IRA statements on 28 July 2005 stating that they are ready to lay down their arms forever, gives hope for a new start. Whatever "is struggling to be born,"[212] at the present time, a way out of the log-jammed talks must be found.

The Text

It is often taken for granted that the Northern Ireland conflict must be solved by rational means. There is no argument against that, but as text 13 shows, this conflict

---

208 Brendan O'Leary and John McGarry, *The Politics of Antagonism*, p. 351.
209 O'Leary and McGarry, p. 352.
210 Figures taken from Bettina Schulz, "Der Terror in Nordirland lähmt die Wirtschaft", *Frankfurter Allgemeine Zeitung*, 17 January 1994.
211 John McGarry and Brendan O'Leary, *Explaining Northern Ireland*, p. 307.
212 Brendan O'Leary and John McGarry, *The Politics of Antagonism*, p. 364.

is just as much an emotional phenomenon, and this has to be taken into consideration. In Ireland, as Michael Elliott explains in his article, history is a major source of never-ending self-stimulation in defining one's own national identity, in belonging, and, in particular, in drawing the borderline between "us" and "them". It may be that the notorious marches of the Orange Order in Northern Ireland, which are not so much meant to "remember 1690" as to provoke Catholics by marching through their areas or the "'eight-hundred-years-of-struggle version of Irish history'" (ll. 9f.) that Nationalists (especially in the far-away Irish diaspora in the United States) cherish, are all products of a romantic glorification of the past which is counterproductive to any rational solution to the violence. When Gordon Wilson, whose daughter was killed in an IRA attack at Enniskillen in 1987, managed to meet IRA representatives to convince them to stop the violence, he was told as a justification of the deed: "History is on our side."[213]

Michael Elliott's shrewd meditations on the devastating effects that overemphasising history and tradition have on any form of mutual understanding, not only in Ireland, help us to see such an attitude as a danger to the peace process and a lasting reconciliation in Ireland and also to relativise the Irish preoccupation with history. The article, an expository text, unfolds its argument in a logical progression.

To catch the reader's attention, the **first paragraph** refers to Ireland's distinguished and internationally renowned poet, W. B. Yeats, by quoting his famous lines "Romantic Ireland's dead and gone, it's with O'Leary in the grave" from his volume *Responsibilities* (1914). Yeats, who had been involved in creating a cultural nationalism, laments that his hope for a heroic Ireland has not been fulfilled. Elliott focuses on the term 'romantic' to qualify Irish-American reactions to the 1994 IRA ceasefire announcement, which, he criticises, was immediately called one of the many "'historic moments'" (l. 5) that "draws an unbroken line" (l. 11) to the many other references to Irish history when talking about the country. Thus he has named the issue he is going to talk about in the rest of the text.

The **second paragraph** asks the slightly ironic question "Did any country ever suffer from history as much as Ireland?" (ll. 16f.), only to drive its point home that both communities have their immediate answers by pointing to historical events which remind us of "today's smaller men of yesterday's 'delirium of the brave'" (ll. 19f.).

In the **third paragraph** the author shows the difference between this Irish way of referring to history and tradition and that of other cultures, in this case the Jews. In Ireland, "history has not brought people together; green and orange, it has torn them apart" (ll. 30–32).

[213] Gina Thomas, "Die Geister fordern große Taten", *Frankfurter Allgemeine Zeitung*, 8 March 1996.

In the **fourth paragraph** the accent is put on other countries, namely Cuba and Canada, to demonstrate that "it isn't just Ireland that's damaged by history" (l. 34). But it does not matter which country; his question is: what are slogans like "I remember" good for, "for God's sake?"

The **fifth paragraph** looks at the criticism often uttered by Europeans that this view of the phenomenon is typical of Americans who "don't understand" (l. 55) the "complexity" (l. 52) and "significance" (l. 56) of such historical occurrences.

Then, in the **sixth paragraph** Elliott defends this easygoing American attitude towards history by pointing to the Walt Disney Co. and its takeover of the interpretation of American historic highlights and puts forward the down-to-earth argument that "the two communities are going to have to spend the future living together" (ll. 71f.). To do so "they will have to keep (the past) locked away in history books" (ll. 74f.).

The **final paragraph** takes South African president Nelson Mandela as an example. He decided to lock away in history books what happened to his people and to himself during the long period of white rule in that country and now looks forward in a constructive way to a common, peaceful future. He rounds off the article by quoting another poet, John Dryden, the extract of whose poem reminds the reader not to look to the past but to the future.

Employing a sometimes slightly ironic, but obviously critical matter-of-fact tone, Elliott offers a straightforward exposition of a problem the acknowledgement of which might, indeed, help understand the Irish question better. Its key sentence could be, "For both communities on that island, Roman Catholic and Protestant, the heroes of the past sit on a collective shoulder, reminding today's smaller men of yesterday's 'delirium of the brave'" (ll. 18–20). The quoting of Yeats, again ironically commented on as "inevitable" (l. 21), is meant as a hint at the use of pathetic language to underline one's position and to derive its justification from history. The same irony can be detected in ll. 57–59, where the author criticises the attitude often assumed by Europeans that Americans "'don't understand' why Irish Protestants revere King Billy 304 years after he defeated a Catholic army on the Boyne. Historic events, Elliott wants to indicate, may once have been of great importance but after 304 years there are better things to do than to base a common future on them.

The author is fair enough to state that Ireland is not the only place in the world to be trapped by that wrong understanding of history. He puts it side by side with Cuba, Quebec, and Serbia, whose peoples also have to suffer from that notorious slogan "I remember". To attain a better future for Ireland, his message is that history has to be put where it belongs: "in history books" (l. 75).

The question whether or not Elliott's assertion might help to bring an end to Ireland's problem can spark off a controversial discussion, especially, as is intended with task 13, if this question is put into an intercultural context. To provide students with a counter-argument, Sinéad O'Connor's song "Famine" should be taken into consideration. It represents the Irish voice and demands precisely the opposite of what Elliott wants, namely

> [...] if there ever is gonna be healing
> There has to be remembering
> And then grieving
> So that there then can be forgiving
> There has to be knowledge and understanding.[214]

The question remains: how should the task of remembering be carried out?

For more material on various aspects of Northern Ireland and for more in-depth work on task 16 the teacher or students might contact The British Council.

The Oliver Cromwell Mural

Against the background of what has been said in the above section, the Oliver Cromwell mural can now be judged less by its artistic merit but by its role in political communication. It shows the English general, politician and Puritan, Lord Lieutenant and later Lord Protector Oliver Cromwell (1599–1658) and some of his roundhead soldiers killing an Irish Catholic. The English flag and the flag of William of Orange are waving in the background. (This last flag together with a blue star in the lower right corner is now used by the Orange Order when on parade.) The text written around the Cromwell picture says: "Oliver Cromwell –Lieutenant General – Lord Protector – Defender of the Protestant faith." And the text on both sides in the lower parts of the mural tells the beholder (left): "Catholicism is more than a religion. It is a Political Power therefore I'm led to believe there will be no peace in Ireland until the Catholic Church is Crushed – Oliver Cromwell," (right) "Our Clergy persecuted and our Protestant churches desecrated. Also our Protestant people slaughtered in their thousands - Oliver Cromwell."

History tells us that in 1641, while the Civil War was raging in England, the Irish saw a chance to liberate themselves from their English colonial masters. At first they were rather successful as they were supported by the Catholic clergy in their organisation of the rebellion. The Protestant side, both in Ireland and England, was shocked and anti-Catholic reactions were triggered. After the overthrow of King Charles I in 1649 the new political power in England, Parliament, and the new Lord Lieutenant, Oliver Cromwell, did not wait long to crush the Catholic rebellion in Ireland. Their aim was revenge and the abolition of the Irish problem once and for all. Cromwell and his army raged against towns, individuals and the Catholic Church in Ireland with great brutality. His army, it is said, killed one quarter of Ireland's Catholics in the 17th century. Thus, he shattered not only the Counter-Reformation in Ireland but also secured the Protestant Ascendancy for Ireland. A time was to come for the Irish Catholics that is best expressed in the famous phrase "to Hell or to Connacht," which means that the Irish were dispossessed of their land and were only allowed to have land in stony County Clare or Connacht at the West coast. The other 26 counties were exclusively in Protestant hands.

See also *Background to the Text* of chapters 2 and 3 and also Information Sheet 14: "Jet Log: Irish murals illustrate history and tension" which presents a very personal confrontation with these murals

The Projects

Work on the three projects will round off the students' work. Whereas project 16 is more of a research project that takes up the idea of text 14 of probing into possible reasons for the understanding of the Northern Ireland conflict, project 17 challenges students' creative faculties since it demands that they do something constructive. The task has a realistic background and the students' results might even be communicated to the address stated in Information Sheet 16. Project 18 provides some rather simplified yet previously theoretically discussed solutions to the Irish conflict designed to spark off a vivid discussion after a rather short period of preparation.

Information Sheet 16 could provide some interesting new aspects to the topic. This is the background: people isolated in their sectarian communities, each year celebrating traditions which are primarily used as demonstrations against the 'opponent' and in permanent fear of another atrocity by the paramilitary groups of either side – how can this Irish logjam be broken? There have been various attempts at solutions, none has so far resulted in a breakthrough. Yet hope is Ulster's only way forward. Side by side with the high profile attempts by politicians to prepare the ground for peace, efforts are also being made at grassroots level to achieve a better mutual understanding, e.g. in community relation projects that usually go unnoticed by the world. In the case of the Currach Community their area of operation is Shankill and Falls Road in the centre of Belfast. While Shankill is purely Protestant, Falls Road is exclusively Catholic and both roads have been the scene of rioting and bombing. Almost 100 such groups and organisations prove that the people of Northern Ireland are not willing to leave it to the paramilitaries to "solve" the conflict in their region.

[214] Sinéad O'Connor, "Famine" on *Universal Mother* CD (London: Ensign Records, 1994).

15 Interviews with Students from Methodist College Belfast

text type: interview
length: 1277 words
degree of difficulty: *; 9 annotations and 7 explanations
theme: college students talk about their living conditions in Belfast and Northern Ireland

related visual material: two photos of the students and Methodist College Belfast

additional material: three poems on Belfast by young Methodist College Belfast students

Background to the Text : Young People about Their Life in Belfast

Methodist College Belfast, as stated in the introductory remarks to this chapter in the Students' Book, p. 59, is one of the best-known grammar schools in Northern Ireland if not the UK, renowned for its academic excellence, internationality but also its social commitment. It offers academic, sporting and extra-curricular opportunities and has a reputation for its music and drama performances. In 2002 there were 1850 pupils and 140 full-time staff members at that school. It also incorporates two boarding departments. The school is divided into 3 sections: the Junior School (Forms 1, 2 and 3), the Middle School (Forms 4 and 5), the Senior School (Forms Lower 6 and Upper 6).

Methody, as it is often affectionately called, has a long history and tradition dating back to its foundation year of 1865. It has always been interdenominational and co-educational. Among many others, one of its major activities is its participation in the inter-schools peace and reconciliation movement (PRISM), "a movement formed in 1982, following an initiative by the then Minister of Education for Northern Ireland, to encourage young people from different backgrounds and communities to meet socially and exchanges views. The group aims to challenge how sixth-form students perceive themselves, their own prejudices and intolerance and how they perceive others."[215]

Academic matters are important at Methody. At the highest educational level in the UK school system, the A level, "almost 73% of grades awarded were either A or B, an outcome which compares favourably with any school in the UK."[216] [217] As guest speaker, Professor McKenna from the University of Ulster points out: "Whatever else you do, identify some way in which you can be of public service or somehow contribute to the public good. It does not particularly matter what you do: but it is immensely important for this society, struggling out of decades of social and political convulsion, that you do it. The future is more in your hands than in those of my generation."[218] [219]

The Text

It is obviously the spirit of that school and those last words uttered by Professor McKenna which are displayed in the interviews. The interviewees of all grades are intelligent young people, well informed, highly interested and very responsive to the questions. There is no sign of self-consciousness or shyness. The students display an intellectual freshness and open-mindedness and a mature opinion or attitude to all the questions asked. Combined with a natural sense of humour the interviewees provide the reader with a young and unbiased attitude towards life in a place in the world that many people still do not want to visit for fear of dangers unknown. We are also given a view of a city (Belfast) which is home to these young people and accordingly a place they love and like to be. Maybe, of course, it is because these students attend a prestigious school and therefore probably come from better-off families with a more differentiated view of things. Yet this did not come out in the interview and because of the school uniforms, clothing gave no indication of social class.

The linguistically easy text, which contains many juvenile colloquialisms, deals with four different aspects of young people's lives in Belfast: "Living in Belfast", "Catholics and Protestants", "Politics", "What others think of us". The four sixth form girls demonstrate an obvious, proud patriotism in their answers, at least they are looking for fairness and an understanding that they, their city and their country are in no way different from other people, cities or countries in the world. Especially Rebecca, in **"Living in Belfast",** complains that people, mainly Americans, have a totally wrong and exaggerated perception of how it must be to live in a place like Belfast. Her plea is to be recognized as "normal" ("We're normal", l. 14), when she ridicules any comparison by foreigners of Northern Ireland and Iraq (l. 5) and states,

[215] *Peace and Reconciliation Movement*, CAIN Web Service, http://cain.ulst.ac.uk/othelem/organ/porgan.htm.

[216] "Senior Prize Distribution, Headmaster's Address", *M.C.B. magazine*, Vol. LXXXIX, December 2002, p. 33.

[217] The school system in Northern Ireland follows mainly Great Britain's current system of secondary education.

[218] PG McKenna, "Response" in: *M.C.B. magazine,* Vol. LXXXIX, December 2002, p. 39.

[219] based on: *Introduction to Methody*, http://mcb.methody.org/about/about.html.

"I have never seen a building blown up" (ll. 7–8). Emily, when she goes abroad, is afraid of saying she is from Northern Ireland and instead says she is Irish, because people might immediately associate her with "terrorists and stuff" (l. 20). She, too, demonstrates a slightly hurt pride when she finishes: "It's nothing like the country that we grow up in at all" (ll. 23–24). Rebecca adds that she has never ever felt unsafe in Belfast and compares it to any other city in the world as far as safety is concerned, and Alana adds, "It's a friendly city!" Statistics show that "between 2001–02 and 2002–03, the overall level of recorded crime in Northern Ireland increased by around two percent."[220] One explanation for the slight increase may be that crimes were not reported to the police but more to the paramilitaries during the times of the Troubles and that this has changed after the Troubles declined.[221]

Turning to the second section of the interviews **"Catholics and Protestants"**, the reader is confronted with an astonishing observation: in the general perception of the Northern Ireland problem people often feel (or are told by the media) that the conflict is an issue between Protestants and Catholics. The four girls, however, make clear right from the beginning that those are the wrong categories, as has often been claimed by people who know the situation better. Thus, Laura, for example, states that she has no problem (l. 45) at all with Protestants or Catholics: "There is no difference" (l. 40), she has noticed. Alana confesses that it is difficult to know the difference because people get confused between Catholicism and nationalism, i. e. the religious and the political categories. There are even, she says, Catholics in Northern Ireland who want to remain in the U.K., something that is not too well known. And Kathrin is actually annoyed about the fact that the people who create all that trouble call themselves Protestants or Catholics while they are definitely not acting in accordance with any religious belief (ll. 56–63). Another aspect that is often forgotten in the "black-and-white" judgement of many people and the media is the fact that although 53.1% of the population in Northern Ireland are Protestant and 43.8% are Catholics, quite a number of people in Northern Ireland are neither Catholic nor Protestant. Some are members of the Church of Ireland, "which is like in the middle between Protestant and Catholic" (ll. 67–68),[222] and some belong to other religious groups or do not have any religion at all. Emily even says that at "Methody" it is important who you are and it does not matter which religion you have. In this context, Nicola refers to something of great importance: she remembers that when she was in primary school, her Catholic school visited a Protestant school and they sang together in a common choir of Protestant and Catholic school children (ll. 34–37). In fact, there is a long-lasting and serious effort to make education the key to peace-building. Based on the insight that fundamental divisions exist in society in Northern Ireland in many fields such as housing, sport, the media and that "over 90% of all schools are either Catholic or Protestant in ethos and practice"[9] the Integrated Education Fund (IEF) think that "the reality of segregated education is that, in the main, Catholic and Protestant children do not meet each other. Catholic children attend Catholic schools and Protestant children attend state schools which are mainly Protestant. We believe that, irrespective of shifts in power base or political compromise, unless the children in Northern Ireland meet and learn about each other's traditions at school, the odds are against a peaceful and secure future in their own country."[224]

Indeed, as can be read in *The Irish News* of Friday, January 9, 2004, "schools remain shy of cross-community links"[225] although Ms Marion Matchett, chief inspector of schools for Northern Ireland said at the North of England Conference (the largest conference of educationalists in Britain and Ireland) that "understanding of pluralism was a key purpose of education, and a 'special need' of society in Northern Ireland."[226]

Apart from the IEF's efforts to bring an end to segregated education through inter-school activities and government-backed courses on education for mutual understanding (EMU) (see also Information Sheet 17: "Education for Mutual Understanding and Cultural Heritage") there already exists a lot of inter-church and cross-community youth work of that kind.[227] One of the even simpler means of cross-cultural "education" is reported by a former youth work tutor:

---

220 *Northern Ireland Annual Abstract of Statistics 2003*, Northern Ireland Statistics & Research Agency, The Stationary Office, 16 Arthur Street, Belfast, www.nics.gov.uk/press/dfp/031031a-dfp.htm.

221 See Ken Pease and Gemma Cox, University of Manchester, "Northern Ireland: Crime Statistics", *The World Factbook of Criminal Justice Systems*, U.S. Department of Justice, Bureau of Justice Statistics, 1993 (2002), www.nics.gov.uk/press/dfp/031031a-dfp.htm.

222 The Church of Ireland is an independent Anglican church in the Republic of Ireland and Northern Ireland.

223 The Integrated Education Fund, History: Northern Ireland - A Divided Society, www.ief.org.uk/files/history/dividedsociety. asp.

224 The Integrated Education Fund, History: Northern Ireland - A Divided Society.

225 *The Irish News*, January 9, 2004, p. 7.

226 *The Irish News*, p. 7.

227 See John Lampen, *Building the Peace. Good Practice in Community Relations Work in Northern Ireland*, Community Relations Council, Belfast, 1995, pp. 123–130.

> The school buses in many rural areas are mixed, and I often used to travel to work by bus. I saw a lot of mixing by the kids. Someone from a state school would regularly sit beside someone from a Catholic school on the bus. They certainly all know each other on first name terms throughout the bus route – not just those who get on at the same stop. It's not just a superficial knowing who the other person is; they stop and chat to each other, they have a lot of social contact through the bus ride.[228]

Yet things are not always as easy as that. Even though the Belfast Agreement of 1998 states that an "essential aspect of the reconciliation process is the promotion of a culture of tolerance at every level of society and includes initiatives to facilitate and encourage integrated education and mixed housing,"[229] sectarian intimidation and punishment attacks seek to prevent reconciliation.[230] These acts of violence hinder the efforts of private cross-community groups and government-sponsored initiatives as well as legislative provision for integrated education[231] and the voluntary work of the Northern Ireland Council for Integrated Education (NICIE). This organisation, whose slogan is "taking the fear out of difference" has helped bring about a rapid increase in the number of integrated schools.[232]
Nevertheless, Northern Ireland has no other chance but believe the then Minister of Education, former IRA chief Martin McGuiness, when he said in 2000, "I will be considering how all schools can be supported and reinforced in their work in promoting a culture of tolerance and respect for diversity."[233]

It is here that one can see how intermingled things are in Northern Ireland and once talk centres on religious matters, politics are immediately included. This can also be seen in the third part of the interview called **"Politics"**. Again, we meet young people who are facing a serious problem with the freshness and light-heartedness of youth. It sounds so easy to solve the Northern Ireland conflict when Andrew says "that the best way forward for Northern Ireland is for all the politicians to get together and decide on a future that is bright for all" (ll. 75–78). He feels that being governed from Westminster, with "English Labour MPs coming over and doing things they actually don't know anything about" (ll. 80f.) cannot be the solution. Leave it to the people here, he says; they only have to cooperate to "make things work" (l. 84). Maybe this is a little naïve, but it is as simple as that. However, there are too many people who pursue their own interests in the Northern Ireland "business." Kathrin approves of Andrew's opinion and adds that she is "sick and tired of all this" (l. 88) as is, she reckons, her whole generation. And Rebecca is of the opinion that political figures like Gerry Adams (Sinn Féin) and Ian Paisley (DUP), the leaders of the main confronting parties in Northern Ireland, "are like really satirized" (ll. 94), which means they cannot be looked at as serious politicians. She uses adjectives like "childlike" (l. 97) and "stupid" (l. 99) and compares them to "fighting children" (l. 99). There is a lot of anger and disapproval of adults who try to solve problems this way. Her only hope is her own generation who, if they ever gain political power, will, hopefully, "wise up to it" and will find better solutions than the current ones because "it's so sickening." This perception by young people of their country's most challenging problem and its possible solution can be left to speak for itself; it may spark off an interesting classroom discussion.

What becomes evident in **"What Others Think of Us"** is a certain sadness if not hurt pride that the world does not recognize the positive sides of Northern Ireland and Belfast. Just like other events it is too often only the bad news that draws attention to this part of the world like the 12-week-dispute in the summer of 2001 over children attending a Catholic school who had to walk through a Protestant street.[234] Alana was outside Northern Ireland, in the United States, when the story was on the national news there and she felt very ashamed at that. She thinks the affair was "blown out of proportion" (l. 121) and blames the media for that, and Kathrin adds that it is only "a small percentage of the community" who "just have to have their arguments" (ll. 127–130). Emily, too, blames the press for this, as the effect of such sensational reports is that "even in England they don't want to come over here, because they are scared, too." (ll. 133f.). Nobody, the girls complain, ever tells people about the positive things about Belfast, the culture it has to offer, its wonderful architecture and the beauty of the landscape of Northern Ireland. "Northern Ireland's got so much to give" (ll. 147f.).

---

228 John Lampen, p. 123.

229 The Belfast Agreement, Strand 3, Section 13.

230 See, for example, BBC News, Northern Ireland, 31 August 2005: "An arson attack on a Catholic primary school in County Antrim is being treated as sectarian by police", news.bbc.co.uk/go/em/-/1/hi/northern_ireland/4199646.stm.

231 See, for example, Ulidia Integrated College in Carrickfergus, County Antrim (no website; Email: ulidia.college@excite.com) and the Millenium Integrated Primary School in Carryduff, County Down (www.carryduffprimaryschool.ik.org) which are both receiving government funding.

232 A chronological history of the efforts to establish integrated education in Northern Ireland can be found here: www.ief.org.uk/files/history/chronological.asp.

233 Speech at a visit to NICIE: Fiona Stephen, "Promoting a culture of tolerance: education in Northern Ireland," Michael Cox, Adrian Guelke and Fiona Stephen, *A farewell to arms? From 'long war' to long peace in Northern Ireland,* Manchester University Press, Manchester and New York, 2000, p. 176.

234 See BBC News, Northern Ireland, http://news.bbc.co.uk/1/hi/northern_ireland/1518025.stm .

The Poems

The poems written by young Methodist College Belfast students (form 2) for the 2002 MCB School Magazine display a fairly naïve approach towards the problem under discussion here, yet, one should not forget they are written from a child's point of view at an impressionable age. In **Mark Davison's poem "Belfast"** it is again the media that are made responsible for the bad reputation of Mark's home town. All the negative aspects are mentioned like "fights and drugs and all things bad" that do not allow Belfast to be compared to Hollywood, the place where the beautiful and the rich live and which the world looks at with admiration and envy for the good luck those people have had in their lives. Nothing good can be expected from Belfast. The only good thing, Mary Peters' unexpected 1972 Olympic pentathlon victory in Munich, which united the opposing factions at the height of the Troubles in a common celebration of this great sporting success of Northern Ireland, happened long ago. The outside world only sees the Belfastians "drink and smoke, and shout and fight and row." Mark is sick and tired of this cliché and shouts out proudly:" We are the new generation, we are the hope for the future" and Belfast will be another, a better place then.

Hannah Morrison's "Belfast" poem characterizes the city as a very normal, everyday place, where people are "hurrying" and "worrying", "having fun" or are "looking for some sun" just like in any city. She does not avoid the negative characteristics that Belfast is well-known for like being "damp" and "cold," but she is able to present the image of a place that is just as normal as can be: "Belfast is new, Belfast is old, city of work, city of play" in order to finally point out what she thinks the real worth of this city is: "A great place to be at the end of the day." It is a kind of love declaration that takes up the idea of the beginning of the poem where she stated: "Belfast is home, a home to love and leave, Belfast is cool, a real celtic jewel," which refers to the golden Celtic times of Ireland far, far before any Troubles started. A warm, unpretentious way of saying she loves that place and likes to be there.

Uzman Rashid's poem about Belfast, **"It's what they all say,"** is of particular interest as Uzman's family may not be native Irish. However, his poem does not show any difference in commitment to the city. He, too, is very unhappy about "what they all say", that is to say that there is only rioting and bombing in the streets of Belfast every day. In the second stanza he starts to defend his city: "But Belfast isn't like that" and blames the people to "exaggerate so blatantly". And he always sees that "sceptic stare" when he tells people that Belfast is great. He admits that the city "has her dark sides" and "the side against the law" but that is just like every city. He finishes with an invitation to come over to the place and see that Belfast is "no lion's den." It seems this is a special poem in so far as a young boy, presumably from a different cultural background, wants the place where he lives to be recognized as something positive, something he can be proud of. It seems astonishing, as racial tensions have been increasing during the last few years in Northern Ireland. Even so this is not part of our reflections here, but we might have a premonition of a new dimension of the Northern Ireland problem: the involvement of ethnic minorities.[235]

16 | A Farewell to Arms? From Long War to Uncertain Peace in Northern Ireland

text type: article from non-fictional book
length: 727 words
degree of difficulty: **; 18 annotations and 3 explanations
theme: introduction to a non-fictional book which prepares the ground for a detailed analysis of the Irish peace process and its chances of realization

related visual material: a photograph of an unusual road sign; a photograph of the Peace Memorial in Belfast

for additional reading see Info Sheets 10, "IRA Statement in Full," and 11, "Independent International Commission on Decommissioning" (Chastelain Report).

Will there ever be peace in Northern Ireland? This crucial question must be asked as we now draw to the end of this section and of the whole anthology on Ireland. The students have been given a wide range of information about the origins of and the endeavours to reconstruct a divided Ireland and (hopefully) bring peace to this troubled part of Europe. The concluding text is therefore offered as one possible answer, among many others, to the above question and as an appropriate point of departure for some final stocktaking.

---

[235] The Northern Ireland Human Rights Commission sees clear signs of scapegoating of ethnic minorities and the increase of the potential for racial tensions in Northern Ireland. See The Northern Ireland Human Rights Commission, Response of the Northern Ireland Human Rights Commission to the Consultation on Political Party Advertising, § 18, Temple Court, 39 North Street, Belfast BT1 1NA, March 2004, see also www.nihrc.org/documents/landp/134.doc.

Background to the Text: Has Peace a Chance in Northern Ireland?

Eleven years after the historic IRA Ceasefire Statement of 31 August 1994 (see Text 11) and seven years after the Good Friday Agreement of 10 April 1998 (see Text 12), the two decisive documents for a brighter, peaceful future in Northern Ireland, it is time to take stock, at least for the time being.

What has happened in the meantime? With 71.12% of the people of Northern Ireland endorsing the Good Friday Agreement and only 28.88% against it[236], hopes were justified for an end of armed conflict and lasting peace in the troubled province. On December 10, 1998 moderate nationalist SDLP leader John Hume and Ulster Unionist Party leader David Trimble were awarded the Nobel Peace Prize for their commitment to the realization of the Belfast Agreement and their long-lasting efforts to find a peaceful solution to the conflict in Northern Ireland. But reality continued to show its ugly face: One of the most dreadful attacks happened on 15 August 1998 when an IRA bomb killed 29 people in Omagh and on 15 March 1999 human rights lawyer, Rosemary Nelson, was assassinated by loyalists. In spite of this the official powers of Great Britain, the Republic of Ireland and the U. S. were willing to take the initiative and in December 1999 power was passed to a power-sharing executive with David Trimble as First Minister. Soon, however, on 12 February 2000 the Northern Ireland Assembly was suspended again by Northern Ireland Secretary, Peter Mandelson because of decommissioning problems with the IRA. When the republicans finally agreed to verifiably put their weapons beyond use, devolution was restored on 30 May 2000. A little more than a year later, on 1 July 2001, David Trimble resigned in protest at the IRA's failure to disarm. This issue remained the greatest problem of the peace process of the following years as unionists were not willing to accept anything less than complete disarmament of the IRA. Again on 10 August 2001, on 21 September 2001 and finally on 14 October 2002 John Reid, then the Northern Ireland Secretary, suspended devolution and reintroduced direct rule from Westminster. The Northern Ireland Assembly has since been suspended. The uncertainty about the IRA's clear will to end their armed struggle and to fully disarm overshadows the peace process and let it run into a deadlock. In addition, the November 2003 elections made Ian Paisley's hard-line DUP become the largest unionist party and also Northern Ireland's largest party and Sinn Féin the strongest nationalist party. Many political experts call this a stalemate and expect the peace process to stagnate, which has, in fact, happened. The sad case of Robert McCartney's brutal death, which his family claimed to be the IRA's deed, gained international attention and put the IRA under enormous international pressure. Finally, on 28 July 2005 the IRA announced the sensational end to its armed campaign and agreed to lay down their arms forever.

[236] Cf. www.cain.ulst.ac.uk/issues/politics/election/rev1998.htm.

The IRA statement of 28 July 2005 about the end of its armed struggle

As this document seems to be of a more serious nature than the many statements that have been made in the long story of the peace process, it has been added as Information Sheet 10. Students can attempt to decipher its meaning on their own and embark on a discussion as to how seriously it can be taken.

Although, in general, an optimistic attitude prevails among most political commentators of this sensational statement it has not been received favourably by everyone.

U. S. President George W. Bush, for example, states:

"This IRA statement must now be followed by actions demonstrating the republican movement's unequivocal commitment to the rule of law and to the renunciation of all paramilitary and criminal activities. We understand that many, especially victims and their families, will be sceptical. They will want to be certain that this terrorism and criminality are indeed things of the past."[237]

Peter Hain, the Northern Ireland Secretary, calls for caution but also expresses his great hopes:

"The clarity of this statement is in contrast to its predecessors. It states in plain language that the armed campaign is at an end. Nevertheless, the way that the conflict has played out in Northern Ireland means that there will be some caution. But caution should not become obduracy. Since the IRA has stated it is relegating physical force to history and dedicating itself to exclusively peaceful and democratic means, I hope that all democrats will acknowledge the significance of that commitment. It opens up the prospect that devolved government can be re-established in Northern Ireland and on an inclusive basis."[238]

Ian Paisley, the leader of the largest Unionist party in Northern Ireland, the DUP, said:

"I am saying now the proof of the pudding is in the eating and digesting of it ... We've heard it all before. You can wrap it up anyway you like ... put a new bit of ribbon on the package but we want the action, the proof this is happening" (to BBC).[239]

[237] "Reactions to the IRA statement renouncing violence," George Bush, *Times Online*, July 28 2005, http://www.timesonline.co.uk/article/0,,2-1711946,00.html.

[238] "Reactions to the IRA statement renouncing violence," Peter Hain.

[239] "Reactions to the IRA statement renouncing violence," Ian Paisley.

And even among the nationalists there are enough dissidents who do not agree with Gerry Adams's "closing-down sale," as former IRA activist Anthony McIntyre, who spent eighteen years in prison, calls it.[240] Bernadette McCaliskey (formerly Bernadette Devlin, in the 1960/70s a well-known figure in the Catholic Civil Rights Movement in Northern Ireland and the youngest woman ever to be elected to the British parliament), for example, still dreams of the armed struggle against the British. And what about the more radical IRA splinter groups like the Real IRA or the hard-line Continuity IRA, who are violently opposed to anything but a united Ireland?

However, even Anthony McIntyre must admit: "Ohne bewaffneten Kampf kann die irische Einheit nicht gewonnen werden, aber mit Gewalt lässt sie sich auch nicht erreichen."[241] As to the main aim of the Northern Irish nationalists, a united Ireland, journalist Jürgen Krönig's conclusion seems bitter: "Demografische Trends in der Provinz, der Widerstand der protestantischen Mehrheit und die Abneigung eines Teils der katholischen Minderheit, den britischen Rechts- und Sozialstaat gegen die irische Republik aufzugeben, deuten auf eine sehr viel längere Geduldsprobe für die Verfechter der irischen Republik hin."[242]

In a Guardian Unlimited newsblog of Thursday July 28, 2005 called "The booby trap in the IRA statement" the Observer's Belfast correspondent Henry McDonald criticized the fact that the word "disbandment" is missing in the IRA statement and suspects that "the most lethal paramilitary organisation in western Europe remains intact" and, as in loyalist communities, will strengthen "IRA-controlled underground economy" and "the IRA's control of working class areas across Ireland."[243] His remarks were followed by an acrimonious discussion of other contributors to this forum and can be read at http://blogs.guardian.co.uk/news/archives/2005/07/28/the_booby_trap_in_the_ira_statement.htm. Another debate about the IRA statement was started on August 01, 2005 on the internet platform of Times Online which invited its readers to give their views on the statement. The following are extracts from this website and demonstrate very impressively what people think about this document and the conflict in general. These contributions are fairly representative and might spark off a fertile classroom discussion. They can be found at http://www.timesonline.co.uk/article/0,,564-1711947,00.html.

[240] Jürgen Krönig, "Revolutionäre Nostalgie", *Die Zeit*, 4. August 2005, S. 6.

[241] Jürgen Krönig, *Die Zeit*, S. 6.

[242] Krönig, S.6.

[243] Henry McDonald "The booby trap in the IRA statement", Guardian Unlimited: Newsblog, Thursday July 28, 2005, http://blogs.guardian.co.uk/news/archives/2005/07/28/the_booby_trap_in_the_ira_statement.htm.

The IRA is known for its discipline. By not disbanding, it retains control over its members and so limits the numbers who might otherwise move to dissident groups. Implementing the terms of the Good Friday Agreement is not a concession to republicans. Not fully implementing them is a breach of an International Treaty. All sides should now comply with their outstanding obligations under this Treaty.... *McGrath, Mojacar, Spain.*

It's a widely held opinion that the IRA has been forced into this position by Blair and Ahern, who were sick of the Sinn Fein demanding concessions without giving anything up. Unionists insist the entire peace process has been one concession to Republicans after another. Sinn Fein signed the Good Friday Agreement, which stated that there could be no change to NI's constitutional position without majority consent – the essence of Unionism. They then began decommissioning, which they swore they would never do. The peace process then stalled. On both a practical and an ideological level, the IRA has made huge sacrifices for peace and progress. They weren't enough for the Unionists. This statement won't be either. *Hugh Collins, London.*

I have never desired a Catholic Ireland [Philip Habib and DSA Murray], nor have I ever craved a 'socialist united Ireland'. All I have ever wanted was a peacefully united Ireland, with no ulterior motive. And I believe most nationalists are of a similar mind. There is nothing underhand about it, and it is no attack on the English. Allowing nationalists/republicans a seat in the government that controls them is no sell-out, simply a recognition that society is made up of many disparate elements, all of which should be equally valued and represented. Only by giving people a chance to control their own destiny do you ever allow a society to grow and mature and do people begin to take responsibility for their actions. Forgiveness is needed – but by all sides. If you try to see yesterday's events from the perspective of the other 'side' can you not understand how those involved effectively gave up their desire for retribution for all the wrongs done to them, their people and their ancestors? That's not quite forgiveness, but it's a step in the right direction. I believe that yesterday's announcement was a major step forwards that took great courage on behalf of those involved. I hope now that the Good Friday Agreement will be implemented and that all concessions aren't one-sided as they appear to have been up until now. I hope with all my heart that I didn't vote to give up my country's claim on the North for nothing. *Sinead Nic an Ri, Stirling.*

Why the preoccupation with the IRA? When are people going to start asking the UDF, UDV and other unionist paramilitary organisations about their weapons? What about their murders? Perhaps when the unionist organisations conform to civilised behaviour also there will indeed be peace in all Ireland. *David Courtney, Grolejac, Dordogne.*

Without the threat of violence, who or what are the IRA? There is obviously a role for Sinn Fein as a political representation of nationalist ambitions in Northern Island but the real focus will be on those hard men who were willing to kill, threaten, kneecap and torture and who now – according to the latest "historic statement" – will be disarmed and expected to live as normal, hard-working citizens. There has to be hope that this is a new beginning but it is difficult not to expect the strengthening of break-away movements and the increase in criminal activities as some of these hard-liners try to come to terms with their leadership's change of direction. *Keith Downer, London.*[244]

The Text

The extract chosen for the Students' Book is the introduction to "A farewell to arms?" Apart from this introduction and a conclusion, the book contains twenty essays written by academics and political practitioners who offer their particular analysis of the notable transition of Northern Ireland "from 'long war' to long peace." The main occupation of this book is with the Good Friday Agreement and its background but it also covers the history of the peace process, Northern Ireland politics and the role of the main groups participating in this process. And it weighs, of course, the chances of a lasting peace. The academic approach saves the authors from a possible suspicion of taking sides, although, depending on one's convictions one might always be accused of being partisan – especially in Northern Ireland. A new perspective is introduced when especially Michael Cox in his essay "Northern Ireland after the Cold War" puts the Northern Ireland peace process into a wider international context, for example the integration of Ireland into the European Union, but also other conflicts like the Middle East, South Africa or the Basque country are analysed and compared to the Irish Question. In their conclusion the three editors acknowledge the Good Friday Agreement as the only basis of lasting peace in Northern Ireland as there is no alternative. In view of the difficulties in fully implementing the Agreement, especially those coming from the unionists and nationalists, it is clear that the Agreement is the best compromise that could have been reached at the time. Although the objective of the nationalists, a united Ireland, and that of the unionists, that Northern Ireland should remain part of the UK, are mutually exclusive according to the authors the realisation of both these aims is still not out of reach. If any of the solutions should ever become reality, it will be a democratic solution with the people of Northern Ireland wishing so in a true act of self-determination. "What can safely be concluded," the three editors write in their conclusion, "is that the success of the Agreement presents the only foreseeable alternative to Irish unity which is capable of bringing about the closure of the Irish Question."[245]

[244] All the quotes have been taken from http://www.timesonline.co.uk/article/0,,564-1711947,00.html.

[245] Michael Cox, Adrian Guelke and Fiona Stephen, "Conclusion: closure for the Irish Question?", Michael Cox, Adrian Guelke and Fiona Stephen, *A farewell to arms? From 'long war' to long peace in Northern Ireland,* Manchester University Press, Manchester and New York, 2000, p. 296.

The article, an expository text which unfolds its argument in logical progression, is the beginning of the introduction to a collection of essays which all try to give answers to the question asked in the title of the book, *A farewell to arms*? In this extract from the introduction, the authors Michael Cox, Adrian Guelke and Fiona Stephen, who are, at the same time, the editors of the volume, confront the reader with the unexpected fact that peace in Northern Ireland is possible after all and then explain how this surprising situation came about.

As the extract has only two paragraphs, students have to identify the structural elements and the main arguments by themselves (see Analysis 8). The authors start from the general statement that "all wars ... must one day come to an end." (l. 1) and lead into the particular Northern Ireland situation by remarking that the pace "may be agonizingly slow" (ll. 2 f.). They reason that from a cynical point of view, one could believe "that many within the North either did not care for the peace or had become so used to the conflict that they preferred its certainties to the uncertainties of the new world order" (ll. 10–13). Another reason why the peace process was so tentative "was not the people of Ireland but certain politicians and parties at Westminster" (ll. 16 f.) implying that some British officials might not honestly have been interested in peace in Northern Ireland. What counts most, according to their point of view, however, is the fact that it was not a sudden feeling of harmony (l. 21) which made the conflicting parties suddenly come to reason but the fact that "they were finally impelled to the rather unpalatable conclusion that neither "armed violence" (l. 25, refers to the IRA, P. R.) nor "no surrender" (l. 26, refers to the Loyalists, P. R.) were means of a possible solution to the Irish Question. On the contrary, there was no "middle ground" (l. 30) or "Road to Damascus" (l. 32) that would have shown political wisdom or a "meeting of minds" (l. 28) but the painful "recognition that the old means of achieving desired ends either did not work or were no longer acceptable" (ll. 35f.) to the two parties' respective supporters. The authors call the Irish peace process "a jigsaw puzzle" as there has never ever been a straightforward development from war to peace but only small successes, setbacks, side movements, surprising third-party interventions, deadlocks, breakthroughs, etc. Some people even fear this might only be "an inter-war period" (l. 41f.) until one day one side finally triumphs over the other side. In an aside against more liberal-minded people who might think that peace has come naturally to Ireland the authors point out that "when peace did finally come to Ireland it did so for perhaps the least idealistic of motives" (ll. 58f.). It came as an unexpected surprise even to the experts. In the early 1990s the IRA's firm will was "long war" (l. 68) but certainly no peace. Peace and its necessary consequences such as "Unionists (...) sitting around the same table with republicans, would have been regarded as mere fantasy" (ll. 72–74). Compared to that, the peace process has been a success so far.

In the following paragraph, which is not part of this extract, the authors disclose their credo about the origins of the Irish peace process, namely that it must be put into a wider international setting: " [...] we were prepared to learn, and possibly accepted earlier than most that changes both inside and outside Irland as a whole – the ending of the Cold War, European integration, regional settlements in places like the Middle East and South Africa – were beginning to redefine the political landscape in the North and therefore made possible that which would have once seemed inconceivable."[246]

As a whole, text 16 may contribute to the students' deeper and more differentiated insight into the genesis of the Irish peace process in the aftermath of the Belfast Agreement. The article can be discussed and arguments for and against the authors' view can be developed, in particular with some deeper knowledge of the international situation in the 1990s.

Internet Project

When the website of the Bloody Sunday Inquiry opens, the following words appear:

> *".... that a Tribunal be established for inquiring into a definite matter of urgent public importance, namely the events on Sunday 30 January 1972 which led to loss of life in connection with the procession in Londonderry on that day, taking account of any new information relevant to events on that day."*[247]

These words were uttered by Mr Tony Blair MP, the British Prime Minister, to the House of Commons on 29 January 1998. It is an acknowledgement of the necessity of investigating an incident that has come down in the history of the Troubles as Bloody Sunday, one of the blackest days in Northern Ireland and perhaps one of the most disastrous events in this violent conflict.

On Sunday January 30, 1972 the Bogside area of Londonderry (Derry) was the scene of a massacre by the British Army. During a Civil Rights demonstration against the continuation of internment without trial, soldiers of the Parachute Regiment shot dead 14 demonstrators and wounded many more. The official army version was that the soldiers had suspected IRA terrorists of throwing bombs and of firing guns and had only fired at people carrying guns. Many witnesses, however, denied this and claimed that soldiers had fired indiscriminately into the crowd. The international shock at the brutality of this use of state power was enormous and support of the IRA increased remarkably. A first inquiry under Lord Chief Justice Widgery, which supported the army's interpretation, left many who had been witnesses to the event (demonstrators, locals, journalists) dissatisfied. From this time on Northern Irish Catholics and nationalists deeply distrusted the British Army and certainly did not consider it to be their protector. On the contrary, it became a most hated enemy, which again strengthened support for the IRA's great aim which was to free Ireland from the British. More radical splinter groups of the IRA such as the Provisional IRA or the Irish National Liberation Army (INLA) gained support. Their violent campaign over the next few years was directed against Britain and they declared a "war against the British" with many brutal attacks against the soldiers of the British Army but also against many innocent civilians.

As the events of Bloody Sunday had always been an emotive issue and many people, the relatives of the victims in particular, demanded a fair inquiry, a second tribunal, the so-called Saville[248] or Blood Sunday Inquiry was set up on the basis of Prime Minister Tony Blair's statement of 29 January 1998 (see above). This Inquiry was much more comprehensive and received statements from about 2,500 people among them civilians, military personnel, journalists, scientists, priests, and former members of paramilitaries. For security reasons the tribunal temporarily moved to London when they interviewed former soldiers who had been involved in the operation on Bloody Sunday. The Saville Inquiry submitted its report in 2005.

For direct correspondence with the Inquiry write to The Bloody Sunday Inquiry, PO Box 18031, London SW1Y 4WG or write an email to enquiries@bloody-sunday-inquiry.org.

For comprehensive information on Bloody Sunday, including personal accounts of the events, photographs and audio clips see also CAIN Web Service: Key Events – 'Bloody Sunday', Derry 30 January 1972 at http://cain.ulst.ac.uk/events/bsunday/bs.htm.

---

[246] Michael Cox, Adrian Guelke and Fiona Stephen (eds.), *A farewell to arms? From 'long war' to long peace in Northern Ireland*, Manchester University Press, Manchester and New York, 2000, p. 2.

[247] www.bloody-sunday-inquiry.org.

[248] Lord Saville of Newdigate is the chaiman of the second commission of Inquiry.

Teachers might as well want to consider using the popular U2 protest song "Sunday Bloody Sunday" or the 2002 film *Bloody Sunday*.

Against the background of what students have now learned about Ireland they should not only be able to engage in the general discussion of the historical and contemporary situation in Ireland and Northern Ireland and make their personal judgement about it but also develop their own more objective ideas about the Northern Ireland conflict and even possible solutions to it.

The following pages provide 20 **Information Sheets** which can be photocopied and distributed in class. The detailed background knowledge they offer is related to specific topics in the Students' Book and can be used to complement them if and when required (for example for project and/or group work).

Info 1: Swift's Ireland

The Protestant Ascendancy[1]

The city's remarkable resurgence began at the end of the 17th century, when thousands of refugee Huguenot weavers from France settled in Protestant Dublin [...]. Flemish weavers came in their wake, and soon the cloth trades were flourishing. [...] In the course of the 18th century, economic prosperity led to the development of Georgian Dublin. Development spread beyond the old medieval walls; more bridges were erected over the Liffey; and splendid new suburbs arose to the north and east. The city that emerged was, in essence, that of the Dublin of today. Culturally, the century was one of the richest periods in the city's history. Jonathan Swift was dean of St. Patrick's Cathedral between 1713 and 1745, and other noted literary figures – Oliver Goldsmith, Sir Richard Steele, and William Congreve – were active in Dublin. In the New Musick Hall, Handel conducted the first public performance of his Messiah in 1742. For members of the Protestant Ascendancy, as the English establishment was called, Dublin was a gay, fashionable city of elegance and wit. It was something less than that, however, for Roman Catholics, who constituted the majority of the population. At the beginning of the century the Irish Parliament, dominated by the Protestant Ascendancy, passed the Penal Laws, a series of harsh discriminatory measures against the Catholics of Ireland. These laws disfranchised Catholics, placed restrictions on their ownership of property, hindered them from entering the professions, and obstructed Catholic education. The majority of the population was kept in extreme poverty and degradation.

For more information on the Protestant Ascendancy
visit http://www.chapters.eiretek.org/books/Chart/history10.htm.

A Contemporary Report

Any reader setting out to search for Swift's position, whether explicit or implicit, is bound to come, sooner or later, upon Ireland's social and economic plight in the 1720s, a condition which had its roots in English policies [...] in the course of the seventeenth century. As a result of this policy, life in Ireland in the first decades of the eighteenth century had become for the majority of the working population a synonym of poverty and famine, squalor and disease, political oppression and commercial exploitation. [...] For those men who still cared, like Swift's sometime ally, Archbishop William King of Dublin, it was less their horror at the economic woes of the nation than the daunting indifference and casual malice which they were unable to overcome. Writing to an old friend [...] in 1712, King outlined the problems afflicting Ireland in meticulously graphic detail [...]:

> A Gentleman gave me a visit 'tother Day and entertained me with discourse how he had improved his Estate. He told me he had a farm on which there lived about an 100 familys that paid him rent very ill and he lost much every year: that he turned them off and set it dearer to one man who stocked it, lived well upon it and paid his rent punctually. I asked what came of the 100 familys he turned off it; he answered that he did not know. My reply was that those 100 family had at least 500 souls belonging to them, and with what conscience cou'd he send them a begging. He seemed surprized at this, but said that it was their fault: why did they not pay their rent? I desired him to consider that those 500 souls had no other support than what the farms yielded them, and when their maintenance was deducted, it was impossible so much shou'd remain for the Landlord as when only perhaps 10 souls were to be maintained by the produce thereof, and I desired him to consider whether it cou'd be agreable to equity or reason that 490 persons shou'd be turn'd out of their Livlihood without any manner of provision merely that the Landlord might get more rent: that this was just as if an heir shou'd be allowed to murther all his Brothers and Sisters that his Estate might be greater and less incumbered: that this seem'd to me to be the case, or very like the case, of those to whom the Prophet Isayah pronounces a wo. (Is. 5.8.). But the Gentleman still insisted that he might make the best of his own Estate. I answered he might by all Lawful means, but oppressing the poor, ruining familys and sending the familys of whole Baronys to begg were absolutely unlawfull, and so declared by God (Is. 3.14 & 15) and in many other places of Scripture; but I did not find this had any consequence.[2]

---

[1] *Britannica CD 2.0* (Chicago: Encyclopaedia Britannica, 1995).

[2] *See Letters to and from Persons of Quality*, Irish Writings from the Age of Swift, III, ed. Andrew Carpenter (Dublin, 1974), pp. 18–19 (...), quoted from Hermann J. Real, "'A Modest Proposal'. An Interpretation", *Englisch-Amerikanische Studien*, Heft 1, 1988, p. 54.

Info 2: Mercantilism and Laissez-Faire

Mercantilism[1]

economic theory and practice common in Europe from the 16th to the 18th century that promoted governmental regulation of a nation's economy for the purpose of augmenting state power at the expense of rival national powers. It was the economic counterpart of political absolutism. Its 17th-century publicists – most notably Thomas Mun in England, Jean-Baptiste Colbert in France, and Antonio Serra in Italy – never, however, used the term themselves; it was given currency by the Scottish economist Adam Smith in his *Wealth of Nations* (1776). Mercantilism contained many interlocking principles. Precious metals, such as gold and silver, were deemed indispensable to a nation's wealth. If a nation did not possess mines or have access to them, precious metals should be obtained by trade. It was believed that trade balances must be "favourable," meaning an excess of exports over imports. Colonial possessions should serve as markets for exports and as suppliers of raw materials to the mother country. Manufacturing was forbidden in colonies, and all commerce between colony and mother country was held to be a monopoly of the mother country. A strong nation, according to the theory, was to have a large population, for a large population would provide a supply of labour, a market, and soldiers. Human wants were to be minimized, especially for imported luxury goods, for they drained off precious foreign exchange. Sumptuary laws (affecting food and drugs) were to be passed to make sure that wants were held low. Thrift, saving, and even parsimony were regarded as virtues, for only by these means could capital be created. In effect, mercantilism provided the favourable climate for the early development of capitalism, with its promises of profit. Later, mercantilism was severely criticized. Advocates of *laissez-faire* argued that there was really no difference between domestic and foreign trade and that all trade was beneficial both to the trader and to the public. They also maintained that the amount of money or treasure that a state needed would be automatically adjusted and that money, like any other commodity, could exist in excess. They denied the idea that a nation could grow rich only at the expense of another and argued that trade was in reality a two-way street. Laissez-faire, like mercantilism, was challenged by other economic ideas.

Laissez-faire

(French: "allow to do"), policy based on a minimum of governmental interference in the economic affairs of individuals and society. The origin of the term is uncertain, but it is usually associated with the economists known as Physiocrats, who flourished in France from about 1756 to 1778. The policy of laissez-faire received strong support in classical economics as it developed in Great Britain under the influence of Adam Smith. Belief in laissez-faire was a popular view during the 19th century; its proponents cited the assumption in classical economics of a natural economic order as support for their faith in unregulated individual activity. The British economist John Stuart Mill was responsible for bringing this philosophy into popular economic usage in his *Principles of Political Economy* (1848), in which he set forth the arguments for and against government activity in economic affairs. Laissez-faire was a political as well as an economic doctrine. The pervading theory of the 19th century was that the individual, pursuing his own desired ends, would thereby achieve the best results for the society of which he was a part. The function of the state was to maintain order and security and to avoid interference with the initiative of the individual in pursuit of his own desired goals. The philosophy's popularity reached its peak around 1870. In the late 19th century the acute changes caused by industrial growth and the adoption of mass-production techniques proved the laissez-faire doctrine insufficient as a guiding philosophy. Although the original concept had to yield to new theories in attracting wide support, the general philosophy still retains some supporters.

---

[1] Both definitions taken from: *Britannica CD 2.0* (Chicago: Encyclopaedia Britannica, Inc., 1995).

Info 3: Irish Immigration to the United States by Decade, 1820-1970[1]

Decade	Number of Immigrants	Percentage of Total Immigration to United States during Decade
1820–1830	54,338	35.8
1831–1840	207,381	34.6
1841–1850	780,719	45.6
1851–1860	914,109	35.2
1861–1870	435,998	18.6
1871–1880	436,971	15.5
1881–1890	655,482	12.5
1891–1900	388,416	10.5
1901–1910	388,977	4.4
1911–1920	146,131	2.5
1921–1930	220,591	5.4
1931–1940	13,167	2.5
1941–1950	27,503	2.6
1951–1960	57,332	2.3
1961–1970	37,461	1.1
Total, 1820–1970	**4,764,476**	**10.4**

The Irish of the Famine generation composed less than one third of the Irish immigration in the nineteenth century, yet their experience was a formative one in determining Irish response to America and the response of native Americans to them. The peasants who fled the potato blight that ravaged Ireland personified the "tired", "poor", "huddled masses" that Emma Lazarus described in her famous celebration of America's ability to assimilate and transform a diversity of ethnic groups. However, most native Americans perceived the Irish, as Lazarus ambivalently characterized all American immigrants, as "wretched refuse." The Famine-generation Irish were caught in the nineteenth-century equivalent of what Daniel P. Moynihan has termed a "tangle of pathology." Basically unskilled, the Irish were relegated to the most menial jobs – as longshoremen, teamsters, boatmen, and miners or unskilled laborers in a multiplicity of jobs that required strong, untiring backs. They quickly became an urban proletariat, one whose impoverished state and character traits were often invidiously compared to those of black slaves in the South.

The Famine-generation Irish suffered from the most severe ills that afflicted the rapidly expanding urban areas. The slums and tenement quarters in which they lived were among the most congested and squalid in the cities. Because of the crowding, the unsanitary conditions, and the inadequate diet that was available to them, they suffered mortality, morbidity, and insanity rates that were disproportionately higher than those of any other group, whether native or foreign-born. In New York City, arrests of the Irish exceeded those of any other group, and the rate of convictions for Irish criminals was six times that for native Americans. Given these conditions, the Irish became disproportionately dependent upon nineteenth-century welfare – public and private charity – to survive. Poor, illiterate, and prone to high consumption of alcohol, the turbulent Irish "acquired a fearful reputation for ignorance, drunkenness, vice, and violence."

The conflict between native Americans and Irish-Americans was exacerbated by the fact that the two groups differed not only in terms of social class but ethnically and religiously as well. The antipathy of native Americans for the Irish heightened an already deeply embedded opposition to the Catholic faith. The Church, in turn, became identified with the hated Irish, and was perceived as alien to and incompatible with American democratic institutions and values. As they had been the object of tyranny by Anglo-Saxon Protestants in Ireland, so the Irish found themselves the object of persistent discrimination by Anglo-Saxon Protestants in the United States. The forms of derogation were many, ranging stereotypes and epithets through social, educational, and economic discrimination to physical attack and violence. Their social status bleakly reflected in the notorious addendum to "help wanted" notices: "No Irish Need Apply."

Author's Note: The use of the term "native American" in this text is inappropriate. The writer uses it to refer to Americans whose ancestors had settled in America a long time before the great waves of late 19th century and early 20th century immigration.

[1] Qoted from: *Irish History and Culture*, ed. by Harold Orel (Lawrence: University Press of Kansas, 1976), pp. 349; 354f

Info 4: The Great Ulster-Scots

Following[1] dreams of a better life, many Ulster immigrants braved the Atlantic Ocean and settled in America. Their influence was great and they left an enduring legacy that remains strong to this day ...

The Ulster – American link has been thriving ever since the first passenger ship left the tiny port of Groomsport in Ulster for Boston in September 1636. An estimated quarter of a million people emigrated from the north of Ireland to America through the 18th Century, most of them of Scottish Presbyterian stock, whose ancestors had moved to Ulster during the Plantation years of the I7th Century.

Tempted by tales of a new life, rich in wealth and comfort, these Ulster-Scots were prepared to face a hazardous journey across the Atlantic in simple wooden sailing boats. The journey took around six to eight weeks and conditions on board were often appalling with overcrowding, disease and lack of fresh food and water resulting in a number of deaths.

However, the majority of these hardy immigrants survived the journey to become the first citizens of America's frontier lands, cutting their way through dense forest and across formidable river and mountain barriers to create settlements that became the backbone of the United States.

By 1790 the Ulster-Scots accounted for 14% of the white population in America and today an estimated 44 million people in the United States are of Irish extraction, 56% of which can trace their roots back to the 18th Century Ulster immigrants.

Colloquial Ulster-Scot dialect and terminology in the US, with its distinctive patterns of pronunciation, enjoys remarkable parallels with speech patterns in Northern Ireland today and there are other personal characteristics which define people who may live far apart, but are intrinsically linked in the passage of history. It has been said of the Ulster-Scots that they were the first to start and the last to quit. This vigour and grit was reflected in their pioneering instinct and these sterling qualities have become deeply engrained into the American psyche.

Regions of the United States where the social and cultural inheritance of the Ulster -Scots has become firmly embedded include Pennsylvania, New Hampshire, West Virginia, Shenandoah Valley of Virginia, western Virginia, east and middle Tennessee, North Carolina, Kentucky, North Georgia, Alabama and parts of Texas.

Americans from Ulster-Scots family background have contributed much to the social, economic and literary life of the United States over the last 200 years. Famous names such as Samuel Langhorn Clemens (novelist Mark Twain), Thomas Mellon and Davy Crockett all had roots in Ulster. But it is on the political front that the Ulster-Scots have left their most impressive legacy. 17 of the 43 American Presidents are generally accepted as being of Ulster ancestry.

[1] Information taken from *Northern Ireland Visitors Journal*, 2003, p. 99.

Info 5: Folklore in Ireland

The[1] speaking voice of Irish tradition comes to us from many sources. Its richest base lies in the heritage of the Irish language, but all the peoples who settled in this island – Norsemen, Normans, Scots, and English – have made their own contributions. Furthermore, since striking narratives and curious ideas are transmitted easily from one culture to another, a great wealth of international folkloric materials has been borrowed into Ireland down through the centuries.

In mediaeval Ireland, responsibility for preserving cultural data devolved upon a special learned caste. Such data included accounts of mythological heroes and of the important figures of ancient history, together with detailed genealogical and onomastic traditions. The range and scope of this learned lore is well represented in the older Irish literature, which abounds in descriptions of personages, septs and locale. The literature originated in the 6th century AD and continued to flower until the suppression of native institutions a thousand years later. The period from the 17th to the 19th century witnessed a great weakening in the Gaelic culture, and this was accompanied by an increasing decline in the use of the language itself. Some of the old heroic tales were, however, preserved in readily available manuscripts and, through being read aloud in the peasant environment, were given a new lease of life in oral storytelling and have survived among speakers of Irish to our own time.

[...] From time immemorial, the poet or *file* was a leading personage in Irish culture. The poets specialised in praise and satire, and their verses were thought by many to contain mystical knowledge and to have magical effect. Being the leading representatives of the learned caste, they were professionals and enjoyed the lavish patronage of Gaelic, and later Norman-Gaelic, lords. The traditional poetry survived the demise of the Gaelic social order. Living among the ordinary people and themselves often reduced to penury, the later Gaelic poets made a significant contribution to the sense of style and accuracy of expression which remains a distinctive trait of the Irish language. The poets also became themselves the subjects of folk legends, in which they are portrayed as vanquishing with the keenness of their verses those who indulged in authoritarianism, pomposity, or stinginess.

[1] "Folklore in Ireland" in *Ireland* (Dublin: The Department of Foreign Affairs, Fact Sheet 1/96, 1996).

Info 6: Celtic Mythology

Most[1] of our information on Celtic mythology is about mythical characters and events in the British Isles, particularly in Ireland. During the Middle Ages, Irish monks preserved many ancient Celtic myths in several collections of manuscripts. The most important collection of manuscripts is the *Lebor Gabala* (Book of Conquests), which traces the mythical history of Ireland. [...]

The Irish Cycles. A great deal of Irish Celtic mythology concerns three important cycles (series of related stories). These cycles are (1) the mythological cycle, (2) the Ulster cycle, and (3) the Fenian cycle.

The Mythological Cycle, the oldest cycle, is preserved in the *Lebor Gabala*. The cycle describes the early settlement of Ireland through a succession of invasions by five supernatural races. The most important race was the Tuatha De Danann, or People of the Goddess Danu. [...] The Tuatha De Danann were the source of most of the divinities that the Irish people worshipped before they became Christians in the A.D. 400's.

The Ulster Cycle centers on the court of King Conchobar at Ulster, probably about the time of Christ. The stories deal with the adventures of Cúchulainn, a great Irish hero who can also be considered a demigod. In some ways, he resembled the Greek hero Achilles. But unlike Achilles and other Greek heroes, Cúchulainn had many supernatural powers. For example, he could spit fire in battle. He was also a magician and poet. [...]

The Fenian Cycle describes the deeds of the hero Finn MacCool and his band of warriors known as the Fianna. Finn and the Fianna were famous for their great size and strength. In addition, Finn was known for his generosity and wisdom. Although divine beings and supernatural events play a part in these stories, the central characters are human. Some scholars believe the events in the Fenian cycle may reflect the political and social conditions in Ireland during the A.D. 200's.

The most famous **Welsh myths** concern King Arthur and his knights. The mythical King Arthur was probably based on a powerful Celtic chief who lived in Wales during the A.D. 500's.

---

[1] Qoted from *Information Finder*, (World Book, Inc., 1995).

Info 7: A Province of Myth and Legend

Northern[1] Ireland is steeped in superstition and folklore that has been handed down from generation to generation. Some stories have been in written form since the 8th Century, but most originated over 2000 years ago when the Druids passed on stories orally from one generation to the next.

Fairies & Leprechauns

The existence of spirits and in particular the 'little people' plays a large part in Irish folklore. Centuries ago it was believed that fairies lived under mounds of earth or fairy forts and that touching one of these tiny figures brought bad luck. The most famous of the little people is the leprechaun.

Legend has it that these little men dressed in green tunics sat under trees mending fairies' shoes and that if you caught one, he would lead you to a crock of gold, but take your eyes of him for an instant and he would vanish into thin air with the gold.

The Banshee

The Banshee is a female spirit with long flowing hair whose wailing presence outside a house is said to signal the imminent death of someone within. Many people, especially in rural areas, still believe in the banshee today and dread hearing wailing.

The Children of Lir

One of the best-known legends concerns the four beautiful children of King Lir. Their mother died when they were young and the King, wanting to give them a new mother, married his wife's sister, Aoife. But Aoife, seeing the King playing with the children became jealous of them and using magic she turned them all into swans, who would only be set free from the spell in 900 years when St. Patrick came to Ireland and they heard the first Christian bells.

And so, after 900 years, they heard the sound of distant bells and followed them until they came to the house of a Christian man called Caomhog and told him what happened to them. They were lovingly cared for by the people of the house and people came from near and far to see the talking swans. Then one day a princess sent her servants to try and steal the swans, but just as they laid hands on them, the time came for the swans to become children again.

Now the swans were human again, although 900 years old, Caomhog had them baptised and the bells rang out at their christening. Soon afterwards they died of old age and that night four beautiful children were seen flying out over the lake and straight up to heaven. To this day it is illegal to kill swans in Ireland.

The Shamrock

The shamrock symbolises the cross and blessed trinity. Before the Christian era it was a sacred plant of the Druids because its leaves formed a triad.

The well-known legend of the Shamrock connects it to St.Patrick. Preaching in open air on the doctrine of the trinity, he is said to have illustrated the existence of Three in One by plucking a shamrock from the grass and showing it to his congregation. The legend of the shamrock is also connected with that of the banishment of the serpents from Ireland by a tradition that snakes are never seen on shamrock and that it is a remedy against the sting of snakes and scorpions.

[1] Information taken from *Northern Ireland Visitors Journal*, 2003, p. 68f.

Finn McCool and the Creation of Lough Neagh

Finn McCool was a giant who, according to legend, created the Giant's Causeway and Lough Neagh. The story goes that Finn got into a fight with another giant from Scotland. In order to chase him away, Finn reached down and pulled a sod from the ground and threw it at the Scottish giant. If you look at a map of Ireland, you will see the hole which was left when he pulled out this sod of earth. It later filled with water and is known as Lough Neagh, the largest lake in Ireland.

The place where the sod landed is in the middle of the Irish Sea, just between Ireland and England, and is now called the Isle of Man.

Finn McCool and the Salmon of Knowledge

One day Finn was sent to a wise old man who lived at the banks of the River Boyne. For seven years he had been trying to catch the sacred Salmon of Knowledge, because it had been foretold that the first to taste this salmon would possess all the wisdom in the world. That day Finn caught the salmon but the old man warned Finn that he was not allowed to taste the salmon, but should give the first piece to the old man. Finn agreed and began cooking the salmon over an open fire. When Finn went to turn the salmon over to cook it on the other side, he burnt his thumb and immediately stuck his thumb into his mouth to cool it. Of course, when he did this he tasted the salmon and so possessed all the knowledge of the world. Every day after that, whenever Finn wanted to solve a problem, all he had to do was suck his thumb!

Cuchulainn

Cuchulain is described as a small black-browed man, beardless and full of fun. When he is in battle a remarkable change comes over him; he increases in size and his body trembles and whirls about inside of his skin so that his frontal features are turned to the rear. He can draw one of his eyes back into his head and his hair bristles on end, with a drop of blood on the end of each hair. When he is in warrior frenzy, he attacks anyone in vicinity – friend or foe.

Info 8: Irish Bilingualism

Until[1] the nineteenth century the common vernacular was Irish (Gaeilge or Gaelicóa Celtic language, cousin to Welsh and to the ancient tongue of the Gauls). It had been so since before the dawn of history. Neither Vikings nor Anglo-Normans nor – until the time of the first Queen Elizabeth – the English had maintained their linguistic independence. Systematic plantation (i.e. land-robbery by the English) in Ulster and the Midlands created English-speaking "islands" from the seventeenth century onwards, but even some of these as well as the cities and towns (all old strongholds of English power) were often partly gaelicised through intermarriage with the Irish and the need for "native labour". Not until the end of the eighteenth century [...] did the native Irish set about having their children taught English.

Long before English became Ireland's new spoken language, it had reigned high in the domain of the written word. Yet it never penetrated the Gaelic literary world, unlike Norman-French which brought to the English literary tradition a precious cargo from Provençal and from French itself. (The glittering impedimenta of Courtly Love, which the bilingual Hiberno-Norman lords refashioned into Gaelic verses and which were later re-forged into the popular love songs, are still sung in the Irish-speaking countryside.) English, I say, remained outside the Gaelic bardic circle. Even when that circle was broken with the collapse of the Gaelic aristocracy and its patronage at the beginning of the seventeenth century, only an occasional antiquarian acknowledgement [...] showed that even the most cultivated of the colonists had been at all aware of the cultural hinterland beyond the English Pale. Swift is sometimes said to have been an exception but, I believe, on very doubtful evidence. Not until bilingual Irish scholars emerged and could meet their peers on something like terms of equality was the work of publication and serious translation begun. Hardiman's *Irish Minstrelsy* (1831) is a landmark.

But if the Irish remained almost untouched by English and Hiberno-English literature until Tom Moore's time (1779–1852), they had long been all too aware of the written word of the colonists in another sphere. With the breakdown of Gaelic institutions in the early seventeenth century, spoken Irish lost all public function. English became the language of law and order, of commerce and communication, of "improvement" rural and urban, of schooling both established and informal and even of the Catholic Church (outside of the Latin liturgy). All over the country, grave-stones from the seventeenth and eighteenth centuries record in English the passing of men and women whose only tongue was Irish.

And so was born a tension, a linguistic relationship which changed radically as the vernacular balance tipped from Irish to English. It was both guilt-ridden and liberated and charged with enormous creative capacity. The guilt, conscious or subconscious, came from the apparent rejection of the past and the attendant breakdown in communication between the generations – often, literally, between parent and child – which resulted from the widespread adoption of English as the spoken word. Balanced against this was the liberation which a second language always brings: the liberation from the automatic identification of word and thing, of idea and expression. Irish bilingualism does not mean that all or even most of us are equally at home in both languages. Indeed, as the vernacular shift from Irish to English took place, entire communities were left with only the vaguest memory of the speech of their grandparents, and today strenuous efforts to restore and revive Irish have only partially succeeded. Nevertheless it is important to recognise that the nation as a whole is bilingual, historically and actually (however imperfectly so) – in contrast to the situation of Belgium, say, or Canada, or Switzerland.

[1] Quoted from *Irish Life and Traditions*, ed. by Sharon Gmelch (Syracuse: Syracuse University Press, 1986), pp. 211f.

Info 9: The 1994 Ceasefire Statements

IRA Statement[1]

Recognising the potential of the current situation and in order to enhance the democratic peace process and to underline our definitive commitment to its success the leadership of Oglaigh na hÉireann have decided that as of midnight Wednesday, August 31, there will be a complete cessation of military operations. All our units have been instructed accordingly. At this historic crossroads the leadership Oglaigh na hÉireann salutes and commends our volunteers and other activists, our supporters and the political prisoners who have sustained this struggle against all odds for the past 25 years. Your courage, determination and sacrifice have demonstrated that the spirit of freedom and the desire for peace based on a just and lasting settlement cannot be crushed. We remember all those who have died for Irish freedom and we reiterate our commitment to our republican objectives. Our struggle has seen many gains and advances made by nationalists and for the democratic position. We believe that an opportunity to secure a just and lasting settlement has been created. We are therefore entering a new situation in a spirit of determination and confidence, determined that the injustices which created this conflict will be removed and confident in the strength and justice of our struggle to achieve this. We note that the Downing Street Declaration is not a solution, nor was it presented as such by its authors. A solution will only be found as a result of inclusive negotiations. Others, not least the British Government, have a duty to face up to their responsibilities. It is our desire to significantly contribute with energy, determination and patience.

Statement by the Combined Loyalist Military Command, Belfast, Oct. 13, 1994[2]

After a widespread consultative process initiated by representations from the Ulster Democratic and Progressive Unionist parties, and after having received confirmations and guarantees in relation to the Northern Ireland constitutional position within the United Kingdom, as well as other assurances, and, in the belief that the democratically expressed wishes of the greater number of people in Northern Ireland will be respected and upheld, the Combined Loyalist Military Command will universally cease all operational hostilities as from 12 midnight on Thursday, Oct. 13, 1994. The permanence of our ceasefire will be completely dependent upon the continued cessation of all nationalist/republican violence; the sole responsibility for a return to war lies with them. In the genuine hope that this peace will be permanent, we take the opportunity to pay homage to all our fighters, commandoes and volunteers who have paid the human sacrifice. They did not die in vain. The Union is safe. To our physically and mentally wounded who have served Ulster so unselfishly, we wish a speedy recovery and to the relatives of these men and women, we pledge our continued moral and practical support. To our prisoners who have undergone so much deprivation and degradation with great courage and forbearance, we solemnly promise to leave no stone unturned to secure their freedom. To our serving officers, NCOs and personnel, we extend our eternal gratitude for their obedience to orders, for their ingenuity and good humour in the most trying of circumstances, and we commend them for their courageous fortitude and unshakable faith over the long years of armed confrontation. In all sincerity, we offer to the loved ones of all innocent victims over the past 25 years, abject and true remorse. No words of ours will compensate for the intolerable suffering they have undergone during the conflict. Let us firmly resolve to respect our differing views of freedom, culture and aspiration and never again permit our political circumstance to degenerate into bloody warfare. We are on the threshold of a new and exciting beginning with our battles in future being political battles, fought on the side of honesty, decency and democracy against the negativity of mistrust, misunderstanding and malevolence so that together we can bring forth a wholesome society in which our children and their children will know the meaning of peace.

---

[1] Information taken from *Belfast Telegraph*, 31 August, 1994.
[2] Qoted from http://cain.ulst.ac.uk/events/peace/docs/clmc131094.htm.

Info 10: IRA Statement, 28 July 2005

The Belfast Telegraph Digital[1]

The IRA has said it will stand down all units from 4pm today. A statement said it would put an end to 'armed struggle' and devote efforts towards peaceful solutions.

It instructed all members to "assist the development of purely political and democratic programmes through exclusively peaceful means". The statement also invites a representative from the Protestant and Catholic churches to witness the disarmament.

STATEMENT IN FULL

"The leadership of Óglaigh na hÉireann has formally ordered an end to the armed campaign. This will take effect from 4pm this afternoon.

All IRA units have been ordered to dump arms. All Volunteers have been instructed to assist the development of purely political and democratic programmes through exclusively peaceful means.

Volunteers must not engage in any other activities whatsoever. The IRA leadership has also authorised our representative to engage with the IICD[2] to complete the process to verifiably put its arms beyond use in a way which will further enhance public confidence and to conclude this as quickly as possible.

We have invited two independent witnesses, from the Protestant and Catholic churches, to testify to this. The Army Council took these decisions following an unprecedented internal discussion and consultation process with IRA units and Volunteers.

We appreciate the honest and forthright way in which the consultation process was carried out and the depth and content of the submissions.

We are proud of the comradely way in which this truly historic discussion was conducted. The outcome of our consultations show very strong support among IRA Volunteers for the Sinn Féin peace strategy. There is also widespread concern about the failure of the two governments and the unionists to fully engage in the peace process. This has created real difficulties.

The overwhelming majority of people in Ireland fully support this process. They and friends of Irish unity throughout the world want to see the full implementation of the Good Friday Agreement. Notwithstanding these difficulties our decisions have been taken to advance our republican and democratic objectives, including our goal of a united Ireland.

We believe there is now an alternative way to achieve this and to end British rule in our country. It is the responsibility of all Volunteers to show leadership, determination and courage. We are very mindful of the sacrifices of our patriot dead, those who went to jail, Volunteers, their families and the wider republican base. We reiterate our view that the armed struggle was entirely legitimate.

We are conscious that many people suffered in the conflict. There is a compelling imperative on all sides to build a just and lasting peace. The issue of the defence of nationalist and republican communities has been raised with us. There is a responsibility on society to ensure that there is no re-occurrence of the pogroms of 1969 and the early 1970s.

---

1 *The Belfast Telegraph Digital*, 28 July, 2005, http://www.belfasttelegraph.co.uk/news/story.jsp?story=654393.

2 Independent International Commission on Decommissioning.

There is also a universal responsibility to tackle sectarianism in all its forms. The IRA is fully committed to the goals of Irish unity and independence and to building the Republic outlined in the 1916 Proclamation. We call for maximum unity and effort by Irish republicans everywhere. We are confident that by working together Irish republicans can achieve our objectives.

Every Volunteer is aware of the import of the decisions we have taken and all Óglaigh are compelled to fully comply with these orders. There is now an unprecedented opportunity to utilise the considerable energy and goodwill which there is for the peace process.

This comprehensive series of unparalleled initiatives is our contribution to this and to the continued endeavours to bring about independence and unity for the people of Ireland. Irish Republican Army orders an end to armed campaign. The IRA is fully committed to the goals of Irish unity and independence and to building the Republic outlined in the 1916 Proclamation.

Our decisions have been taken to advance our republican and democratic objectives, including our goal of a united Ireland. We believe there is now an alternative way to achieve this and to end British rule in our country.

Info 11: Chastelain Report on IRA Decommissioning, 26 September 2005

INDEPENDENT INTERNATIONAL COMMISSION ON DECOMMISSIONING

Brigadier Tauno Nieminen *General John de Chastelain* *Andrew D. Sens*

Address in Dublin

Dublin Castle
Block M, Ship Street
DUBLIN 2

Tel No: (01) 4780111
Fax No: (01) 4780600

Address in Belfast

Rosepark House
Upper Newtownards Road
BELFAST BT4 3NX

Tel No: (028) 90 488600
Fax No: (028) 90 488601

REPORT OF THE INDEPENDENT INTERNATIONAL COMMISSSION ON DECOMMISSIONING

To:
The Rt. Hon. Peter Hain, MP
Secretary of State for Northern Ireland
BELFAST

To:
Mr. Michael McDowell, TD
Minister for Justice, Equality and Law Reform
DUBLIN

1. Over the past number of weeks we have engaged with the IRA representative in the execution of our mandate to decommission paramilitary arms.

2. We can now report that we have observed and verified events to put beyond use very large quantities of arms which the representative has informed us includes all the arms in the IRA's possession. We have made an inventory of this materièl.

3. In 2004 the Commission was provided with estimates of the number and quantity of arms held by the IRA. These estimates were produced by the security forces in both jurisdictions and were in agreement. Our inventory is consistent with these estimates and we believe that the arms decommissioned represent the totality of the IRA's arsenal.

4. The manner in which the arms were decommissioned is in accordance with the remit given us by the two governments as reflected in their Decommissioning Acts of 1997.

5. A Protestant and a Catholic clergyman also witnessed all these recent events: the Reverend Harold Good, former President of the Methodist Church in Ireland, and Father Alec Reid, a Redemptorist priest.

6. The new single inventory of decommissioned IRA arms incorporates the three we made during the preceding IRA events. This lists all the IRA arms we have verified as having been put beyond use. We will retain possession of this inventory until our mandate is complete.

7. We can report, however, that the arms involved in the recent events include a full range of ammunition, rifles, machine guns, mortars, missiles, handguns, explosives, explosive substances and other arms, including all the categories described in the estimates provided by the security forces.

8. In summary, we have determined that the IRA has met its commitment to put all its arms beyond use in a manner called for by the legislation.

9. It remains for us to address the arms of the loyalist paramilitary groups, as well as other paramilitary organizations, when these are prepared to cooperate with us in doing so.

Tauno Nieminen   John de Chastelain   Andrew Sens

26 September 2005

Info 12: A Short History of the Conflict in Northern Ireland

The outside observer is often under the impression that what happens in Northern Ireland is an incomprehensible religious conflict. Yet, it is not religion alone that has contributed to the inextricable situation in Northern Ireland. It is as well a question of power politics, economics and social life – and the key to the understanding of the conflict in Northern Ireland today lies in Great Britain! Irish history (and Northern Ireland is a part of it) has always been the history of Anglo-Irish relations – at least for the last 800 years and with a nation divided as its result.
The following timeline is based on John Mc Hugh, "Ireland: A chronology of key events" in Bill Jones (ed.), *Political Issues in Britain Today* (Manchester: Manchester University Press, 1989), pp. 296–98; and James Walsh, "A History of the Troubles", *Time*, 12 September 1994, pp. 26–31.

Origins of the conflict

1170	Henry II of England begins conquest of Ireland.
1542	Henry VII proclaimed King of Ireland. Ulster remains Gaelic and unsuppressed.
1603	Ulster now comes under firm English governmental control. Gaelic order vanquished and settlement of Ulster by 175,000 mostly Scots Presbyterians begins.
1641	Catholic revolt involving massacre of Ulster Protestants (Portadown). Cromwellian suppression follows (1649–50).
1688	James II deposed by Parliament who ask William & Mary ('Glorious Revolution') to become King and Queen. But James still recognised as King by Catholic Ireland.
1689	Siege of Londonderry protestants by forces of James II.
1690	James defeated at the Battle of the Boyne: Protestant ascendancy now assured.
1782	Irish Parliament set up in Dublin under Henry Gratton, inspired by the American Revolution.
1790s	Birth of Irish Republicanism by Wolfe Tone, inspired by the French Revolution – attempt at French revolutionary intervention.
1798	Insurrection of Tone's 'United Irishmen' suppressed in a particularly savage fashion.
1801	Act of Union: Dublin Parliament disappears and Ireland becomes an integral part of the U.K.
[Mid 19th century]	Growing agitation for Home Rule for Ireland is resisted by successive British governments.
[Late 19th century]	attempts to introduce Home Rule by the Liberals under Gladstone resisted by unionists in Northern Ireland
1916	Dublin Easter Rising. Fifteen leaders executed. Sinn Féin now overtakes the Nationalist party as the voice of 'Catholic' Ireland.
1918	Sinn Féin wins a majority of seats at the General Election and in 1919 sets up the First Dáil as an alternative Parliament. IRA formed in 1919 from IRB.
1919–21	Anglo-Irish War between IRA and 'Black and Tans' – military auxiliaries.

Ulster: emergence of a 'mini-state', 1920–88

1920–21	The Government of Ireland Act 1920 and Anglo-Irish Treaty 1921 establish the boundaries of the partitioned island. The Ulster 'State' consists of six of the nine historic counties which make up the Province of Ulster.
1922–72	The Unionist Party dominates the politics of Northern Ireland. The Roman Catholic minority is represented by the residual elements of the old Nationalist party but a portion looks to the remnants of Sinn Féin and the IRA who have not accepted the 1920/21 Anglo-Irish arrangements. Politics seem to be frozen in a permanent religious / cultural / nationalist time warp. 'Normal' politics based on class / economic / social issues are marginal.

The 'Troubles'

1968 The Civil Rights Movement emerges with new demands related to jobs, housing and discrimination which starts the process of destroying the Stomont Parliament and the monolithic Unionist Party. The IRA re-emerges and the British government reluctantly gets sucked into the Ulster Crisis.

1969–72 British troops deployed in Belfast and Londonderry as peacekeepers, ostensibly to protect Catholics from Protestant forces of 'law and order'. The position quickly changes and British troops find themselves confronting the IRA as well.

1972 Londonderry civil rights marchers scuffle with British soldiers, who fire into the crowd, killing 13 Catholics. The clash, known as Bloody Sunday, intensifies Catholic opposition to Britain's presence. London assumes direct rule of Northern Ireland.

1981 Republican martyr Bobby Sands dies in Belfast's Maze prison after a 66-day hunger strike in protest against the British refusal to grant special political-prisoner status to 700 IRA prisoners.

1983 A Christmas-shopping day at Harrods in London turns to terror when a car bomb explodes outside the store, blasting glass and debris into the crowds. Five die; more than 80 are hurt.

1985 Margaret Thatcher and Irish PM Garrett Fitzgerald sign the Anglo-Irish Agreement, giving the Irish a voice in Northern Ireland matters; in return, Dublin recognises the loyalist hopes of Ulster Protestants.

1988 Protestant fires into a crowd of Catholic mourners, killing three. A week later, Catholics at another burial pull two British soldiers from their car and slay them with their own weapons.

1993 IRA bombing of an English shopping mall leaves two children, ages 12 and 3, dead. A Dublin peace march draws 20,000, and 100,000 sign condolence books for the children's mothers.
IRA bombing of a Shankill Road fish shop in Belfast kills seven. Within days, Protestants retaliate spraying a pub with bullets while shouting "Trick or Treat!" Seven are killed.
British Prime Minister John Major and Irish Prime Minister Albert Reynolds sign the Downing Street Declaration, a blueprint for self-determination in Northern Ireland.

1994 Sinn Féin announces a ceasefire, pledging "complete cessation of all military operation."

1995 A Framework for Agreement released by the British and Irish governments for the future governance of Northern Ireland.

1996 (Feb) End of ceasefire with renewed bombing campaign of the IRA.

1997 (July) Restoration of the 1994 IRA ceasefire helps Britain's new Labour government to allow Sinn Féin to take part in new peace talks.

1998–2006 see Students' Book, p. 16. For more detailed information on the Irish Peace Process as the Northern Ireland conflict was gradually called after the 1998 Good Friday (or Belfast) Agreement see *Times Online*, "Timeline – Key events in peace process", http://www.timesonline.co.uk/article/0,,-1711759,00.html.

Info 13: Who Is Who? The Four Major Players

Although there have been various groups with different aims involved in 'The Troubles' in Northern Ireland, there are four main parties : Catholics / Republicans; Protestants / Unionists; the Irish government; the British government. Of course, it is the main aim of the peace process in Northern Ireland to find a way of reaching a compromise between the divergent positions of the various parties and groups participating in the peace process – or the continuation of the conflict. For historical reasons and in order to realize the difficulties in the process of securing lasting peace in Northern Ireland, here are the traditional positions taken by the four major players:
For more detailed information on the key players in the Irish peace process go to http://www.infoplease.com/spot/northirelandwho1.html.

IRA

The Irish Republican Army's aim is to unite Northern Ireland and the Republic of Ireland. The Provisional IRA is its paramilitary wing (see extra information on p. 52, Study Aids). The following text is taken from *The I.R.A. Speaks*, No. 3, A Repsol Pamphlet, p. 9:

> *Those who think that political means alone are sufficient for the Re-Conquest of Ireland are closing their minds to the lessons of history, not alone in Ireland but in every other country struggling for national liberation.*
> *If freedom can be won without violence then by all means let us win it that way, but, let us not allow victory to be snatched from us by those who will have no scruples about the use of violence when they see power and wealth and privilege slipping from their grasp.*
> *Only an armed, determined people will be listened to with respect. While Britain claims the right to legislate for Ireland and upholds that claim by armed force, then Irishmen must be trained and ready to resist her claim by armed force.*

UDA

Unionists (mainly protestant defenders of Northern Ireland as a part of the United Kingdom) are split into different groups. The UDA, the Ulster Defence Association, is an extremist paramilitary organization in Northern Ireland which takes violent action in opposition to the actions of the IRA. This is what a UDA spokesperson said in an interview to the student paper *Gown*, 22 (7) 1976:

Gown*: How long will the civil war last? UDA: We would like it to be over in a week.*
Gown*: What about those Catholics who have no arms? UDA: How do we know they've no arms? We will assume that Catholics are fully armed and on that assumption we will take action against them.*
Gown*: Can anybody surrender? UDA: We cannot take prisoners. They are a liability.*
Gown*: Will you win? UDA: While there are Protestants here, there will be a NI as a part of Britain.*
Gown*: What will be the conditions under which Catholics will stay? UDA: There will be no room for RCs in a new state.*

British Government

from: *Statement of Security Policy*, November 1990.

1. *Northern Ireland is part of the United Kingdom because that is the will of the majority of people who live there. It will not cease to be a part of the United Kingdom unless that situation changes. Majority desire for a change in status clearly does not exist at present. There is no reason to expect this to alter in the foreseeable future.*
2. *The Government's aims are:*
   (a) to maintain the rule of law; (b) to ensure that all the people of Northern Ireland are free to express their political opinions without inhibition, fear of discrimination or reprisal; (c) to defend the democratically expressed wishes of the people of Northern Ireland against those who try to promote political objectives, including a change in the status of Northern Ireland, by violence or the threat of violence.

BUNREACHT NA hÉIREANN (Constitution of the Republic of Ireland)

Article 2: The national territory consists of the whole island of Ireland, its islands and the territorial seas.
Article 3: Pending the re-integration of the national territory, and without prejudice to the right of the Parliament and Government established by this Constitution to exercise jurisdiction over the whole of that territory, the laws enacted by that Parliament shall have the like area and extent of application as the laws of Saorstát Éireann and the like extra-territorial effect.

Info 14: Jet Log: Irish Murals Illustrate History and Tensions

I[1] stared at the masked man whose automatic rifle was pointed straight at me, raised my camera to my eye and shot a picture. He didn't shoot back; he was frozen mid-aim, larger than life, painted on the side of a house in Protestant West Belfast.

It was only one surreal moment among many during my program-sponsored trip to Northern Ireland. I came with my head filled with facts from my class about the "troubles," the period of political violence from 1969 onward that has left 3,556 people dead.

I learned from our professor about the two deeply divided sides of the struggle: the Protestant unionist community, which sees itself as British and wants to remain part of the United Kingdom, and the Catholic nationalist community, which sees the Northern Irish state as a failed partition attempt and wants to create a united Ireland.

I read about the escalation of violence between the Irish Republican Army and loyalist paramilitaries that has killed army officers and unarmed children. I listened to lectures about the peace process, the Good Friday Agreement of 1998 and the struggle to make the agreement work in the years since then.

But nothing prepares you for the murals. My classmates and I piled into a black cab for a tour of the "trouble spots" of Belfast, and we first went to the Protestant neighborhood of Shankill Road. We pulled up to an area that looked completely normal except for the enormous paintings on the sides of the houses.

The murals are cartoonish, but their images are deadly serious. A painting of Oliver Cromwell is paired with the quote, "There will be no peace in Ireland until the Catholic Church is crushed." Another showed members of paramilitaries, with a masked man holding a machine gun front and center.

We traveled next to the Catholic area near Falls Road, only minutes away from Shankill. Murals now showed events like the Bombay Street firebombing in 1969, and paid tribute to Bobby Sands and other IRA members who died on hunger strikes for prisoner rights in 1981.

The only thing separating the two communities is an enormous concrete wall topped with barbed wire. It's monitored constantly by cameras, and it's covered in scrawled messages of peace from people all over the world.

There's something extremely uncomfortable about standing around as a gawking tourist, taking pictures of what is essentially someone's neighborhood. I can leave when I've seen enough, but they can't.

Since the Good Friday Agreement, there's been little secular violence in Northern Ireland, but when the symbols of the underlying hostility between the two sides are so visible in everyday life, it's not hard to understand why the emotions are still strong.

Gerry Adams, the president of Sinn Fein, the IRA's political wing, called on the group last Thursday to end its violent activities permanently and choose a purely political path to a united Ireland. The country has been on edge since the $50 million bank raid in December that has been blamed on the IRA, and the IRA murder of a Belfast man, Robert McCartney, that brought the group's criminality back into the spotlight.

There is a sense of being on edge, teetering between what could be seen years down the road either as a mere blip in the peace process or the compilation of events that brought it to a standstill. And there is a sense of resignation, that it's just the way things are and the way they will be for a long time.

When we were on our tour in Belfast, one of the girls in my cab asked our driver if he thought the IRA would ever return to violence after its 1997 ceasefire. "I don't think the IRA will go back to war," he said. "But when you're in this country, who knows?"

---

[1] This text is an excerpt from Katie Maslanka, "Jet Log: Irish murals illustrate history and tensions," *The Ithacan Online*, (72/26), www.ithaca.edu/ithacan/articles/0504/14/accent/3jet_log.htm.

Info 15: What Foreigners Think of Ireland

With tens of thousands of people moving to Ireland each year, Jane Lyons asks some "blow-ins" what they think of Ireland in her article "Ireland? Sure we don't know how great it is." *Irish Independent*, 2 January 2004, p.18.

LEA GOSSART, 24 (FRANCE)

Length of stay: Three-and-a-half years, **Occupation:** Front of house coordinator **Likes:** "Dublin is small enough and big enough – it is not a huge city where you get lost and it is not like a village with one street You've got enough entertainment and enough attractions. In general, Irish people are really warm people. They live up to the reputation that they have. Irish people tend to speak to people in the streets and pubs while in Paris you don't do that because it is so big." **Dislikes:** "Ireland can be quite frustrating because there is no margin for difference. If you are not part of the Standard, you feel like you are not going to belong. Sometimes people are quite limited in their way of seeing things."

EMILY LIDSTROM, 22 (SWEDEN)

Length of stay: Two years **Occupation:** Photography student
Likes: "I like the intimacy of the people. It is very easy to move here by yourself and it's a little bit easier to get to know people than in other places I've been to. "It feels like it is possible to do things here now, while in other countries things might be very established. There are many young people who are doing things. It feels like there are more possibilities to start a band, a record company, magazine, clothes label – stuff like that"
Dislikes: "I don't like the weather: the damp and cold. The prices are also very expensive."

MARTA GARCIA TASCóN, 26 (SPAIN)

Length of stay: Three months **Occupation:** Bar attendant **Likes:** "The weather in these last three months has been very nice. The humour of the Irish is similar to the Spanish people – it is friendly and happy – and the personality is very open. There are also more jobs and money here."
Dislikes: "I don't like the taxes. In Spain everything is public – the health, medical, hospital. Here you have to pay for these services and you have to pay more taxes. You have to pay for everything. It is very expensive."

AVERY JOHN, 28 (TRINIDAD)

Length of stay: Four years **Occupation:** Professional football player **Likes:** "One of the greatest things I have experienced is the friendliness of the people. When I came here four years ago there weren't very many black people (compared to now) and, at least for me, I have never experienced any racial tension. I found the people very genuine, very helpful and very nice. They reminded me of people from home: very easy-going, love to party, love to drink."
Dislikes: "The hardest thing has been the weather."

GIUSEPPE CONTI, 31 (1TALY)

Length of stay: Six months **Occupation:** Bar attendant **Likes:** "I usually don't talk about a place, I talk about the people. I find Irish people, in a way, similar to Italian people. I've met some really good people."
Dislikes: "I think they drink too much. I usually don't drink but since I've been here I go drinking because that is the only way you can socialise with people. They also don't care as much about food as Italians do."

CIARAN MURPHY, 34 (AUSTRALIA)

Length of stay: Four years **Occupation:** Sub-editor **Likes:** "I like the ease of companionship, the vigour of an argument over a few pints, the beauty of the countryside and the real Ireland that lies behind the hi-diddly-i facade."
Dislikes: "I dislike the political shadow games which are allowed to continue with a nod and a wink while the nation frays. I also dislike the contentment in, and rabid pursuit of wealth and the plain tackiness of the manner in which it is displayed."

JAMES ARMSTRONG, 52 (AMERICA)

Length of stay: Six years **Occupation:** Photojournalism lecturer **Likes:** "It is a very interesting time to be here with what has happened with the economy in the last six to eight years. It is a period where the young Irish are plugged in and connected and are as contemporary as any other group anywhere else. It is an absorbing time for them in terms of an international culture and it probably has to do with developing a contemporary or, dare I say, a post-modern Irish sensibility – who they are and what they are." **Dislikes:** "I dislike the moral vanity of the upper-middle class or the intelligentsia. I think the Irish love to take the higher ground. There is a certain way of looking at the world where a lot of the educated Irish are very critical about things in world politics that have not been resolved on their own door-step."

MIRELLA MECHITA, 20 (ROMANIA)

Length of stay: Three years **Occupation:** Business Student **Likes:** "It has always seemed more normal for me to consider Ireland in terms of advantages and disadvantages, ups and downs. What Ireland stands for, for me, is the opportunity to achieve something, to fulfil a set of dreams that would be far more difficult back home. The things I like best are the people – they are friendly, outgoing, full of life, 'can-I-help-you', 'le'ts-go-out-for-a-drink' people." **Dislikes:** "I have met some hypocritical people who have been sweetness and light to my face but, as soon as I have turned my back, they have clenched their teeth and called me a f***ing immigrant and f***ing foreigner'."

GAYLE WIUJAMSON, 33 (SOUTH AFRICA)

Length of stay: Two-and-a-half years **Occupation:** Journalist **Likes:** "I know locals will say that Dublin isn't like it used to be but, having come from South Africa (where I lived for 20 years), I find it very friendly and safe. I love that you can go into shops here, especially in the smaller towns, and shopkeepers talk to you and get to know you. Or even when you're standing in a queue in Tesco and the person next to you starts a conversation. There's a real sense of community." **Dislikes:** "The only things I don't like are the traffic congestion, how much everyone seems to drink and the high cost of living."

SHINYA OKAWA, 29 (JAPAN)

Length of stay: Three-and-a-half years **Occupation:** Multimedia expert **Likes:** "The people and the atmosphere of Dublin, I like that. It is not too big, it is not too small and so it is a nice cosy city where I can have fun. The place and people are also easygoing." **Dislikes:** "Sometimes people here are a bit unsophisticated and not so cosmopolitan. I don't like the 'lad' culture or the new rich Irish people who splash money about in so-called exclusive places."

REMCO DE WIT, 31 (HOLLAND)

Length of stay: Four years **Occupation:** Manager of an internet café, **Likes:** "I like the people – they are nicer than in Holland. At home the people are not nice any more; they are not friendly and they are always in bad moods. The Irish people are easygoing. I also like the countryside very much." **Dislikes:** "In the supermarkets they don't have as big an assortment as in Holland. The rent is also too high."

Info 16: Building the Peace. A Community Relations Project in Belfast

Currach Community[1]
Address: 2 Workman Avenue, Belfast BT13 3FB
Tel: (0232) 312658

Contact person: Noreen Christian
Date established: 1992
Total membership: 6

Origins

The Community is the result of a search of a small group of Christians from both traditions to establish a meaningful community in West Belfast.

Aims/objectives

- To provide a setting on the interface of the Shankill/Falls areas of the city in which people from both traditions can choose to live out their lives together in a Christian context.
- To be supportive presence to local families.
- To facilitate the gathering together of local people to share their common life-experience and struggles.
- To help local people discern their needs.
- To encourage local people through self-empowerment for their own good and that of the wider community.
- To establish projects relevant to the stated aims.

Geographical area of operation

Immediate Shankill/Falls area of Belfast.

Affiliations/networks

No official links but there is a close relationship with the Cornerstone Community and the Belfast Central Mission.[2]

---

1 "Currach Community", in *A Guide to Peace, Reconciliation and Community Relations Projects in Ireland,* compiled by Joe Hinds (Belfast: Community Relations Council), p. 40.

2 In the meantime, Currach Community has become a member of Forthspring, an inter-community partnership between the Currach Community, Cornerstone Community, and Springfield Road Methodist Church and serves the communities of the mid-Springfield Road + Woodvale areas of West Belfast.

Info 17: Education for Mutual Understanding and Cultural Heritage

Most[1] Protestants and Catholics in Northern Ireland have been educated apart from each other and have had few opportunities to meet and to learn to trust each other. Some people have seen this as a significant obstacle to community peace and reconciliation in this part of Ireland.

Over the past few years, however, various educational projects have grown up to provide children and young people with new opportunities to build up relationships based on confidence and friendship.

Separate Schools

Knowing what school someone went to in Northern Ireland is an effective means of discovering whether someone is from a Protestant (unionist/British) background or a Catholic (nationalist/Irish) background. (Protestant and Catholic are often used in Northern Ireland as shorthand terms to describe people's cultural and community background, and they do not necessarily indicate a specific religious affiliation.) Catholic parents are strongly encouraged by the Catholic Church to send their children to Catholic Schools (the vast majority of which are now fully state funded), and almost all do. Protestant parents normally send their children to Controlled schools which are not "Protestant Schools" as such but in which the influences and ethos are fundamentally Protestant (in the broadest cultural sense). Although there has been a small number of local areas where shared schooling is taking place, the predominant reality has been that of two parallel separate school systems. Government figures indicate that 95% of children still attend the schools of "their own community".

In recent years a number of planned Integrated Schools – for Protestants and Catholics together – have grown up. The first of these was established in 1981, and at the time of writing (June 1997) there are 33 – eleven for Secondary-age pupils and the others for Primary-age children – with more due to open in the next few months. So far, however, these schools account for only around 2%–3% of the school population (about 7,000 children), although their influence is growing slowly.

Mutual Understanding

Building on the work of individual teachers and schools of voluntary (not-for-profit) organisations and of experimental curriculum projects over many years, the Department of Education for Northern Ireland (DENI) has since the early 1980's promoted in all kinds of schools the development of educational programmes to encourage better community relations. Since 1983 the umbrella title of Education for Mutual Understanding has bee adopted to cover these various activities. This work relates closely to programmes found in other countries, such as multicultural or intercultural education for citizenship and peace education.

In 1987 DENI introduced a voluntary inter-school Cross Contact Scheme which provides funds to support planned and long-term contact programmes between controlled and maintained schools. Presently between one-third and one-half of all schools in Northern Ireland are taking part in this scheme, although the numbers of pupils involved varies considerably from place to place.

---

[1] Source of the text: Norman L. Richardson, "Education for Mutual Understanding and Cultural Heritage," *CAIN Web Service*, http://cain.ulst.ac.uk/emu/emuback.htm.

Educational Themes

In the Government's Education Reform (Northern Ireland) Order of 1989, six mandatory educational (cross curricular) themes were introduced, including the two complementary themes of Education for Mutual Understanding (EMU) and Cultural Heritage (CH). These formally came into statute in September 1992.

EMU and CH have been defined as being fundamentally about "learning to live with differences in a spirit of acceptance, fairness and mutual respect" (Richardson, 1996). This definition is elaborated by four shared objectives which may be summarised as follows:

1. Fostering Respect for Self and Others and Building Relationships.
   Pupils have opportunities to develop knowledge and understanding of themselves, and how to handle and react appropriately to a range of personal and social situations.
2. Understanding and Dealing Creatively with Conflict.
   Pupils should have opportunities to develop knowledge and understanding of conflict in a variety of contexts and of how to respond to it positively and creatively
3. Awareness of Interdependence
   Pupils should have opportunities to develop a knowledge, appreciation and understanding of interdependence, continuity and change in the social and cultural process as it relates to individuals, families, local communities and the wider world.
4. Understanding Cultural Diversity
   Pupils should have opportunities to develop an informed awareness of the similarities and differences between the cultural traditions which influence people who live in Northern Ireland, and of the international and transnational influences on contemporary culture.

As compulsory themes in the Northern Ireland Curriculum, EMU and CH must be addressed by all teachers of all subjects throughout each stage of education although the content of certain subjects is clearly more relevant that that of others. EMU is also very significant as a whole school process in relation to ethos and pastoral dimensions of school life. Voluntary cross-community contact programmes between separate schools are encouraged as a valuable dimension of EMU, but they are not required by law. If they are to be effective, EMU and CH must relate to the broad curriculum within and between schools.

Some excellent work has been carried out in recent years in relation to EMU and CH, but those involved in this field recognise that what is required is a long term commitment and continuity if there is to be any hope of widespread benefit from the various programmes.

[For official details on the promotion of education for mutual understanding see: *Towards a Culture of Tolerance: Education for Diversity,* Department of Education Northern Ireland (DENI), 1999, http://www.deni.gov.uk/community_relations/documents/consultationdocument2.pdf .]

Info 18: Millward Brown Ulster: Opinion Poll, March 2005

1. Introduction and background

In May 1998 an Inter-party Political Agreement was endorsed by Referendum: 71% voted in favour of the Agreement and 29% voted against. Subsequently, an election was held to return 108 members to the new Assembly, which in turn internally elected the Executive, comprising 12 members, headed, as at October 2002, by David Trimble (First Minister), and Mark Durkan (Deputy First Minister).

In October 2002, it was alleged that Sinn Fein had been carrying out political spying, an act regarded as a clear breach of the Agreement. The Northern Ireland Assembly was thereafter suspended by the Secretary of State. (There had also been a previous suspension in February 2000.) On suspension, the government of Northern Ireland reverted to "Direct Rule", by a ministerial team appointed by the Prime Minister, Tony Blair. Further informal talks ensued, and in October 2003, it was announced that an Assembly election would be held on November 26th. (Postponed from its scheduled date of May 2003). On the day of the announcement (October 22nd) a series of statements was made, firstly by Gerry Adams, leader of Sinn Fein, and then by de Chastelain, who verified that a further (third) act of decommissioning had occurred, but that he remained bound by the IRA injunction not to provide quantitative or other details. Very shortly thereafter, David Trimble made a statement in which he asserted that the non-provision of such details was unsatisfactory, and that he would therefore "put the process on hold", by not committing to reforming the administration, i.e., the Executive government. Nevertheless, the decision to hold the election was maintained.

The election results revealed considerable polarization towards the 'hard-line' parties on either side, with the SDLP for the first time being eclipsed by Sinn Fein, whilst on the unionist side, Ian Paisley's DUP came in ahead of David Trimble's UUP. This meant that in the event of the Assembly being restored and a new Executive formed, that the DUP would provide the First Minister and Sinn Fein the Deputy First Minister.

Nevertheless, the Assembly remained in suspension and informal talks ensued with a view to reconciling the positions of Sinn Fein and the DUP. Whilst these talks, which focused on the issue of IRA decommissioning, appeared promising, they foundered on the means of verification: the DUP required photographic evidence, a process rejected by the IRA.

Direct rule continued indefinitely, but a number of events sharply focused attention on the intentions and activities of the IRA and the relationship of Sinn Fein and its leaders with that organization. Specifically a well-orchestrated robbery involving intimidation of staff and their families relieved the Northern Bank of £26.5m. The Chief Constable of the PSNI, Hugh Orde, shortly made a statement declaring his belief, on the basis of investigations and intelligence, that the robbery hade been carried out by the IRA. This position was shortly affirmed by both the British and Irish governments, and by the fourth report of the Independent Monitoring Commission. The IMC also stated that Sinn Fein must bear a share of responsibility for the abductions and robberies, and that some of its senior members were members of the IRA and involved in sanctioning the series of robberies.

In January 2005, the murder in Belfast occurred of Robert McCartney, known to have strong Republican sentiments. His sisters shortly made a series of statements to the effect that IRA members had been involved in this murder and that the IRA and Sinn Fein were inadequately facilitating the identification, charging, and prosecution of the perpetrators. Amongst other responses to this initiative, the IRA firstly reported dismissing some members, and then projected an offer to shoot them.

Against this background, Millward Brown Ulster carried out a wide-ranging opinion poll to ascertain the state of public opinion in Northern Ireland, focusing on attitudes to the activities and intentions of the IRA, and what might be required to encourage support for the restitution of the Assembly on an inclusive basis. A representative sample of 1010 adults (18+) was interviewed from 7th to 8th March 2005 by fully trained and experienced interviewers, according to the definitive quality standards of the IQCS (Interviewer Quality Control Scheme). All interviewing was carried out face-to-face at 56 sampling points selected at random throughout Northern Ireland.

2. Commentary and analysis

At the time of the Agreement Referendum in May 1998, a weakness emerged in that the Agreement failed to achieve proportionate cross-community support: whereas Catholics were virtually universally in favour, only 51% of Protestants were in favour and 49% were opposed. It was also clear that this opposition was overwhelmingly predicated on anxiety about the intentions of Republican paramilitaries with regard to violence. To gauge these perceptions, respondents were invited to indicate whether they thought that it was the IRA's intention to disarm under the arrangements of the Agreement; only to do so when there was a united Ireland; or never. Amongst neither Catholics nor Protestants was there a majority view that the IRA intended to disarm under the Agreement, and it was very clear that Protestant anxieties remain particularly widespread and profound: 66% thought that they would never disarm, and 22% that they would do so only when their goal of a united Ireland had been achieved. Only 9% felt that they would honour the undertaking to disarm under the provisions of the Good Friday Agreement.

The perceived performance of the 4 main party leaders amongst their own supporters revealed that Gerry Adams continues to enjoy easily the strongest esteem notwithstanding the controversy over IRA criminality and the status of Sinn Fein in this regard. However, compared to November 2003, a small decline in his standing appeared to have occurred. In contrast however, the standing of Mark Durkan (SDLP) fell noticeably, as did that of David Trimble. Regard for Ian Paisley amongst DUP supporters was the only one to have moved in a positive direction. In tandem with this finding, preference for David Trimble as First Minister fell sharply since 2003, with Ian Paisley on the ascendant. Mark Durkan marginally improved his support as First Minister relative to Gerry Adams.

A key parameter of the election (widely conjectured to be held on 5th May) will be the turnout. However, 57% said that they would be certain to vote, and 16% that they would be very likely to do so. On this evidence, it appears likely that the turnout will be along similar lines as in recent elections.

An assessment of voting intentions pointed to an extremely close position between Sinn Fein and SDLP. Whilst interim opinion polls (unlike exit polls) are not specifically intended to afford predictions of forthcoming elections, this finding suggests a moderate adjustment of the SDLP / Sinn Fein share of vote, but by no means points to any landslide dilution of the Sinn Fein vote as result of the recent controversies. However, on the unionist side, the findings point to a further heavy shift in favour of the DUP (Ian Paisley) at the expense of the UUP (David Trimble). When evidence of any overt shifting in party support on behalf of those who voted in the November 2003 Assembly Election was examined, it was found that SDLP and Sinn Fein gains and losses largely balanced out: however, the scale of the respective gains and losses suggests that there may be considerable mobility between these parties. Shifts in favour of the DUP were much higher than for the UUP.

For Nationalists, a crucial component of the Agreement was police reform. Previously, the RUC had been regarded by Nationalists as sectarian and repressive, and major provisions of the Agreement (via the Patten Commission) were the renaming of the RUC to PSNI (Police Service of Northern Ireland); new regulations specifying that recruitment should be 50% Catholic and 50% non-Catholic; and the establishment of the Policing Board and Police Ombudsman. Confidence in the PSNI continues to be stronger among Protestants than Catholics, but on both sides, there was marginal improvement in confidence since 2003.

On both sides, there was considerable unease with the Ombudsman and the Policing Board, and no indication of any improvement over the past year. Even more marked was the decline in confidence in the International Commission on Decommissioning, headed by John de Chastelain. In some contrast, confidence in the Independent Monitoring Commission (IMC) marginally improved in tandem with an uplift in those appearing to be aware of this body.

General confidence in the future prospects for long and lasting peace was also monitored, and indicated a moderate downswing in Catholic confidence since 2003, and no shift as far as Protestants are concerned. Catholic confidence was greatly boosted by the Agreement, and remains significantly stronger than Protestant confidence.

In view of the current suspension of the Assembly, and the factors contributing to the suspension, the poll gauged support for restoring that institution, with the full participation of all parties. As things stood at the time of the poll, only 29% would advocate the Secretary of State proceeding along these lines, but rose to 47% of Catholics compared to only 13% of Protestants, who were much more likely to advocate restoring the Assembly with the exclusion of Sinn Fein (43%). However, in the event of the IRA verifiably decommissioning all weapons, Protestant support for an inclusive Assembly increased to 33%, and increased even further to 45% if the IRA were to disband and verifiably disarm. (In the event of IRA disbanding, Protestant support for Sinn Fein inclusion outweighs support for their exclusion, but decommissioning alone is not sufficient for this balance of opinion to occur).

When nationalist voters were asked to state what they felt the IRA should now do, a majority of 70% thought that they should decommission all weapons, and a majority of 60% thought that they should disband. Specifically amongst Sinn Fein voters, 59% advocated full decommissioning, and 44% disbandment. Thus, whilst this poll reveals substantial support for Gerry Adams amongst Sinn Fein voters, and no more than moderate retrenchment of the Sinn Fein share of vote, there appears to be a substantial body of opinion amongst supporters that the IRA may no longer be of relevance and should as a minimum dispose of the means of violence or even disband.

Overall, a majority of 61% agreed that the IRA was responsible for the £26.5m Northern Bank robbery, a level very similar to an earlier poll in the Republic of Ireland. However, whilst Protestants were almost universal in this belief, Catholics were relatively divided, and uncertain.

In response to the IMC and the Irish Governments statements that Sinn Fein shared responsibility for the Northern Bank robbery and that senior Sinn Fein members may have had prior knowledge, Gerry Adams issued a verbal challenge that evidence be produced or that he be arrested and charged. Overall, the poll indicated that the Northern Ireland populace is divided as to whether such an arrest would be the right course of action (47%), or the wrong one (32%). Whilst unionist parties were generally inclined to the view that such a measure would be appropriate, nationalists took the reverse view, although 13% of Sinn Fein voters were inclined to the view that Gerry Adam's challenge to be arrested should be taken up.

47% were dissatisfied with the response of the Sinn Fein leadership to the killing of Robert McCartney, outweighing the 29% who were satisfied. Amongst Sinn Fein voters specifically, whilst a majority of 65% were satisfied, a significant minority of 25% were not.

When those dissatisfied with the response were invited to say why this was so, the primary reasons were that the Sinn Fein leadership had dissimulated; that they should identify the perpetrators or provide any other relevant information; that they had not done sufficient to bring the killers to justice; and that they were now reacting belatedly to the initiative of McCartney's sisters.

Overall, 70% considered that Sinn Fein's cooperation with the PSNI was inadequate, including 25% of Sinn Fein supporters, and 59% of SDLP supporters.

Lastly, when respondents were invited to state what if anything, they thought Sinn Fein needed to do to demonstrate commitment to democracy and peace, the main declarations were that they should:

- Decommission all weapons
- Break links with the IRA
- Be more honest and truthful
- Get the IRA to cease violence and respect the law
- Cooperate with the PSNI
- 13% thought that there was nothing they needed to do, and had already demonstrated commitment in this regard, rising to 47% of Sinn Fein voters.[1]

[1] Millward Brown Ulster, *Opinion Poll March 2005*, 115 University Street, Belfast BT7 1HP

Info 19: Irish WWW-Sites of Interest

A link list that may be a good starting-point:
http://www.irish-conflict.de/links.html

Heinrich Kessler's comprehensive link list about "anything Irish":
http://de.geocities.com/henry392003/Englisch_Links.htm#Northern%20Ireland

Political parties in Northern Ireland:

Alliance Party, http://www.unite.net/customers/alliance/
Democratic Unionist Party, http://www.dup.org.uk/
Labour in Northern Ireland, http://www.gpl.net/customers/labour/
Northern Ireland Women's Coalition, http://www.pitt.edu/~novosel/northern.html
Progressive Unionist Party, http://www.pup.org/
Sinn Fein, http://www.irlnet.com/sinnfein/index.html
Ulster Democratic Party, http://www.udp.org/
Ulster Unionist Party, http://www.uup.org/

Main political parties in the Republic of Ireland:

Democratic Left, http://www.connect.ie/users/dl/
Fianna Fail, http://www.iol.ie/fiannafail/
Fine Gael, http://www.finegael.com/gohere.htm
Irish Labour Party, http://www.labour.ie/core.htm
Progressive Democrats, http://ireland.iol.ie/pd/

News, opinion and analysis on Irish politics:

An Phoblacht/Republican News, http://www.irlnet.com/aprn/index.html
Belfast Telegraph, http://www.belfasttelegraph.co.uk/
Fortnight, http://www.kerna.ie/fortnight/
Irish News, http://www.irishnews.com/
Irish Times, http://www.irish-times.ie/

Official government Web sites:

Northern Ireland Government Homepage, http://www.nics.gov.uk/index.htm
Government of Ireland (Rialtas na Éireann) Web site, http://www.irlgov.ie/

Other interesting sites:

Grand Orange Lodge of Ireland, http://www.gpl.net/customers/goli/
Hunger Strike Commemoration Web Project, http://larkspirit.com/hungerstrikes
The RUC's Web site (including a 'virtual museum'), http://www.nics.gov.uk/ruc/index.htm

Irish search engine:

Swift Guide, http://swift.kerna.com
This is a revised list of links which were originally compiled by Steve Jones, a Labour Councillor from Oswestry, Shropshire and a member of his party's Agreed Ireland Forum

Other websites of interest:

Nidex – the Northern Ireland search engine
http://www.nidex.com/

Official Site of the NI Tourist Board
http://www.northern-ireland.com

Central online source about the voluntary and community sector in NI
http://www.communityni.org/index.cfm/section/Events/key/954BE867-B0D0-7815-0F69817A7E25680A

The History Guy: Links for the Conflict in Northern Ireland
http://www.historyguy.com/northern_ireland_links.html -

Community Northern Ireland – central online source of information about the voluntary and community sector in Northern Ireland
http://www.communityni.org/index.cfm

CAIN Web Service: Guide to Web Sites Containing Information on the Conflict and Politics in Northern Ireland
http://cain.ulst.ac.uk/bibdbs/newlinks.html

Wikipedia, the free encyclopedia: Northern Ireland
http://en.wikipedia.org/wiki/Northern_Ireland

Northern Ireland Human Rights Commission
http://www.nihrc.org/textonly/links.asp

The Northern Ireland Assembly
http://www.niassembly.gov.uk/

Northern Ireland Statistics and Research Agency
http://www.nisra.gov.uk/census/links.html

Info 20: Glossary and Abbreviations

Anglo-Irish Agreement[1]	Signed by Irish and British governments, November 1985
ANIA	Americans for a New Irish Agenda
Ard Fheis	Conference of Irish political parties
Articles 2 and 3	Articles in the Constitution of the Irish republic which laid claim to the six counties of Northern Ireland
Belfast Agreement	Otherwise known as the Good Friday Agreement, signed in April 1998
Bloomfield Report	May 1998 report by Sir Kenneth Bloomfield into the victims of the Troubles
CAP	Common Agricultural Policy
CCMS	Council for Catholic Maintained Schools
CEAC	Curriculum Examination and Assessment Council
CIRA	Continuity IRA - small splinter group opposed to the peace process
CLMC	Combined Loyalist Military Command; loyalist paramilitary coordinating body formed in 1991 comprising: UDA, UFF, UVF and Red Hand Commando
CRC	Community Relations Council
CRE	Commission for Racial Equality
Dail	Lower house of the Irish parliament
DED	Department of Economic Development
DENI	Department of Education, Northern Ireland
Direct Rule	Introduced in 1972 following the proroguing of Stormont
Downing Street Declaration	Key document of the peace process published jointly by the UK and Irish governments, December 1993
DPPB	District Policing Partnership Board
DUP	Democratic Unionist Party, led by Revd lan Paisley
EC/EU	European Community/European Union
ECHR	European Convention on Human Rights
ECWG	Equality Commission Working Group
EEC	European Economic Community
EOCNI	Equal Opportunities Commission Northern Ireland
FAIR	Families Acting for Innocent Relatives
FAIT	Families Against Intimidation and Terror
FEC	Fair Employment Commission
Fianna Fáil	Constitutional nationalist party in the Irish republic
Fine Gael	One of the two main parties in the Irish Republic
FLNC	National Liberation Front of Corsica (Front de Liberation nationale de la Corse)
Framework Document	Published in February 1995 by Irish and British governments with purpose of bringing about an agreed settlement in Ireland
George Mitchell	President Clinton's special envoy to Northern Ireland
GNP	Gross National Product
HURT	Homes United by Republican Terror, later Homes United by Recurring Terror
IEF	Integrated Education Fund
INCORE	Institute for Conflict Resolution
INLA	Irish National Liberation Army; republican paramilitary group formed in 1974 as a breakaway from the Official IRA
INTERREG	1989 EU initiative to fester economic cooperation between contiguous territories of different EU countries
IRA	Irish Republican Army, also referred to as **Provisional IRA**; formed in late 1969 after a split with the Official IRA
JSA	Jobseekers Allowance

[1] Based on Michael Cox, Adrian Guelke and Fiona Stephen (eds.), "Glossary and Abbreviations", *A farewell to arms. From 'long war' to long peace in Northern Ireland,* Manchester United Press, Manchester und New York, 2000, p. xviiff.

LVF	Loyalist Volunteer Force
Mitchell Report	Published February 1996 laying down six conditions for inclusive political discussions, including the renunciation of force and no resort to anything other than democratic and peaceful means
NICE	Northern Ireland Centre in Europe
NICIE	Northern Ireland Council for Integrated Education
NIO	Northern Ireland Office, British government department
NITVT	Northern Ireland Terrorist Victims Together
NIWC	Northern Ireland Women's Coalition
Northern Ireland Forum	Public initiative in the Irish republic taken in 1983 to explore different possible 'solutions' to the 'Irish Question'
Omagh	Town in Northern Ireland where twenty-eight were killed in 1998 by a bomb after the signing of the Good Friday Agreement
PAFT	Policy Appraisal and Fair Treatment
Patten Report	1999 commission report drafted by Chris Patten advocating reform of RUC
PMVD	Politically motivated violent offenders
PR(STV)	proportional representation (single transferable vote)
PUP	Progressive Unionist Party, loyalist party closest to the UVF
Real IRA (RIRA)	Splinter group opposed to peace process
RIR	Royal Irish Regiment (formerly UDR)
RTE	Radio Telefis Eireann, radio and TV network in the Irish Republic
RUC	Royal Ulster Constabulary, Northern Ireland police force
SACHR	Standing Advisory Committee on Human Rights
SAS	Special Air Services, elite regiment of the British Army
SDLP	Social Democratic and Labour Party, largest nationalist party in Northern Ireland led by John Hume
Sinn Fein	Political wing of the IRA
SSPR	Special Support Programme for Peace and Reconciliation initiated in Northern Ireland after 1994 ceasefires
Sunningdale	Location in UK where agreement was reached that led to the formation of a power sharing executive in 1974
Tanaiste	Official title of the deputy prime minister of the Irish republic
Taoiseach	Official title of the prime minister of the Irish Republic
TD	Member of the Dail
TSN	Targeting Social Need
UDA	Ulster Defence Association, largest loyalist paramilitary Organisation
UDP	Ulster Democratic Party
UDR	Ulster Defence Regiment, locally recruited and based regiment of the British Army (renamed Royal Irish Regiment in 1992)
UFF	Ulster Freedom Fighters, proscribed loyalist paramilitary Organisation
UKUP	United Kingdom Unionist Party, led by Bob McCartney and opposed to the Good Friday Agreement
UTU	Ulster Teachers' Union
UUP	Ulster Unionist Party
UVF	Ulster Volunteer Force, proscribed loyalist paramilitary Organisation
UWC	Ulster Worker's Council, loyalist committee that planned the collapse of the power sharing agreement of 1974
Washington 3	The three conditions laid down by the British government in March 1993 for Sinn Fein joining all party talks, which included 'actual decommissioning of some arms as a tangible confidence-building measure'